Internationa
and the Development
of International
Relations Theory

Edited by
B. A. Roberson

Continuum
The Tower Building, 11 York Road, London SE1 7NX
370 Lexington Avenue, New York, NY 10017-6503

First published by Pinter in 1998

Revised paperback edition published by Continuum 2002

British Library Cataloguing-in-Publication Data
A catalogue record for this book is available from the British Library.

ISBN 1-85567-403-3 (hardback)
0-8264-5224-8 (paperback)

Library of Congress Cataloging-in-Publication Data
International society and the development of international relations theory / edited by B. A. Roberson.
p. cm.
Includes bibliographical references and index.
ISBN 1-85567-403-3 (hardcover 0-8264-5224 -8 (paperback)
1. International relations. I. Roberson, B. A. (Barbara Allen)
JZ1305.158 1998
341.2-dc21 97-27669
CIP

Typeset by BookEns Ltd, Royston, Herts.
Printed and bound in Great Britain by
Bookcraft (Bath) Ltd, Midsomer Norton, Somerset

Contents

Contributors

Fulvio Attiná is Jean Monnet Professor of European Comparative Politics and Professor of International Relations at the University of Catania.

Tim Dunne is Lecturer in International Politics at the University of Wales, Aberystwyth.

Andrew Hurrell is University Lecturer in International Relations at Oxford University and a Fellow of Nuffield College.

Yale H. Ferguson is Professor of International Relations at Rutgers University, Newark.

Robert H. Jackson is Professor of Political Science at the University of British Columbia.

R. J. Barry Jones is Professor in International Relations at the University of Reading.

Richard Little is Professor of International Relations at the University of Bristol.

James Mayall is Professor of International Relations at the London School of Economics.

B. A. Roberson is Lecturer in International Relations at the University of Warwick.

Ole Wæver is Professor at the Institute of Political Science, University of Copenhagen.

Adam Watson is Emeritus Professor of International Relations at the University of Virginia.

Nicholas J. Wheeler is Lecturer in International Politics at the University of Wales, Aberystwyth.

Preface to the Hardback Edition

The majority of the papers comprising this book emerged from a European Consortium for Political Research Workshop held in Limerick, Ireland, in 1992. Additional contributions by scholars concerned with current perspectives on international society and international relations have been included. The original purpose of the workshop was to 'reconsider', in the wake of a disintegrating old order exemplified by the Cold War, the idea of international society. It was to be a contribution to an alternative perspective for the study of international relations embodying the concept of an 'international society' which contains elements of co-operation and common values. This was what the participants in the workshop set out to do. The first revisions resulted in the aftermath of the discussion and work of the workshop. Further revisions are the result of the very useful advice of Pinter's readers, one of whom urged the contributors to explore the influence of the idea of international society on international relations theory. We are grateful to Pinter's readers for their very positive approach to our manuscript. I particularly would like to acknowledge the valuable assistance of Richard Devetak in the editing of Ole Wæver's chapter. Initial work on the endnotes and creation of the bibliography was carried out by Stephen Calleya, supported by the Warwick Research Fund. The bibliography in its final form is the result of the much appreciated efforts of Linda Bromley and Margaret Roberson. Lastly, I want to warmly thank Pinter's editors, Nicola Niinikka and, latterly, Petra Recter, for their support, care and concern shown throughout without which our spirits would have surely withered.

B. A. Roberson
London, March 1997

Preface to the Paperback Edition

For some time, there has been a sustained and growing interest in the question of international society: its conception, methodology, function and praxis, the process of its change and its expansion into the wider world. The stimuli for this interest lie in the pragmatic concerns of governments and others with the level of violence in the international system, and for a way of devising institutional arrangements amongst states that would serve as a mechanism for the resolution of international conflict. For academics in particular there is a need to account theoretically for cooperative developments in an international system of sovereign states that is devoid of a central authority. This undertaking is thus a search for reality, for an in-depth understanding of the complex of activity comprising the international system, with the prospect of discovering the nature of international society, how it develops and how it is held together.

The European system and states has been viewed as an emerging society of states, and has served as a foundation for the institutionalization of international relations based on common and enduring understandings of the interests, rules and values embodied in a constitutionalized international order. The process by which the European state began to take shape had its origins in the gradual development of the modern states system following the turbulent developments of the Middle Ages. The European state system itself was a product of the Holy Roman Empire, a loose confederation of kingdoms, principalities and other political formations, with power and authority dispersed amongst the Emperor, ecclesiastical authorities and alliances of lesser powers. With the centres of power and authority spread out in this way, the political formations within the Empire existed in symbiotic relation to each other. None was able to achieve dominance. Order, within the constellation of these powers, had to be negotiated. This negotiation of differences led to the establishment of formal rules not only of political conflict but also of military engagement. This in turn led to the establishment of structural foundations for the institutionalization of relations between political formations: a system that provided a rudimentary model for a society of states.

One of the most significant results of these developments was the establishment of international law. Modern international law emerged from the desire of states to bring about some degree of order in their relations with each other, while at the same time preserving their sovereign independence. A cooperative international order was maintained coterminously with the ability of individual states to determine their own internal affairs. It is this process that has determined the development of international society. The notion of society is inherent in the concept of international law. At the national level it accommodates a degree of solidarity that provides substance to the particular nature of that order. Consequently, progress towards cooperation amongst states proceeds like the random movement of an amoeba. Despite this, it is generally the case that those states that accept the acquis of international law adhere to its principles and obligations. It is the states themselves that have acquiesced to the establishment of rules and values (whether through consent, coercion, or a combination of the two), and norms thus emerge from the sovereignty of states themselves, binding them to cooperative relations in the international system, creating a framework of expectations for future relationships, giving continuity to those relations, and subjecting them, when disagreements arise, to a response involving rational analysis and hence the possibility of change and accommodation.

International law becomes not only a mechanism through which changes in relationships can occur, but also a means of incorporating states into an acquis of cooperative expectations. It is clear that power politics is oriented to the establishment of state relations on a competitive and conflictual basis; it is also clear that the function and logic of international law is to ameliorate or resolve the difficulties that surround the relations of states existing in an essentially anarchic environment. Although its aims are clear, it is less evident how international law functions to bring about a particular order through cooperative means. This is a subject on which there needs to be further empirical research. What is important is that the consensus in international law is not the consensus of states but of those responsible for the decision process in the state. The decisions of the more powerful states have a disproportionate effect on the development of international law. Where the lesser powers are involved in international cooperation, a judicious adjustment of interests is often required as part of the development of the societal characteristics of the international system.

The end of the cold war accelerated a reconstruction of the notion of international society following trends that had been quietly developed in the 1980s. The new millennium saw the intensive questioning and revision of established international relations theories, by scholars impatient with their previously held 'truths' and former insights, and with new perspectives and theories to present. Such reconsideration of an important notion for international society, as put forward in the writings of Bill, Wight, Manning and others (presented at an ECPR workshop in Limerick, Ireland) led to the publication of this volume in hardback in 1998.

We hope that this updated paperback edition will bring our ideas to a wider audience, especially to those students interested in on-going developments in the concept of international society, and in the prospect of a less conflictual world through the historical expansion of cooperative relations amongst nations.

B. A. Roberson
London, December 2001

1

Probing the Idea and Prospects for International Society

B. A. ROBERSON

The intention of this volume is to re-examine the current position of the international society tradition that has emerged out of the deliberation of the English School and other academics. The contributions to this study will examine the conception and implication of the international society concept within international relations theory more generally and in light of current theoretical concerns.

The English School of international relations had some of its roots in the concerns generated by the seemingly mindless slaughter of the First World War. Its theoretical foundations lay in the classic writings of European political philosophy reaching back into the Middle Ages and beyond. It was the trauma of the First World War that brought into sharp focus the need for a solution to conflict among states, its nature, causes and ways of organizing the system of states to promote peace in a world in which 'faith and sentiments' that held Christendom together no longer existed.[1] What did exist was an awareness of an international community.[2] What finally emerged in the aftermath of the war was the creation of an international organization, the League of Nations, to maintain a legal order that would promote general peace. The hopes, however, that the League would be able to manage international conflict through international law and international institutions eventually foundered on the power politics of the 1930s.

To some academics, notably E. H. Carr, the policies of governments in the aftermath of the First World War neglected the lessons of history in their belief in the possibility of an emerging new moral world order. This hope for a new moral age in international relations dissipated in the Japanese invasion of Manchuria, the Italian invasion of Abyssinia and the inability of the League to respond effectively to international crises where the great powers were involved. The idealism of this period became submerged in power politics, bringing into question the utopist perspective, setting off a realist-idealist debate.[3]

Carr derided approaches that sought solutions to the problem of international conflict through the application of international law and the creation of international organization which were predicated on the acceptance of what were assumed to be international norms and offered a power-based perspective for the analysis of international relations. The idealist–realist debate came to dominate international relations theorizing, reinforced in the early 1950s by Morgenthau's advocacy of the primacy of power in the politics of survival against the pursuit of values in international relations. Neither Carr nor Morgenthau abjured morality in international relations. Carr noted that 'realism devoid of morality lacks meaningful action, therefore, for realism to work it must contain both elements of morality and reality'.[4] However, where moral interests form part of policy objectives, it was the national interest that was to be pursued.

British academics in general were in agreement as to the realist view of the central role of the state and the anarchical and hierarchical character of the international system which was the driving force that guided the actions of states to pursue policies of power politics. This formed the hostile environment of insecurity within which international politics developed. They also observed that despite the nature of the international system there was clear evidence of some degree of co-operation and what appeared to be an order of sorts. In the late 1950s, the British Committee on the Theory of International Relations[5] met to reflect: on the nature of the international state system; what constituted the degree of order that appeared to exist; what was the basis for this order; how did it develop; and what were the prospects of an international society emerging from the current order in the international system. The founding members of the British Committee were Herbert Butterfield and Kenneth Thompson. The rest of the Committee comprised William Armstrong, Hedley Bull, Michael Howerd, Geoffrey Hudson, Donald Mackinnon, Adam Watson, Martin Wight and Desmond Williams. Not all were academics. Watson was from the Foreign Office, and Armstrong from the Treasury represented the practitioners in the formulation of government policy. They all felt that the criticism levied against the idealist approach to international relations theory was largely valid. But while accepting much of what realists described as the international system, they found this perspective wanting as an explanation of how this system worked.

How is one to incorporate the co-operative aspect of international relations into the realist conception of the conflictual nature of the international system? But there is more to this theory building. The realist perspective was intent on understanding how international politics worked and why it worked the way it did. Their conclusion left them with a perspective that viewed the relations of states as driven by power politics. Idealists had been concerned with how international order could be organized to bring about a more peaceful and just world. The international society theorists, in their turn, agreed with the realists that the international system resembled a Hobbesian world in a state of nature and that states were the prime actors in the international system. They also observed that there existed a semblance of order among states: through their recognition of international law and, to a considerable extent, the adherence of states to international law in their relations with each other; diplomatic practices which allowed states to discuss mutual concerns in a spirit of compromise; and international regimes and institutions which were created to allow states to deal with common problems. For international society theorists, these relations comprised an incipient form of an international society. It was a third way of looking at the international system that contained elements of both realism and idealism.

For C. A. W. Manning, a professor of international relations at the London School of Economics and Political Science, along with Martin Wight, the seeming paradox of the nature of the international system invited an explanation. Manning was not committed to any particular view of international relations but taught the subject as an observable phenomenon to be explained for an understanding of its behaviour. He took an open-ended approach to his teaching that liberated students to explore freely various ideas and seek their own explanations of the phenomena being studied. In many ways, it was an intellectual exercise. His ideas and style of writing can be seen in his publication *The Nature of International Society*, published in 1962.[6] His writing was at times distractingly idiosyncratic, with his ideas often emerging more clearly on second reading.

For Manning, the existence of international society was predicated on the existence and practice of international law that emerged from the relations among states and it was this that comprised the society of states. For him, international society, as with other international relations notions, was an abstract concept. Notionally, it was a society of states. It was essentially an ideational construct with the reality of the notion existing in the structure of state relations. It was a concept designed to correspond with phenomena that had some congruence with the empirical world. The empirical world, though viewed as an objective reality in his time, today is in fact encumbered by the cognitive limitations of human abilities and affective experience from which would emerge abstract conceptions that would only allow human beings to view the external world in probabilistic terms.[7] However, though Manning accepted the notional character of both international society and the states that comprised it, he asserted that in another sense states and hence international society were a reality in that they comprised real structures and people. These had an impact on those who held the notional view of the state. The reality of the notion existed in the effect that the ideational state had on people and on society.

For some international society theorists, considerations went beyond the attempt to understand societal developments in the international system of states. They also contemplated, but quite ambiguously, the possible eventual emergence of a world society that would be based on common values of humanity.[8] This brought the role of the state into question and put the focus of the objectives of society on the individual. The dynamics of this process would link both the individual and the institutions in complex relationships.

Though the international society approach retains its potential in international relations studies, it remains conceptually underdeveloped, particularly in regard to two key concepts that underlie international society theory - society and state.[9] Domestic society is a highly organized collectivity, to a considerable extent centralized and institutionalized. It embodies cultural attributes and a value system that make it distinct from other collectivities. As for international society, the problematique contains significant differences. It exists in a diverse, decentralized multicultural system and consists of territorially defined sovereign states as prime referents. It functions in an anarchic international system which is believed to foster the conflictual nature of the international system. Despite this, however, the international system is not entirely disordered but is one where some degree of order does exist, though it is an order that is fractured and incomplete. In some ways, international violence mimics domestic violence and which, in the past, used to be somewhat proportionate to domestic violence but with today's considerably enhanced munitions and delivery capabilities with mass effects, international violence is developing an ominous potential. However, there are other processes underway in the international system which mitigate the effects of its anarchic character, that is, the co-operative efforts that are continually forming (and disintegrating) among states. Co-operation among states is believed to involve interests and values - that is, belief about what constitutes that which is good - that are expressed in rules that become embedded in international institutions and agreements that emerge from co-operation. In the hierarchy of state concerns and changing conditions in the international system, the values of co-operation can and do change. Not only can changing circumstances alter the advantages of co-operation, but the international system allows states in pursuit of sovereign interests to withdraw from co-operative arrangements. The question arises: where there is evidence of co-operation among states, can we attribute it to common values which are embedded in a common understanding? Values, rules and regulations, or, for that matter, interests, as part of agreements, are not engraved on stone. They are not necessarily enduring or changeless. Nor are they necessarily crucial aspects of co-operative agreements. This is not to say that values can not have important effects but only to suggest that other effects can also be instrumental in bringing about co-operation. For example, when an issue is deemed by one or more states to be important enough for international consideration, the response to the issue will depend on what the primary concern of the international organization is, the extent of membership in the organization, and the structure of power that exists there. An organization that is hegemonic or oligopolistic will produce results that would be different if equality prevailed.[10]

It is this development in co-operation among states that is said to form an incipient international society that is expected as it develops to transform the relations among states. Developing a concept of society, defining its nature, distinguishing its differences and its expanse, in general, clarifying the ambiguities embedded in current notions of the term is a first step in understanding the problematique of society; how it functions and the processes of its development and change. To what extent are the rules and values enfolded in co-operative agreements effective and durable in advancing and preserving international order? Can this order be attributable to the development of societal characteristics? In light of the different status among states, can power politics be eliminated as a factor? Considering the diversity of issues in foreign policy and the hierarchy of values contained in these issues and the sovereign nature of the state which allows it considerable autonomy within the limits of its status, what is it about these agreements that generates values and gives them their durability? The dynamics of the international system is of a complexity that puts considerable obstacles to developing meaningful abstractions that can produce concepts that are definitive and, within the limits of social science methodology, corresponds to the phenomena being observed. It is at the level of theory construction and conceptual development that the usefulness of the idea of an international society concept is limited.

Initially, instigation for international society theorizing came from the observation that the realist perspective of the international system was much too stark, putting overwhelming emphasis on the conflictual nature of the system at the expense of considerable evidence of co-operative relations among states. This suggested to theorists that there was a strand of development in the international system that appeared to ameliorate the anarchical nature of the system. But what did this indicate about the dynamics of the international system, about the processes going on in the system, and about the prospects for the system itself, and so on? The idea was brought forward that the degree of co-operation among states was the beginnings of the formation of an international society, which as it progressed could significantly alter the conflictual nature of the international system, to produce a new and better international and possibly a world order based on societal values. This is the long-term aim of international society theorizing. Whether this would be a natural development or one that is, to some extent, subject to rational management (as some believe) is as yet to be determined. What does need to be determined is the exact nature of the international system: why do co-operative efforts among states arise; what determines their extent and durability; and what is the effect of asymmetrical co-operation in a general anarchic environment?

One of the key concepts that needs further study is that of society. Concepts are mental constructs and as such tend to have definitional deficiencies and indistinct boundaries. Society, as with most concepts, is a problem concept, particularly when it relates to the international system. It needs to be definitionally distinct, relate adequately to empirical phenomena and serve some purpose or have some significance in elaborating a principle or theory, in our case, one that is exemplified by the hypothesis that the formation of an international society will mitigate the conflictual nature of the international system. The purpose in conceptualizing international society is to deal with the problem that exists in the international system.

There are other definitional problems contained within the society concept. Though differences abound among societies particularly those between domestic and international society, common to most descriptions of society is the idea of a social bond, binding elements both subjective and institutional, that draws people into distinct collectivities. The binding elements differ among societies. In domestic society where the societal referents are people and institutions, the binding elements are found in shared values and understandings, common institutions, institutional compulsions, structural influences, etc. In contrast, in international society, the constituent elements, ordering principles and values differ considerably from those found in domestic society. The point is that the profusion of differences, the complex and dynamic nature of the phenomena, makes it difficult to abstract those factors that would reflect the distinctive character of the phenomena that would provide its usefulness in theory formation. Perhaps as an alternative emphasis rather than focusing on society, an expanded perspective examining the question of order in the international system would admit a wider variation of hypotheses to emerge.

Since the concept of international society was first considered as a possible clue to understanding the paradoxical nature of the international system, it also emerged as a way of studying the possible manifestation of a global international order that would be based on universalistic principles and rules of association - becoming known as the English School. The contributors to this volume have emerged from this school or have been inspired by the intellectual discourse surrounding it and are furthering the analysis and assessment of this school and its key concept.

Andrew Hurrell remains convinced that the international society approach, though it is not attempting to develop its own overall theory of world politics, is relevant to international relations analysis. He examines the international society approach through an examination of Hedley Bull's thinking on the subject, bringing into sharp relief the growth and evaluation of his ideas and the ambiguities in his analysis. From his analysis of Bull, Hurrell presents three categorizations of international society, the minimalist, the pluralist, and the solidarist conceptions. For the minimalist view, only a general awareness of a common interest among states is required. This is possible through the existence of general rules informally held by states. The pluralist view embodies deeper relations of co-operation among states that provides a minimum degree of order between states but also provides a 'sense of shared moral values'. The solidarist view goes beyond the focus on the components of international society - the sovereign state - and focuses on the society of states itself and is based on relations that have arrived at a deepened degree of solidarity.

In his later writings, Bull's conception of international society, while retaining aspects of the minimalist view, placed greater emphasis on the need for international society to limit the sovereignty of states asserting that 'whatever rights are due to states or nations or other actors in international relations they are subject to and limited by the rights of the international community'.[11] Bull further noted that the common good of humanity would be advanced by going beyond the common interests of governments in international society. This drift in Bull's thinking towards a sense of the common good of humanity emerged from the transformations occurring in the world, those resulting from the increasing complexities of the problems facing the world involving environment, population explosion, ethnic and human rights concerns, etc.

Hurrell questions the common values that are said to underpin the existence of international society while there have been positive effects resulting from the post Cold War changes involving globalization, the declining emphasis on conflict in the solution of international problems and greater emphasis on issues of economic well-being and human rights, etc., these have also engendered controversies among states in the values embedded in many of these issues.

In conclusion, Hurrell discusses the utility of the international society approach for the solution of problems engendered by world politics. He observes that the strength of this approach lies in its concern with moral issues and the recognition of the crucial effects of states on international affairs. It is an approach that attempts to 'integrate the desirable with the practical'.

Hurrell argues that, though conditions in the international arena have become intensely more complex and densely active and even though a whole range of international theorists have shown an impatience with the state, viewing it as perhaps the main obstacle to progress on norms, particularly moral questions, in world politics, the international society approach presses forward sets of questions which, practically, keep us focused on where the action is. In other words, in effect, this requires being aware of and analysing the fumbling and grappling for the 'procedural consensus on the nature of international institutions and a broader consensus over the substantive issues'. This is the focus of the international society approach of the 1990s.

Nick Wheeler and Tim Dunne have explored the question as to Bull's vision and his understanding to the potential for the formation of a universal moral community. Though Bull is associated with a classical approach to international relations, there were aspects of his thinking which departed from this mode, one that assumed a crucial basic mould in which reason or natural law inhered and upon which the philosophical basis of West European political, social and economic institutions evolved. Bull took a constructivist approach which argued that the moral or ethical principles emanating from this eighteenth century classical position were not primordial or inherent but constructed by people and reproduced. Wheeler and Dunne see this position posing particular difficulties for Bull's theorizing when investigating the possibility of a world moral community. While expounding international society's ability to promote and encourage common interests or common values among states, he also stated that in world society the 'ultimate referent was the individual'. The question of what the ethical basis of world order would be if it was not founded on reason or natural law becomes important in understanding Bull's view of the possibility of a universal moral community.

Bull did not accept the assumption of a primordial natural law foundation for modern society. By identifying what is required for society to exist - security against violence, respect for agreements, stability of possessions - Bull questioned the natural law tradition and assumptions. He also referred to universal goals, meaning basic human rights, but Wheeler and Dunne ask how can one be sure that state leaders share a moral community among one another. Further, how can one assume that there are universal values throughout humanity as a whole which one could assume would project a shaping affect on state leaders. If natural law was not primordial, then one could not assume that the basis for society, a moral community or universal goals, was in place. How did one go from the individual being the ultimate moral referent to a universal moral community in world order and society.

However, given that states define goals, including universal goals, influenced by their own societal culture and values, how can one assume that these variations or divergencies, as there surely will be, marry up amicably with universal goals or produce a universal consensus on the basic requirements of social life which Bull had indicated is necessary for world order?

The second aspect of this problem is whether one assumes compatibility between the notion of 'the individual as the primary referent in world order' and the fact that it is states who are expected to achieve the universal goals producing the universal moral community. Taking one of Bull's basic preconditions - security from violence - of society, it is states who will decide whether this is determined in terms of the rights of the individual or the collective or public. Even if a state internally regards the individual as the ultimate referent, it cannot be assumed that their international behaviour will be such as to produce the sort of world order envisaged by Bull.

Bull saw that trans- or cross-cultural solidarities would be necessary for the emergence of global human rights. This would happen through cosmopolitan moral consciousness in the West that would lead to empathy for the problems of humanity elsewhere. But this would require the West to appreciate the cultural stances of other states and societies as regards human rights. If they did not, then it was unlikely that the West could be persuaded to engage in a global redistribution of wealth felt to be so necessary to Third World needs.

The conundrum here is that Bull saw that through international society some states could pursue the creation of a consensus toward the universal goals. But since states and societies and their cultures give different meanings to human rights, if some set themselves up as arbiters, what happens to the fundamental basis of the sovereign state system - that of recognition of each other's sovereignty, and thus the principle of the coexistence of states?

Richard Little clarifies some of the criticisms of the English School made by English academics not in sympathy with, or who are not part of, the English School. These criticisms have flowed specifically around the three key concepts of international system, international society and world society. In the process, Little sets out to clarify crucial assumptions made by the English School which go some way to clarifying misconceptions and mitigating some of the criticisms. He focuses on three critics who have made these concepts a prime concern in their analysis of the efficacy of the English School contribution to the understanding of international relations: Alan James, Barry Buzan and Martin Shaw. Each of these critics levelled their critiques around the question of boundaries. Little, first of all, sets out the vagaries within these discussions in the English School which have contributed to the arguments surrounding these concepts. These arguments have not been helped by the inconsistent or different uses of these ideas by Wight and Bull, key members of the English School. Little's basic thrust is to analyse some of the key assumptions and implications of English School thinking. He focuses on two areas which he describes as the methodology and ontology of the English School. Clarification of the assumptions in these areas, in his view, would enhance the utility of the English School contribution to the understanding of international relations. Because members of the English School, by and large, have not been explicit in setting out their own methodology, Little maintains that they have nonetheless had a methodology which should not be neglected. First, he argues that there is a strong impulse to understand the particular situation and explain the general levels as well as the link between the two. Further, seeing the international arena as complex as well as amorphous, he suggests it is best viewed from a number of differing perspectives. For the English School, these are categorized into the anarchical international system, the co-operative and value-laden international society and world society which takes into account actions and activities of individuals captured in the term 'transnational'. As regards ontology, this refers to the English School focus on discovering the nature or essence of the three categories or 'levels of analysis', the linkages between them and the implications of both English School methodology and ontology in the analysis. Each of the three critics of the English School is viewed in turn and an attempt is made to 'reconcile the differences' each has with the English School. Of the three critics, Buzan's is found to have more positive resonance with the effort to clarify these concepts and, in particular, to explore the linkages between his use of the sociological concepts of *gemeinschaft* (community) and *gessellschaft* (society).

From Ole Wæver's perspective, the concept of international society as viewed by the English School could contribute more significantly to international relations theory if it is explored more meaningfully, if it possessed a greater theoretical coherence and further buttressed its perspective with empirical evidence. Terms need to be defined more precisely, to define what the nature and constituent elements are of an international society. What are the actual rules that would contribute to the formation of an international society? When do common rules such as those embodied in diplomacy, international agreements, etc. generate common interests and shared values? When shared values emerge, do they emerge as beliefs or conventions? Are the definitive actors in an international society states or the political and other élites that operate within the state? Is cultural homogeneity a factor in the bonding of states?

With the view that US international relations theory is capable of contributing significantly to a discourse on international society, Ole Wæver advocates the integration of US and English School thinking while avoiding the dominance of the American approaches. He briefly analyses the current debates in the US carried on by the institutionalists, constructivists and post-structuralists on the question of international society. In the process, he outlines the intermittent dialogue between American international relations academics and those of the English School. In his own understanding of the international society problematique, he constructs a typology of four meanings of international society.

The international society idea currently is conceptually weak with little explanatory power. However, it is an approach to the study of the international system that is amenable to the historical context and to an analysis of law and culture in the formation of society. International society can also potentially contribute to the study of international relations through attempts at establishing the boundaries of international society. It is through this approach that the present barriers to the understanding of the international society idea can be breached: an understanding of the content and process of co-operation; and the study of collective identity among states and its translation into recognition and acceptance within states; theoretically re-engaging the state to redefine the basis of recognition and legitimacy.

Adam Watson argues that by the Peace of Westphalia creating and confirming independent states, the anti-hegemonial principle is instituted in international society. Concomitant with this was the emergence of the principle of non-interference in the internal affairs of other states. Within a comparatively short period, this international order was put in jeopardy by the ambition of Louis XIV who sought to impose a hegemonic order in Europe through the process of co-optation of other rulers and skilful use of diplomacy. This allowed him to exercise a near hegemonic role 'within the legitimacy established by the Westphalian treaties'.

The reality of international politics is that hegemons have continued to emerge. Today, states, in most cases, are juridically equal with rules and international institutions operating to preserve this juridical equality. States, however, vary considerably in their economies and in their power capabilities. This allows the more successful states the opportunity to manipulate the anti-hegemonial framework of international society in ways that encourage other states to accept this dominance.

He goes further to point out that the reality has been that rather different hegemons have continued to emerge. The more successful being those who in general show the ability to manipulate the anti-hegemonial framework in ways that encourage other states to accept this dominance.

In Robert Jackson's view, international borders provide the juridical identities of community constructs that form an international society of states. These borders exist through mutual recognition and provide a logic for the existence of an international society concept. It is an historically constructed international order. Where realism sees the international system as anarchical in nature, there is very little room for co-operation and commonality of interests and values. Revolutionism, in focusing on universal values of humankind that bind humankind into a world community, views boundaries as an impediment to these ends. Rationalists see those relations among states that involve shared values and interests. Boundaries, in this perspective, are viewed as shared structures embodying shared values.

States are not value-free institutions but possess norms and values that transcend those embodied in their populations. In this sense, states can be seen as political communities. What exists today is an international society on a global scale. State boundaries allow for considerable diversity in institutions and values to exist in the developing international society of states.

Robert Jackson is arguing that international boundaries are a key fundamental value in international society, that they are highly respected by the states who have them in common and rarely violated. Moreover, he argues that of the three approaches to the international theory of the English School, rationalism offers the more accurate theory and operation of international boundaries, because in general they have acquired moral and legal status such that there is an international obligation on the part of states to observe them. This is underlined by his discussion of the cases of Croatia and Bosnia, not so much the actions of Serbs, Croats and Muslims but the response of the international community which has called on all parties to respect the existing international boundaries and the rights of minorities.

Essentially, Jackson is elaborating the evolution of the particular character of international boundaries that emerge with the Westphalian peace. Wight had observed that territory belonged to rulers and, hence, sovereignty, and by implication the boundaries were set in this way. Even when the principle of self-determination came in to determine sovereignty, it did not affect the position of international boundaries. Jackson points out that Germany was not allowed to redraw the boundaries of Europe on the basis of self-determination and the Asian and African states had to use 'pre-existing subordinate territorial jurisdictions'. Likewise, the new states arising from the collapse of the Soviet Union and Yugoslavia. Their arrival on the scene may have been announced in terms of the principle of self-determination but it was the pre-existing boundaries which became the international boundaries. Inherited boundaries have been legitimated. In effect, this is a version of prescription to which Wight referred.

The larger point which Jackson makes from this analysis of international boundaries is that international society allows for the possibility of the 'good life', for people to construct in their own time, that international society allows for and accommodates the plurality of human endeavour, that this is made possible if international boundaries are observed and non-intervention respected.

James Mayall analyses the theory, practice and problems of intervention in the affairs of other states via international society perspective. In this way, he is able to point out the practical and theoretical features of international society, its shortcomings as well as the real point of international society. Indeed, he doubts that the rising tide of criticism of international society theory by cosmopolitans and communitarians has yet to find a way forward on the question and ethics of intervention.

The origins of non-intervention come out of the Peace of Westphalia with the emergence of sovereign states and mutual recognition. In effect, this was an agreement to leave each prince in charge of ideology in his territory free from outside intervention. This is the principle that was later stated in UN Charter Article 2.7; that intervention can only occur if there is a threat to international peace and security.

Today's problems are complicating traditional responses to international crises. The main reason for this is that the crises concern an area with which the UN Charter does not concern itself. This is the problem of civil conflicts, particularly those in failed states where public authority of any kind is lacking.

Mayall traces the evolution of the theory and practice of international intervention. In the cases of Yugoslavia, Somalia, Rwanda and Haiti, interventions have been conducted so as to conform to Westphalian principles. As Mayall puts it, these are the principles of internal legitimacy and external sovereignty. With failed states, it is wellnigh impossible to apply these principles. In circumstances where public authority has collapsed and humanitarian concerns have become paramount, Chapter 7 of the UN Charter does not provide a clear rationale for intervention. These circumstances also pose a theoretical problem to international society theory as envisaged by its founders. The concept of international society accepts the notion of sovereign states and the immunity of their domestic affairs from external interference. This, however, does not provide a theoretical basis for humanitarian intervention in what Mayall refers to as 'collapsed states'. More to the point, the practice of the international society of states in these circumstances indicates a reluctance to intervene.

The point about international society which is underlined by this analysis is that it is the emergence of a society of states that creates a degree of order and certain rules potentially to handle problems that might require intervention under circumstances which have the possibility of success. In turn, it is domestic order that is necessary for the state to endure. An international society based on the sovereignty of states as one of its main pillars cannot exist if domestic disorder prevails to the extent that state authority is said to be lacking. Imperial solutions might be revived to restore order in collapsed states but this does not find support in today's international climate, nor does the notion of breaking the rules under which intervention is currently allowed by resorting to support of particular factions in a civil struggle. As it now stands, international society appears reluctant to move beyond humanitarian intervention which would violate the traditional principles embodied in the concept of an international society of states.

Yale Ferguson engages in an appreciation of Bull and his Anarchical Society which both praises aspects of Bull's argument and ideas and strongly questions or criticizes other parts of it. He observes that the elegance and persuasion with which Bull argued his case blunted the impact that American academic behaviouralism might have had in Britain and the Commonwealth countries, and preserved an analytical approach to the classical tradition derived from an appreciation of philosophy, history and law.

Ferguson notes the well-known distance of Bull's thinking from realism and is particularly attracted to his remarks in which he alluded to the possibility of an international order not based upon the state but on the whole of humankind. Ferguson was led to his reservations concerning the concept of international society through his view of the ambiguity of the state as a concept in international relations. State sovereignty exists as an established legal doctrine with validity in international law. The state itself is not a coherent, centralized agent. While the state does exist, it is not the only actor in the politics of a society. Other actors exist that function outside the control of the state that form part of the governance of society. If the patterns of governance in societies are fairly widely dispersed, this brings into question the validity of the concept of an international society based on the notion of sovereign states. Ferguson sees all polities having authorities that 'govern' in their space but are not necessarily governments in the traditional sense. It is his conclusion that focusing one's analysis of international relations theory based on the notion of international society will not lead toward 'true understanding' of international relations.

Fulvio Attiná explores an alternative way of viewing the international system and international society by looking at the effect of social cleavages which translate onto the international political scene. As in the international society approach which focuses on states, these societal cleavages at the international level also concentrate on states as they aggregate into like-minded groups with common perspectives regarding the issues on the global agenda affecting the 'governmental coalitions in multilateral negotiation'. Attiná's critique of the international society approach concerns its concentration only on the common values, institutions, etc., ignoring the concomitant disorder, obstruction and separation that are also present, whether looking at the domestic or international scenes, and their effect on the character of the global issues that emerge. His concern is to focus on international change which is more easily discerned by not only taking into account the power configuration and diplomacy but the groupings of states that form around social difference and structures which influence the alignments of states over issues on the global agenda. It is this dominating aggregate of states that is inspired by Europe and of European expansion elsewhere, which has provoked a reaction at many levels.

R. J. Barry Jones questions the ambiguities of the conceptualization of international society by the English School. Some, notably Bull and Watson, view international society as a natural phenomenon. Others, such as Manning, see international society as a normative construct. In Jones' view, this dichotomy in effect limits the analysis of political events. In most cases, the political nature of international relations, in his view, is defined by both empirical factors and the normative foundations of this phenomenon. Therefore, to arrive at what constitutes international society, it will be necessary to discover the nature of political activity and the political order that provides the environment for this activity. In this context, the complex relationship between empirical analysis and normative theory needs to be understood.

International society theorists view political phenomena as occurring at the level of states. It is essentially at the level of élite decision-makers within states. International society, however, at the level of élites, does not necessarily translate into international society at the public level. There is no reason to assume that international society at the élite level will endure. What international relations theorists should consider is the extent that international society contributes to anti-systemic impulsions, that is, that international society itself generates within states an antipathy towards international society.

Notes

1 Brice, James, *International Relations* (London, Macmillan, 1922), p. 245.
2 Ibid., pp. 267-8.
3 Carr has used the term 'utopian', rather than 'idealistic', to avoid confusion with the ideological contrast of idealism with materialism then prevalent in Marxist discourse.
4 Carr, E. H., *The Twenty Years' Crisis 1919-1939* (London, Macmillan, 1946), p. 92.
5 The best discussion of this is to be found in Dunne, T., 'International relations theory: the invention of an international society tradition', D.Phil. Thesis, Oxford University (1993).
6 Manning, C. A. W., *The Nature of International Society* (London, G. Bells and Sons Ltd, 1962).
7 Despite our inability to know anything with certainty, enough of the 'real' world

can be discerned and validated to allow a sufficient understanding of the phenomena that would allow for creativity, manipulation and reproduction.

The idea that we cannot know reality with certainty emerged out of the study by W. K. Heisenberg of sub-atomic particles and the Uncertainty Principle (1927) that this inspired. This, however, did not bring about an end to sub-atomic particle research. The imaginative development and application of vector analysis allowed for continued research in this area of quantum physics and the validation of hypothesis on a probabilistic basis.

8 Bull, H., *The Anarchical Society: A Study of Order in World Politics* (London, Macmillan, 1977), pp. 20–2.

9 A particularly interesting discussion of the problem of the state can be found in a book by Ferguson, Y. H. and Mansbach, R.W., *The State, Conceptual Chaos, and the Future of International Relations Theory*, GSIS Monograph Series in World Affairs, University of Denver (London, Lynne Rienner, 1989). 'The state has little substance as an empirical concept and virtually no utility as an analytic concept; it obscures far more than it clarifies' (p. 81).

10 For an example, compare issues placed before the UN Security Council and similar issues that come before the UN General Assembly. The power structure in the former is oligarchic; in the latter, widely dispersed.

Of particular interest in this regard, see Schoenbourn, T. J., 'International trade and protection of the environment: the continuing search for reconciliation', *The American Journal of International Law*, April 1997, pp. 288–313.

For a discussion of co-operation based on interest and in the context of regimes, see Keohane, R. O., *After Hegemony: Cooperation and Discord in the World Political Economy* (Princeton, NJ, Princeton University Press, 1984), pp. 49–64.

11 Bull, H., 'Justice in international relations', in *The 1983–84 Hagey Lectures* (Waterloo, Ontario, University of Waterloo, 1984).

2

Society and Anarchy in International Relations

ANDREW HURRELL[1]

Writing in the late 1960s, Hedley Bull argued that realism had run its course, that its truths had been absorbed, and that it was time to move on and focus not on power politics but on the nature of order and on the idea of international society.[2] Today the same question may be asked of theories built around the concept of international society. Have the ideas of the international society theorists now run their course? Traditionalist approaches, such as those expounded by Bull and other members of the British Committee may well have raised fundamental issues, provided much-needed historical depth, and opened up suggestive lines of enquiry. But do they continue to represent a valid or viable approach to the study of International Relations? Or does the statism and traditionalism of the 'English School' now lead only to sterile repetition and empty scolasticism?[3] Whilst acknowledging the limitations and criticisms, this chapter seeks to make the case for continuing to take the idea of international society seriously and for believing that, despite the dramatic changes of the late 1980s, it still represents a central point of departure for the study of international relations. It argues that some of the criticisms of the international society tradition are misplaced, and that the moral and political dilemmas that lay at the heart of the tradition remain very much our own dilemmas from which there is little sign of escape or resolution. This chapter addresses three questions:

- Which features of the international society tradition are of most relevance to the academic study of international relations?
- How might we begin to assess the strength of international society in the contemporary international system? How strong is the sense of common interests, common rules and common institutions that Bull saw as so central to the existence of an international society?
- Does the international society tradition provide any guidance for grappling with the moral dilemmas of the post-Cold War international system?

A short chapter of this kind cannot provide answers to these very large questions. But it can try to unravel some of the complexities involved and to sketch out the main lines of the case for continuing to take the idea of international society seriously. In part, then, this chapter looks backward, in particular to the work of Hedley Bull. But it also seeks to take the debate forward by asking how Bull's questions, categories and arguments might be applied to the conditions of the post-Cold War world.

The tradition of international society

Which features of the international society tradition are of most relevance to the academic study of international relations in the 1990s? The starting-point for Bull, as for others writing within the international society tradition, was that a reasonable cohesive international society had developed within the classical European state system but that it was now under challenge. Thus in response to a readers' comments on *The Anarchical Society*, Bull wrote in 1975: 'I am not sure that it is correct to say ... that in the book I see "an international society emerging". I think I rather argue that international society exists but is in decline.'[4] To understand why it might be in decline, it is necessary to review Bull's understanding of the ingredients that together make up the cement of international society.

What might bring states to co-operate in international life? On what might order and co-operation be based? There have been many answers to this question: power and coercion, self-interest and reciprocal benefits, institutionalized habit or inertia, the existence of a sense of community, procedural legitimacy of the process of rule creation, or the moral suasion that derives from a shared sense of justice. The theorists of international society sought to understand order and co-operation in terms of *both* power *and* the operation of legal and moral norms - what Butterfield and Wight spoke of as 'the principles of prudence and moral obligation which have held together the international society of states throughout its history, and still hold it together'.[5] The dual focus, seeking to hold fast to many of the guiding arguments of realism but at the same time recognizing the important role for legal and moral norms, explains why the tradition is in many ways best viewed as a form of liberal realism. It also lies at the heart of many of the unresolved tensions and contributes to the uncertainty (visible on many readings lists) as to whether Bull should be placed in the liberal or realist camp. At its core, the tradition of international society represents a sustained attempt to understand the relationship between the power political order and the international legal order (the economic order is of course seriously neglected), and to argue that no account of order in international life can ignore the complexities and ambiguities that lie at the heart of this relationship.

More specifically, we can isolate three important arguments. First, staying close to realism, there is the continued importance of power and the politics of power. Thus if we take the 'institutions' of international society as analysed by Bull, power remains central: the balance of power, the role of Great Powers and Great Power management, and the institution of war. Indeed there is a very important sense in which the balance of power remains the most important foundation. Without a balance of power and without sustained and stable understandings between the major powers on the conduct of their mutual relations, then the 'softer' elements of international order (international law, international organizations, the existence of shared values) will be so many castles in the air. Order, then, will often be based on hierarchy, on coercion and on power, and the element of 'society' may appear tenuous - especially when seen from the perspective of the weak. For Bull the term 'society' is justified to the extent that such a coercive order rests on a shared set of understandings and mutually recognized interests among the major powers.[6]

The continued acceptance of many of the central tenets of realism is evident in many places in Bull's work. His lectures on theory spoke of the 'truths of realism that each new generation must learn afresh'. He praised Aron's *Peace and War* as 'surely the most profound work that any contemporary has written in the attempt "to comprehend the implicit logic of relations among politically organized collectivities"'.[7] He is clear that Carr's critique of liberal utopianism is essentially justified.

> In the present writer's view the main body of Carr's analysis of what international politics is like, is correct. ... The doubts that arise concern not the truth of the propositions about the world contained in Carr's 'realist critique', but the practical defects of stating them, without at the same time, exploring, in its own terms, the moral aspects of the problem.[8]

The acceptance of many of the central elements of realism is most apparent in the early writings and papers: in his attacks on both the viability and the desirability of general and complete disarmament; in his explicit statements in *Control of the Arms Race* in favour of the centrality of the balance of power; in his early argument against solidarist or 'Grotian' conceptions of international society. But this realist strand remains important and is evident in many discussions of international society in the 1980s: for example, in his criticism of the superpowers for failing to exercise their traditional 'responsibilities'; or in his partial acceptance of the arguments of Robert Tucker that greater equality between North and South had a 'more disturbing side'.

Yet whilst international society might have to start with realism, it could never end with realism. Again there are many examples. Although he praised

Waltz's *Theory of International Politics* as 'an important book', he points to the limits of structural realism:

> If this first, rigorously 'systematic' account of international politics leads to conclusions so much at loggerheads with common sense as that the superpowers are still dominating world politics and that this is in the best interests of all of us, this suggests that an explanation in terms simply of the abstract logic of the system of states is by itself quite inadequate.[9]

These limits partly concern the failure of realism to acknowledge the scope for shared interests and the role of legal and moral obligation. But they are also based on the need for an inclusive order that, at least to some degree, reflects the interests and values of the weaker members of international society. This lies at the heart of Bull's fascination with Carr's arguments for appeasement and is reflected, most centrally, in his concern for an accommodation with the Third World and with those states that have sought to challenge the historic dominance of the West. It is precisely at this point where justice becomes a constituent part of order and where power political and moral arguments come together, but never wholly coincide, that the relationship between order and justice in Bull's work becomes most ambiguous.[10]

> No consensus seems possible at the present time that is founded simply upon the interests of the major powers in international order – or peace and security – and does not seek also to accommodate the demands of the weaker powers, and especially the Third World, for just change.[11]

Second, in addition to its power political underpinning, order is reflected in the international legal system and in the multiplicity of rules, norms and conventions that regulate international relations. The force of the rules and institutions of international society derives partly from considerations of legitimacy (the constitutive function of law and its role in defining the membership rules of the club of states) and partly from considerations of mutual advantages and reciprocal benefit.[12] States co-operate because, however different their values or conflictual their interests, they see the possibility of gain. There is thus the central idea that rules, laws and conventions can emerge without an overarching authority. They are of mutual benefit because they help shape expectations, help increase the predictability of international life, hence reducing the political chaos and uncertainty. Almost all accounts of the role of law on which Bull bases his analysis, describe its political impact in terms of the benefits of order, the costs of violation and the extent to which it provides an order based on the coordination of interests and of patterned expectations.

> Another major weakness of the indictment [that rules depend on the power, interests or values of one group of states] is that the most central rules of

> international intercourse do not depend on their validity on the special interests of one side but on reciprocal interests. The rules that treaties should be observed, that sovereignty should be respected, that states should not interfere in one another's internal agreed frontiers, of immunity or inviolability of diplomatists – to name only a few – can in no sense be viewed simply as instruments of the special interests of a particular group. This, indeed, is why the Third World countries have sought actually to become part of the international order, even while sometimes purporting to denounce it. It is also what makes nonsense of the attempt to account for international law in terms of a class theory of law.[13]

There is therefore a powerful strand in Bull's work that sees cooperation emerging on the back of shared interests and of the functional benefits provided by international institutions. But where Bull differs from more recent US theorists of co-operation is on the importance that he attached to the close study of state practice and to the historical processes by which understanding of common interest evolved and changed through time.[14] Denying that 'Grotian theorists' had any great confidence in abstract human reason, Bull wrote:

> Grotius and other exponents of the natural law theory certainly did have 'confidence in human reason', but the Grotian idea of international society later came to rest on the element of consensus in the actual practice of states, and it is on this rather than on 'human reason' that (in common with other contemporary 'Grotians') I rest the case for taking international society seriously.[15]

This leads to the third, and most distinctive, feature of the international society approach which is to emphasize the role of common values and a common sense of being part of a society. One strand of Bull's work rejects any natural law foundations, or, at least, seeks to develop some empirical equivalent to natural law, some set of general principles without which no society could be said to exist – the influence of H. L. A. Hart is important here. The aim is to identify a conception of international society consistent with self-interest and with the realities of power. Yet, at the same time, there was the awareness that international society could not be understood solely in these terms and had to be rooted within the cultural and historical forces that had helped shape the consciousness of society at any particular time and had moulded perceptions of common values and common purposes. In other words Bull is constantly drawn by Wight's argument that 'International society, then, on this view, can be properly described only in historical and sociological depth'.[16] From this perspective, even the quintessentially realist 'institution' of the balance of power appears in a different light: the balance of power viewed not as a mechanical arrangement, but rather in terms of the common and shared understandings between states as to the meaning of the balance of power and the role that it should play; less as a formal mechanism than as a metaphor that assists power political bargaining and legitimizes agreed outcomes.

The discussion of consensus and shared values has given rise to much misunderstanding. First, the emphasis on normative coherence and on legal and moral obligation can easily lead to a neglect of the more starkly realist elements in Bull's conception of international society. Second, Bull's discussion of consensus rests most importantly on the emergence of an agreed framework of rules and institutions. This is a procedural and not a substantive value consensus. The shared values and the shared framework of understanding have to do primarily with the creation by dialogue and common consent of rules and institutions by which clashes of interests and conflicting values can be mediated.[17] At its heart lies the institutional or diplomatic culture of the classical European state system orchestrated by specialized élites with at least some commitment to shared values and perhaps a shared world-view. This is the dominant line of thinking, not just in Bull but to a still greater extent in Wight and Butterfield. Bull was well aware, first, that co-operation can emerge without any substantive consensus over societal or cultural values; and second, that, as demonstrated by the existence of civil wars, severe conflict can often occur against the background of a high level of consensus over core values.

But running through Bull's work is a persistent, and nagging, question, to which an unequivocal answer never emerges (and perhaps can never emerge): Given that a substantive value consensus did appear to have played an important role in the classical European state system and given that many of the major classical theorists of the state system recognized such a role (for example Heeren, Rousseau, Burke and Vattel), what has been the impact of increased cultural heterogeneity on the workings of international society? According to Bull, a common cultural tradition may contribute to international society in three ways. First, the existence of a common epistemology, a common language and a common cultural tradition will facilitate communication between the members of international society. Second, the existence of such a common culture reinforces the bonds of common interest by adding a sense of moral obligation. Third, the existence of a common value system will help ensure that states place the same relative valuation on such objectives as order, justice, peace, etc.

The problematic relationship between a shared sense of common interest in the workings of common institutions and procedures on the one hand and underlying societal or cultural values on the other was never resolved in Bull's work. One difficulty is that the realist insistence on the separation of the domestic and the international and the heavy statist focus precluded any systematic exploration of the ways in which understandings of international order (in, say, 1815, 1918, 1945 or indeed 1989) were deeply coloured by domestic economic, political or ideological factors. It also precluded systematic study of the transnational processes by which ideas and values are transmitted through the international system, particularly when unmediated by direct state action.

But even within its own terms, Bull's later writings came to no settled conclusion and the case is made for both 'optimistic' and 'pessimistic readings'. In many later papers he examines the idea that the absorption of western political forms has been only superficial or rhetorical, that it is traditional cultural attitudes that determine political behaviour rather than ideas and attitudes imported from the West, and that the deep cultural divide between the West and the Third World will always work against the emergence of a truly global international society. But, as against this, he makes a number of points.[18]

First, at the level of theory he argued that 'it would be difficult to show that rules on international law or diplomacy or conventions of warfare or trade cannot be made to operate across cultural barriers'.[19] He spoke of common rules being improvised 'as a consequence of a perceived interest on both sides in improvising them' and gave as an example the 'rules of the game' developed by the superpowers out of their common interest in avoiding nuclear war.[20] Moreover, in considering the revolt against the West, he saw much evidence of the continued existence of international society based on common interests but without the support of a common culture. Thus, as regards international law, the Third World challenge has to be set against a general acceptance by the majority of Third World states of the advantages provided by the prevailing framework of international law. Third World states have recognized an interest in the benefits that law can provide and, by asserting their rights as states, they have established their place in the international legal order. Similarly, as regards diplomatic conventions, Third World states have generally viewed these as a source of practical benefit and as important symbols of their newly-won statehood and independence. Finally, there is the participation of the Third World in the work of international organizations. 'The clearest indication of the willingness of Third World countries to pursue their objectives within the framework of common rules and institutions has been the importance they have attached to the United Nations.'[21]

Second, there is the question as to whether it is in fact true that the world consists of a limited number of cultures each with its own indestructible and immutable core. If it is not and if cultures develop and change over time, then, Bull argues, 'there is at all events no reason in principle why European or Western norms and institutions of international society cannot be transferred to cultures that are different and display some capacity for resistance'.[22] Given that all cultures are amalgams of various cultural components and influences, he therefore questions the notion that western ideas on international relations should remain permanently outside the experience of other cultures.

Third, given the belief that at least provisional 'rules of the game' can and do emerge between states with very different cultures, there is again no reason why, if they continued to be observed for long enough, these rules should not themselves come to be the focus for a new set of norms and values and, gradually, to draw the cultures of the two sides together.[23] Finally, and perhaps most persistently, there is the question as to whether there are not in fact elements of a new global culture that help to mitigate the divisive impact of increased cultural heterogeneity. At various times Bull considers the process of economic and technological unification and the culture of 'modernization' that this brings with it. He seems reluctant to accord it too great a role, arguing that it could never bring about social or political unification, that its influence is often limited to élite groups and that it has on occasions provoked a serious traditionalist backlash. And yet 'it is a basic fact at work in world politics at present, and it facilitates the workings of international society and its rules'.[24]

Whilst the answers may be elusive, these questions remain important. Indeed they have become ever more important as the normative ambitions of international society continue to expand. As co-operation comes increasingly to involve the creation of rules that affect very deeply the domestic structures and organization of states, that invest individuals and groups within states with rights and duties, and which seek to embody some notion of a common good (human rights, democratization, the environment, the construction of more elaborate and intrusive inter-state security orders), then these questions of society and community re-emerge and the validity of models of co-operation that exclude them needs to be questioned. There are many examples of the increased intrusion of international institutions into domestic affairs: the way in which the focus of efforts to management of an increasingly integrated economy has shifted from trade rules, to investment regimes, to discussions of different forms of capitalism. Or the way in which pursuing global sustainability has moved from conservation issues towards international negotiation of the very 'American way of life' that George Bush was so reluctant to discuss at the Earth Summit in Rio in 1992.

As many critics have pointed out this complex picture of how order is promoted sits uneasily under the single term 'society'. The term 'society' describes a continuum from the barest recognition of common interests on the one hand to the conscious creation of clearly defined rules and institutions through which those common interests can be promoted on the other.[25] Indeed Stanley Hoffmann criticized Bull for not distinguishing between types of international society in the way in which Martin Wight distinguished between various categories of states systems.[26] In a similar way Raymond Cohen argued that Bull failed to show how in different international societies the various individual elements of 'society' relate to each other and together contribute to the maintenance of order.[27] Given this difficulty, it is important to break up the various factors on which order and co-operation might depend and also to identify from Bull's own works three categories of international society.[28]

In the first place, there is a *minimalist* conception of international society which is built around the gradual recognition of common interests between states - the notion that their own interests will be furthered by mutual respect for each others' sovereignty, by recognizing certain limits on the use of force, and by accepting the principle that agreements between them should be honoured. At this level the common rules will be vague, inchoate and ill defined - implicit and provisional understandings rather than formal and widely recognized rules. At this level, too, considerations of power and coercion are also likely to play a major role. The intellectual godfather of this view of international society is Hobbes and can be found in his argument that, even in the state of nature, states and princes are able to recognize and follow - out of considerations of prudence and expediency - certain laws of nature that will help attain peace: rules governing the respect of covenants, the recognition of the immunity of envoys, the willingness to enter into arbitration, etc.[29] On the basis of these conditional and fragile 'articles of peace' Stanley Hoffmann argues that '[W]e can see in Hobbes the father of utilitarian theories of international law and relations'.[30] On this first level, then, Hobbes is pointing to the most basic rules of coexistence without which any conception of international society would be impossible. Indeed, for Bull himself, just as for earlier theorists such as Pufendorf, Wolff and Vattel, the first stage in the argument in favour of international society consists in the application of Hobbes' own arguments about the differences between domestic and international life: that states are less vulnerable than individuals and have less fear of sudden death; that they are unequal in power and resources; and that, if they are rational, they will be less tempted to destroy each other than will individuals in a state of nature and will be able to develop at least minimal rules of coexistence based on self-interest and rational prudence.[31]

Second, there is a *pluralist* conception of international society build around the goal of coexistence and an ethic of difference. Such a conception can be said to exist when these rudimentary rules of coexistence become embodied in more or less explicit and formal rules and institutions, when there exists a shared consciousness of the reality of international society and of the rights and duties of states within it and, finally, where this consciousness is buttressed by the existence of a common language, common culture and a common civilization. This is the conception of international society within Europe embodied in the tradition that runs from Vattel to Oppenheim: the idea that there exists a society able to provide minimal order between states, that this society is different in kind from domestic society, that it is based on what Vattel called the 'natural liberty of states', but that this liberty is tamed, at least to some degree, by a sense of shared moral values. Thus in Vattel the untrammelled freedom of states is balanced by a still strong belief in the residual obligations and restraints derived from natural law. Whilst in Oppenheim an international legal system which accords states great license in waging war was balanced by an implicit belief in the limited ends for which nineteenth-century European states would in fact wage war and by the constraints that resulted from their internal constitution. It was with this tradition that Bull was most directly concerned, both in his theoretical writing on international relations and in his analysis of the 'old' European international order.

Third, there is a more truly Grotian, or *solidarist* conception.[32] Here we are dealing with an idea of international society in which the interests of the whole form the central focus rather than the independence of the states of which it is made up; a view in which the domestic analogy is at least partially accepted; a view in which international society is about more than the provision of the necessary framework for the minimalist goal of continued coexistence between states. The promotion of more extensive goals will inevitably be based on a far broader degree of solidarity and consensus. They might involve the effective implementation of concepts of just and unjust war or of international human rights, or of measures to deal with problems faced by the collectivity of states as a whole (the provision of increased economic development or removing the threat of nuclear destruction).

If we go back to the conclusions of 'The Grotian Conception of International Society', Bull appears to be deeply sceptical of such an extended view of international society. International society is only capable of coming together and agreeing on certain very limited purposes. Attempts to implement a truly Grotian conception would both reduce the efficacy of many of the rules of a more limited international society and indeed possibly threaten its very existence by placing too great a burden on such a fragile structure.[33] Similarly, the main thrust of the argument of *The Anarchical Society* is that the international society of states represents the best, albeit very fragile and imperfect, answer to the dangers of the international anarchy by providing the basis for the promotion of certain basic goals: the survival of the state system itself, the maintenance of the independence of individual states, the setting of limits to use and severity of military force, etc.

If we look, however, at Bull's later writings, the balance has shifted and the emergence of the revolt against western dominance appears to form a central part of that shift. Two points can be made. In the first place, Bull's definition of international society has come to lay progressively more weight on the need to limit the absolute rights of sovereignty of individual states. Rejecting Vattel's view that international law derived from the 'natural liberty of nations', Bull argues:

> whatever rights are due to states or nations or other actors in international relations, they are subject to and limited by the rights of the international community. The rights of sovereign states, and of sovereign peoples or nations, derive from the rules of the international community or society and are limited by them.[34]

Or again:

> It should be clear that whatever case might have been made out at earlier periods in history for such a doctrine of the natural or inherent rights of sovereign states or of independent political communities it cannot be acceptable now.[35]

In the second place, there is a narrowing of the gap which so clearly existed in *The Anarchical Society* between international order on the one hand and world order on the other. In *The Anarchical Society* the focus is firmly on 'the society of states through which such order as exists in world politics is now maintained'. Yet in The Hagey Lectures he writes:

> Measures to avoid these dangers, to advance the world common good, take us beyond the sense of solidarity or common interests among governments that underlines the international society of states, which is rooted in the desire of states to maintain themselves.[36]

What accounts for this shift? First, because the goal of minimal order has become less and less adequate given the range and seriousness of the problems facing international society. Second, because the growth of interdependence and the degree to which individual societies depend on each other for security, prosperity and their ability to control their environment means that the legitimacy of governments now depends on their capacity to meet a vastly increased range of claims and demands. Third, because of the emergence of an albeit still very fragile cosmopolitan moral consciousness that demands that greater attention be paid to questions of individual human rights and the promotion of certain minimum standards of human welfare throughout the world. Despite the obvious limits of this consciousness and the practical difficulties of acting upon it, 'the mere existence of this moral concern with welfare on a world scale represents a major change in our sensibilities'.[37] Equally, there is the reality of an 'emerging sense of a world common good' and increasing recognition that the world as a whole faces certain common dangers in relation to nuclear war, ecological disruption and the global balance between population and resources.

Yet this awareness that the objectives of international society have expanded, that a limited, pluralist conception of international society is no longer adequate adds to the tension between power and law and, more generally, between pluralist and solidarist conceptions of international society.[38] From his early discussion in 'The Grotian Conception' to the Hagey Lectures there is an abiding concern with the disjuncture between the vaulting normative ambitions of contemporary international society and its precarious power political foundations; between a legal order still built very largely around mutual respect for each other's sovereignty and independence on the one hand and attempts to construct far-reaching legal regimes that impinge heavily on the ways in which domestic societies are organized on the other. Despite the increased density of the rules, institutions and organizations that make up international society, there is continued awareness of the dangers of what Bull calls premature global solidarism, of placing too great a strain on the thin fabric of international society.

There are thus four elements to the political dilemmas with which international society theorists have wrestled: first, that a cohesive international society existed within the classical European state system but it has been challenged by developments in the twentieth century; second, that although the state system is under challenge, it remains the primary global political institution; third, that as the foundations of international society have been weakened, so the demands made upon it have grown enormously as a pluralist order of coexistence can no longer be viewed as either morally acceptable or politically adequate; and finally, that in seeking to adapt the state system to these more demanding circumstances and to extend the range of goals, there is a constant danger of undermining the limited gains that have been made. Far from being complacent or optimistic, there is a powerful strand of pessimism that again betrays the influence of realism. The pillars of the Westphalian temple may indeed be in decay but the prospect is not of an alternative form of world order but rather of still more dangerous and divisive anarchy.

Society and anarchy in the contemporary international system

To what extent can the international system in the 1990s still be said to constitute a society? How strong is the sense of common interest, common rules and common institutions on which the idea of international society has been built? There are three arguments around which an optimistic case can be constructed.[39]

In the first place one can point to the enormous expansion in the number, range and scope of international institutions and to the vastly increased density of international society. For liberal progressivists this is leading to a gradual, if uneven and long-term, process of institutional enmeshment in which the 'anarchical' elements of international relations will be gradually tamed, and in which the very notion of the international anarchy is being redefined. Thus, Mark Zacher argues that states 'are becoming increasingly *enmeshed* in a network of interdependencies and regulatory/collaborative arrangements from which exist is generally not a feasible option'.[40] At face value, the sheer growth in the number and range of international institutions seems to give the lie to the idea that international society might in some way be under threat or challenge.

A second argument for optimism concerns the relationship between law and power. In a negative sense, the historic tension between law and power has been lessened by the ending of the deep power political and ideological conflicts and cleavages that have scarred the face of twentieth-century international history and by the apparent decline of great power military rivalry in the post-Cold War period. More positively the revival of the United Nations can be viewed as reducing historic tension that has existed between law and morality on the one hand and effective power and enforcement on the other.

Third, an optimistic reading of the current state of international society would stress the increased signs of normative convergence and the growth of consensus on the fundamental beliefs to which politically dominant groups adhere. Whereas Bull believed 'western values' to be under severe challenge in the 1970s and early 1980s and was sceptical about claims that universal values were emerging and could be acted upon, today we can point to the remarkably broad assertion and acceptance of human rights and democracy, liberal economics, and widely accepted ideas of sustainable development and the spread of unifying culture of modernization.[41] Even without accepting the more extreme forms of western triumphalism, the position of western values has undoubtedly undergone dramatic change. In the economic domain such a position stresses the undermining of the challenges to liberal capitalism with the collapse of the socialist regimes in the former Soviet Union; the widespread move away from statist, developmentalist thinking in very large parts of the developing world; and the increasing power of the global economic system to homogenize the practical range of economic policies and, in effect, to make any notion of 'opting out' of the global capitalist system all but impossible. It has become common for liberal economists to speak in terms of a 'universal convergence'. Or, as John Williamson and Stephan Haggard put it: 'At least in intellectual terms, we today live in one world rather than three.'[42]

A similar story can be told in terms of democracy and human rights: that the previous deep fissures within the human rights regime between North and South and between East and West have been eased; that an increasing number of states proclaim themselves to be democratic and that many of previous opponents of democracy have come to view political democracy as an intrinsic rather than instrumental value; that within international institutions the pursuit of human rights has been broadened to include democracy and good governance; and that, in marked contrast to the 1980s, democratization has become a much more salient feature of the foreign policy agendas of major states. In both Europe and the Americas, democratic governance has emerged as a condition of the membership of regional institutions. International lawyers have begun to talk in terms of emerging international right to democratic governance and to argue that international legitimacy will depend increasingly on how domestic societies are ordered politically.[43]

A further example is provided by the gathering international consensus around the need for concerted international efforts to protect the environment and the crystallization in institutions and international agreements of new normative principles (sustainable development, the precautionary principle, notions of intergenerational equity, of the common heritage, of common concern, the duty on the part of the rich to help secure sustainability in the South through the transfer of technology and resources). Finally the proponents of a cosmopolitan culture of modernization based on a secular, scientific and technological understanding of the world have become increasingly vocal, viewing ideological homogenization as one of the central consequences of the increased pace of economic and technological globalization.

There are, however, five important arguments which lead one to question this picture and which underline the still precarious character of international society in the 1990s. First, the consensus over core values is a good deal less strong than recent rhetoric and indeed many international agreements would suggest. Thus the range of economic policy debates may well have narrowed, but one of the paradoxes of increased interdependence has been to increase the importance of differences between 'rival capitalisms', particularly between 'western' and 'Asian' models. Equally, whilst liberal capitalism may well have defeated its most obvious rivals, it is far from clear that it has an answer to the challenge of global poverty and inequality. In the environmental field the soothing rhetoric of sustainable development continues to cover very deep divisions, not just over means to an agreed end, but also over the choice of ends themselves and the values that underpin them. As the Vienna Conference on human rights showed, there remain deep divisions between western views of human rights and those dominant in the Islamic world and in Asia. Moreover, the alleged natural compatibility of market economics and liberal democracy is under challenge both from the successful economies of East Asia and from the many countries struggling to achieve the political conditions necessary for economic stabilization and reform. The attempt to tie together human rights with the promotion of democracy has brought with it questions of the meaning of democracy, as well as the multiple difficulties of managing the complex relationship between democratization and human rights. Finally, globalization may well press towards greater homogeneity and fusion, but it has also been a powerful stimulus to traditionalist or particularist reactions and to the equally evident processes of fission and fragmentation.

Second, even if values themselves are genuinely shared, there may well be conflict over the political processes and institutional procedures by which those values are to be promoted. In part this has to do with the deep tension between what one might call *consensual solidarism* on the one hand and *coercive solidarism* on the other. The notion of giving 'teeth' to the norms of international society has clearly grown in importance over the past four years. This has been most obvious in terms of the renewed activism of the United Nations, but it has also included the very significant growth of conditionality, whereby flows of resources or membership of organizations are made conditional on the adoption of particular policies. Since the mid-1980s, conditionalities have spread from the traditional field of economics, and now embrace arms spending, nuclear proliferation, human rights and democracy, and environmental protection. Yet, as the tensions within the UN over the powers of the Security Council or between the United States and China over human rights show, moves towards coercive solidarism have been, and are likely to remain, an important source of tension.

But two more fundamental issues lurk behind the arguments for more effective international action to promote 'global values'. In the first place, there are the complex ways in which both the particular kinds of values and the institutional mechanisms to promote them can work to reinforce global inequality between those able to prosper within the globalized world economy and those excluded or left on the margins. Second, any moves towards making international legitimacy and full membership of international society conditional on the adoption of certain models of domestic political or economic practice brings out the tension between pluralist and solidarist conceptions of international society in its sharpest form. It is all very well, for example, to demand international action against particular egregious violations of human rights, but to what extent and with what consequences should international society seek to question the international standing of what John Rawls has called 'well-ordered non-liberal societies' which refuse to conduct their internal affairs according to new 'global' norms.[44] Such debates take us back to one of the central themes explored in the international society tradition, namely the relationship between exclusivist and universalist conceptions of international society.

Third, there is the troubling gulf between the expansion in the scope and claims of international society and its insecure power political foundations, or, put another way, between the 'harder' realist side to the international society tradition and its more ambitious Grotian aspect. There is little sign in the contemporary international system of a stable and agreed set of common understandings between the major powers. Indeed the system may be characterized by the absence of 'Great Powers' willing to exercise leadership and to assume the kinds of broad global responsibilities of which Bull spoke. In marked contrast to 1945 the United States has turned inwards and its commitment to political and economic multilateralism has been called into question, whilst Germany and Japan remain heavily conditioned by post-war patterns of foreign policy behaviour. Perversely the absence of major powers able to formulate and assert any clear notions of national interest, to which others can in turn respond, not only precludes the emergence of any form of great power concert but may also complicate efforts to develop effective collective action in the United Nations and other international bodies. The absence of Great Powers may well have reduced the risk of major war, but it has also undercut the political foundations on which international society has traditionally depended.

The fourth difficulty arises from the erosion of state capacity. As the goals that international society seeks to promote have expanded so it is clear that many of the most serious obstacles do not derive from the constraints of the international anarchy but rather from the domestic weaknesses of particular states and state structures. The problem of states that are states only in name is not of course a new one. The structural weaknesses of many of the new states that were created in the course of the revolt against western dominance was one of the central challenges examined in Bull's work on the expansion of international society. '[M]uch of the world is under the sway of states that are not states in the strict sense of the word, but only by courtesy.'[45] Their own weakness, lack of legitimacy and inability to satisfy demands for economic development constantly threaten internal instability which, in turn, will all too often spill over into the international arena.

But whilst Bull certainly noted the weakness of many individual states, it was still taken as a basic assumption that most (or at least a sufficient number of) states were capable of providing the conditions for local order. The main problem of world order was therefore dominated by the question of how the many islands of localized order could be meshed together, or as Raymond Aron put it, 'under what conditions would men (divided in so many ways) be able not merely to avoïd destruction, but to live together relatively well in one planet'?

Yet, in the post-Cold War world, the old dichotomy between domestic order and international anarchy has therefore been recast in many parts of the world. As international lawyers never tire of pointing out, there is a great deal more 'law and order' internationally than there is on the streets of an increasing number of states, unable to secure even the most minimal conditions of social order and beset by ethnic and communal strife. Indeed, it is becoming a truism of the post-Cold War world that the problem is not the lack of legitimacy between states, but the still greater lack of legitimacy within them. The net result is to debase further the currency of statehood and to move towards a situation in which the empirical claims to statehood of many 'quasi-states' are being gutted of any real meaning.[46]

Understanding these problems is certainly pushing the study of international relations into new areas. More and more is being written on the need for newer and broader notions of security and on the erosion of previously sacrosanct divisions between the 'domestic' and the 'international'. But it is very important to realize that the institutions and norms of international society continue to play a vital role in the management of these 'new' issues: in part through the creation of stable and coherent understandings about the kinds of threats to peace and security that should trigger international action through the UN and justify different forms of intervention; in part by elaborating a new normative structure on the vexed issue of criteria for membership, and, in particular, by seeking to build a new political consensus to replace the previous pragmatic compromise whereby self-determination was lauded in theory but applied only very unevenly in practice. This fundamental question on the rules of membership provides a further example of where the old rules may have ceased to apply but where agreement on new alternatives has yet to emerge.

Finally, an optimistic assessment of international society has to grapple with the extent to which states have lost power to markets and with the implications of globalization. The central difficulty is that states, even very large states acting together, may no longer possess the capacity to manage the international order because of the extent to which power and authority have diffused away from states and towards both markets and the actors that are able to thrive in those markets. Technological change, new patterns of economic competition and the information revolution have strengthened transnational patterns of economic and social interaction between companies, banks, social movements, and scientific and policy communities. As a result, as Susan Strange would argue, states 'are increasingly becoming hollow, or defective, institutions. To outward appearances unchanged, the inner core of their authority in society and over economic transactions within their defined territorial borders is seriously impaired.'[47]

It is certainly the case that earlier statist arguments need to be updated and redeployed against the often exaggerated claims of both theorists of globalization and those who seek salvation in the growth of an increasingly dense and activist transnational civil society.[48] But Bull's rather glib assertions of the state's basic capacity to control its economic environment provide an increasingly inadequate guide to the very complex ways in which the international political system and the increasingly globalized world economy interact. Nevertheless recognizing the importance of these changes need not undermine the validity of the international society approach. Such an approach does not imply that states are the only legitimate objects of study in world politics, nor that they necessarily remain in 'control'. The theorists of international society are not trying to arrive at an overall theory of world politics (whatever this might look like and whatever it might plausibly seek to explain), but are asking a discrete set of questions. There is a critical difference between arguing that transnational relations or dynamics of an increasingly globalized economy need to be 'taken into account' in explaining many important developments and saying that the inter-state system no longer provides an essential framework for promoting world order.

There are, for example, a great many questions that one might want to ask about the workings of the global economy. But there are three that are critical for understanding international society. First, are there institutions or institutionalized structures that exist outside the inter-state system that create or sustain order? Second, what kinds of order and what kinds of values emerge from the dynamics of the world economy? Are there important order-sustaining functions once undertaken by states that are now no longer carried out by anyone? And third, if true, does the declining capacity of states to manage the global economy actually matter? In what ways do these problems complicate the maintenance of order within the framework of inter-state relations? In what ways does the global economy need to be 'managed'?

The institutions of international society are certainly precarious and are under challenge from a range of new forces and factors. The multiple connections between state-society complexes within domestic society and shifting patterns of power and authority globally certainly highlight the need to take very seriously the claim that we may be witnessing a 'centrifugal process of diffusion of authority'.[49] There can be no automatic presumption in favour of a statist perspective. Indeed, it is worth noting that, already in the early 1970s, Bull saw the emergence of a 'neo-medieval order' as the most likely way in which the state system was likely to evolve. Moreover, in contrast to the ahistorical approach of structural realism, the theorists of international society have constantly emphasized the extent to which the state system is an historical oddity that grew out of a particular set of historical circumstances whose norms, institutions and economic 'base' have been subject to constant change and evolution. But the case for international society rests on two still eminently defensible propositions: first, that it is through states, and through states alone, that the global economy has to be managed in the interests of greater stability, justice, or ecological rationality (or whatever values one might wish to promote); and second that alternative or broader structures of world order remain still more precarious and harder to discern.

The normative agenda

If international society still speaks to the political dilemmas of our time, does it provide any firm guidance to the moral problems of contemporary world politics? The use of explicitly moral language has been characteristic of the international society tradition. But this was morality viewed from the perspective of those engaged in practice of statecraft. Speaking of the authors of *Diplomatic Investigations*, Bull argued:

> Far from seeking to exclude moral issues, they placed these at the centre of their inquiries. Above all, perhaps, they saw theory of international politics not as 'models' or 'conceptual frameworks' of their own to be tested against 'data' but as theories or doctrines in which men in international history have actually believed.[50]

This is a view of morality that stays extremely close to the practice of states, that seeks to go with, rather than against, the grain of power politics. Precisely because, to use Martin Wight's words, international relations is the 'realm of recurrence and repetition' and the 'field in which action is most regularly necessitous', it is imperative to concentrate on the ways in which the law of the jungle might be at least marginally deflected; on the kinds of international society that it might be just possible to establish; and on the 'principles of prudence and moral obligation' that might form a part of achieving this goal. Whilst debates and arguments over moral issues form an essential part of the sociology of international society, the theorists of international society are predominantly concerned with the 'morality of states', with prudential ethics, and with the ethics of responsibility.

There are many legitimate grounds on which this view of the normative dimension can be criticized. First, there is the ambiguity surrounding the way in which order and justice are juxtaposed in Bull's work.[51] Second, the range of normative enquiry is constrained by concern for the importance of diplomatic practice, by excessive pessimism about what it might be reasonable to hope for, and by the confusing elevation of prudence to the status of moral principle. Prudential ethics are all very well, but, whilst they speak to the difficulties of going anywhere, they do not give a very clear sense of where we ought to be trying to go. There is no clear point outside Bull's evolving 'consensus of shared values' which can serve as a focus for moral evaluation. Third, it is strange that neither Bull nor Wight were willing to lay out the moral arguments for the statism that they so strongly espoused (in the manner, for example, of Michael Walzer). Finally, the Bull/Wight approach is built on a rather limited view of political theory. If, as Chris Brown argues, we shift the focus of the question, if we alter the way in which we conceive of the divide between the domestic and the international, then we get a rather different set of important normative questions and a rather different set of historical debates and traditions that might help enlighten them.[52]

But whilst it is important to acknowledge these limitations it is also important to remember and to reassert the strengths of this approach. In the first place, the strength of international society's approach to normative issues is precisely that it does stay close to state practice, to the propensity of international relations to frustrate hope for progress, and to the need to integrate the desirable with the practical. It does usefully stress the dangers of moving too far away from the practice of international relations, and of underplaying the difficulties of escaping from the realist logic of recurrence and reproduction. Hence we find Bull's annoyance with Charles Beitz: not only that his critique failed to take the tradition of international society seriously enough, but also that normative theory needed to learn more of the substance of international relations before starting to philosophize about it.[53] Indeed the abstractness of some contemporary international normative theory makes one remember Bull's charge against the model builders and number crunchers of the 1960s: 'as remote from the substance of international politics as the inmates of a Victorian nunnery were from the study of sex'.

Second, and more substantively, the tradition of international society speaks to the fundamental moral dilemma of reconciling the universal with the particular and of resolving the tension between the pluralism and diversity that is such a fundamental characteristic of human life and the moral need to forge an overlapping consensus around which both the rights of individual human beings can be protected and the interests of humankind as whole can be safeguarded.

World society is characterized by profound and abiding human difference. For both prudential and moral reasons, international theory must be sensitive to the claims of difference and diversity and, as postmodernism warns us, must guard against the temptations of 'essentializing' or 'universalizing' discourses. It is not simply that, as both Carr and Marx remind us, there are likely to be good grounds for questioning and unmasking the motives of all those who set themselves up as 'agents of the general good'. Nor that, even when genuinely held, the promotion of global values can work to entrench the special interests of particular states and to exacerbate inequality. It is rather that even if Locke's 'great and natural community' of humankind does exist, it is, to use John Dunn's words, 'an extravagantly variegated natural community'.[54] Or, as Stuart Hampshire has put it:

> The clash of moral and religious loyalties has come to seem, in the light of recent history, much more than a temporary accident of human development, to be dispelled by the spreading of the natural sciences and by healthy enlightenment. Rather the deep-seated spiritual antagonisms have come to seem the essence of humanity, and it is an accident of history if, in some regions and for some period of time, a relative harmony of shared values prevails within a modern society.[55]

Recognition of, and respect for, difference reinforces the very deep-rooted historical arguments in favour of international society based on the mutual respect for sovereignty and an historical tendency to look favourably on the norm of non-intervention – although we should remember that sovereignty has always been a socially constructed and evolving norm and never as rigidly conceived as those who talk glibly of 'a Westphalian model' would suggest. There remains a great deal of force in Bull's insistence that we should question all easy assumptions that going 'beyond the nation state' would necessarily help secure the values that we happen to hold dear. 'It is possible to see the states system as providing a bulwark against greater political and economic injustice in the world than would otherwise exist.'[56]

The moral case for a pluralist order is of course reflected only very imperfectly in the political framework of international society. The claims of many states to represent the interest of their citizens and to embody a sense of national community are often tenuous, if not wholly deceitful. Moreover there is a profound and morally troubling paradox in the use of the unversalizing discourse of statism as the political framework for the protection of the particular. This is particularly true for those groups (such as women, minorities or indigenous peoples) unable to gain any very secure foothold on the basis of the legal categories of an international society still indelibly marked by the statist and western assumptions of its origins.

At the same time there are also many reasons why a simple ethic of difference cannot be sufficient: the manifest failings of many existing states to protect the individuals whose interests they claim to represent and who must stand at the centre of any persuasive ethical code; the extent to which increased global interaction forces previously separate societies into ever closer contact and erodes traditional understandings of sovereignty and non-intervention; the degree to which co-operation on matters of common concern will necessitate some agreement not just on the ways in which states coexist, but also on the ways in which they organize their domestic affairs. It is for these powerful reasons that world society needs political institutions through which respect for pluralism and coexistence can be reconciled with the need for more active co-operation and for an overlapping moral consensus. The most important element of this consensus remains procedural: groping towards a structure of agreed rules by which conflicts between differing moral conceptions and divergent political interests can be decided and within which the calculus of power and interest can be at least marginally deflected by a concern for morality. But as argued earlier, the inevitable expansion in the normative ambitions of international society means that the line between a procedural consensus on the nature of institutions and a broader consensus over the substantive issues to be resolved will often be difficult to draw.

The ways in which the institutions of international society struggle to manage the tension between the ethic of difference and the search for an overlapping but limited substantive moral consensus remain at the heart of contemporary world politics. It is of course not the case that the system of states represents the only framework by which this tension can be mediated. But, whilst global markets and the operations of many groups within transnational civil society are indeed central elements of the world political system, it is around the normative structures of international society and around the significant degree of existing consensus that future tensions between the universal and the particular will have to be resolved. It is in this sense that the rules, norms and institutions of international society do indeed retain their primacy. Beyond the state system the sense of a 'really existing world community' remains both elusive and extremely fragile and the clashes between competing values and cultures continue to run deep. The moral claims of international society are built around its attempt to find a form of international political practice that can bridge the divide between unacceptable moral relativism on the one hand and a utopian and apolitical cosmopolitanism on the other.

Notes

1 I would like to thank Robert Jackson, Tim Dunne, Geoffrey Best, Barry Buzan, Iver Neumann, William Wallace, Mervyn Frost, Andrew Linklater and Benedict Kingsbury for their comments on an earlier draft of this chapter.

2 This is a central theme of '*The Twenty Years' Crisis* thirty years on', *International Journal*, **24**(4) (Autumn 1969). Interestingly, the piece was first entitled 'E. H. Carr and the fifty years' crisis'.

3 See Roy Jones' criticism in 'The "English School" of international relations: a case for closure', *Review of International Studies*, 7(1) (1981). On the existence of

an 'English School' see Grader, Sheila, 'The English School of international relations', *Review of International Studies*, **14**(1) (1988) and reply by Peter Wilson in **15**(1) (1989). Given these debates, it is worth noting Bull's position: 'Someone at BISA said that there was no British School. Nonsense.' Talk on 'The appalling state of IR studies', LSE, 17 January 1980.

4 Letter to Shaie Selzer, Macmillan Publishers, 14 November 1975. Bull Papers, Bodleian Library, Oxford.

5 Butterfield, Herbert and Wight, Martin (eds), *Diplomatic Investigations* (London, George Allen & Unwin, 1966), p. 13.

6 For a criticism of this position see Halliday, Fred, 'International society as homogeneity: Burke, Marx, Fukuyama', *Millennium*, **21**(3) (Winter 1992), p. 442.

7 Review of Aron, Raymond, *Peace and War*, *Survival*, (November 1967), pp. 371–3.

8 '*The Twenty Years' Crisis* thirty years on', pp. 627–8.

9 Review of *Theory of International Politics*, *Times Literary Supplement*, 18 December 1979.

10 See Harris, Ian, 'Order and justice in *The Anarchical Society*', *International Affairs*, **69**(4) (1993).

11 Bull, H., 'Has the sovereign states system a future?', Fryer Memorial Lecture (3 June 1975), p. 17.

12 On legitimacy see Franck, Thomas M., *The Power of Legitimacy Among Nations*, (New York, Oxford University Press, 1990).

13 Bull, H., 'The European international order', undated paper presented to the British Committee, p. 11.

14 For a more detailed comparison of regime theory and the international society tradition see Hurrell, Andrew, 'International society and the study of regimes', in Rittberger, Volker (ed.), *Regime Theory and International Relations* (Oxford, Oxford University Press, 1993).

15 Letter to Shaie Selzer, 14 November 1975.

16 Wight, Martin, 'Western values in international relations', in Butterfield and Wight (eds), *Diplomatic Investigations*, p. 96. See also Nick Rengger's astute comment that Bull's appeals on behalf of international society are a curious blend of the ethical and the self-interested. Rengger, N. J., 'A city which sustains all things? Communitarianism and international society', *Millennium*, **21**(3) (Winter 1992), p. 365.

17 cf. Bull's comment: 'Whether or not there is consensus, I should say, depends not simply on the number or intensity of conflicts, but on what these conflicts are about, and whether they are conducted in a framework of agreed rules'. Letter to Shaie Selzer, 14 November 1975.

18 It is therefore not true, as Nick Rengger suggests, that Bull's understanding of society is 'inevitably' dependent on 'seeing society and culture as locked in parasitic embrace'. Rather, the role of culture opens up questions to which a variety of answers can be given. Rengger, 'A city which sustains all things?', p. 359.

19 Bull, H., 'The Third World and international society', *The Yearbook of World Affairs* (London, Stevens and Sons, 1979), p. 29.

20 Ibid.

21 Ibid. p. 23.
22 Ibid. p. 29.
23 Ibid. p. 30. This evolutionary logic is developed by Barry Buzan in 'From international system to international society: structural realism and regime theory meet the English School', *International Organization*, **47**(3) (Summer 1993), especially pp. 334–6. See also his *People, States and Fear* (London, Harvester Wheatsheaf, 1991), pp. 166–74.
24 Bull, 'The Third World and international society', p. 31.
25 The 'central' stream of the international society tradition is a very broad one. Indeed one of the problems with the Bull/Wight trilectic is that it seriously distorts the evolution of thinking on international society by excluding those such as Hobbes and Kant who can legitimately be included within the tradition. For the best account of the evolution of the idea of international society see Dunne, Tim, 'International relations theory in Britain: the invention of an international society tradition', D.Phil. Thesis, Oxford University, 1993.
26 Hoffmann, Stanley, 'Hedley Bull's contribution to international relations', *International Affairs*, **62**(2) (Spring 1986), pp. 187–8.
27 Cohen, Raymond, *International Politics: The Rules of the Game* (London, Longman, 1981), pp. 2–7.
28 Other criticisms of Bull's use of the term 'society' include Shaw, Martin, 'Global society and global responsibility: the theoretical, historical and political limits of "International Society"', and Halliday, Fred, 'International society as homogeneity: Burke, Marx and Fukuyama', both in *Millennium*, **21**(3) (Winter 1992).
29 On this view of Hobbes see Bull, Hedley, 'Hobbes and the international anarchy', *Social Research*, **48**(4) (Winter 1981); and Hanson, David, 'Thomas Hobbes' "Highway to Peace"', *International Organisation*, **38**(2) (Spring 1984).
30 Hoffmann, Stanley, 'Rousseau on war and peace', *American Political Science Review*, **57**(2) (June 1963), p. 320.
31 Bull, H., *The Anarchical Society* (London, Macmillan, 1977), pp. 46–51.
32 The clearest distinction in Bull's work between the second and third levels of international society is to be found in 'The Grotian conception of international society' in Butterfield and Wight (eds), *Diplomatic Investigations*. Some confusion has arisen because Bull used the term 'Grotian' in two senses: first to describe the doctrine that there is such a thing as international society; and, second, to contrast the Grotian solidarist conception of international society with the more pluralist Vattelian conception. See *The Anarchical Society*, p. 322.
33 Bull's argument at this time against Grotian or solidarist conceptions is apparent in the text of the paper, but still more in the notes of his presentation: 'I had in mind to criticize the conception of International Relations embodied in the League and United Nations and to some extent in Western thinking about international relations. It generally seems to me that the League of Nations picture of the world is criticized on grounds that it is impracticable, but not on the grounds that it is morally unsound, or that it does not constitute even proper objectives to try and bring about. Whereas it seems to me that kind of conception of international relations is open to objections on moral grounds as constituting too simple a view of the moral dilemmas of international politics, and as being a system which it may be dangerous even to try to attempt to put into practice. ... Whereas [in contrast to Lauterpacht] I want to take an

unfavourable view of Grotius, and to try and rehabilitate the nineteenth century positivist international lawyers and the view particularly of Oppenheim.' British Committee discussion of 'The Grotian conception of international relations', 15 April 1962, Bull Papers, Bodleian Library, Oxford.

34 Bull, H., 'Justice in international relations', in *The 1983–84 Hagey Lectures* (Waterloo, Ontario, University of Waterloo, 1984), p. 11.

35 Ibid. p. 12.

36 Ibid. p. 14.

37 Ibid. p. 13.

38 See Wheeler, Nicholas J., 'Pluralist or solidarist conceptions of international society: Bull and Vincent on humanitarian intervention', *Millennium*, **21**(3) (Winter 1992). The fear that the previously clear, if limited, rules of international law are being undermined by excessive normative ambition is also implicit in Bull's essay on Kelsen: 'Hans Kelsen and international law' in Tur, Richard and Twining, William (eds), *Essays on Kelsen* (Oxford, Oxford University Press, 1986).

39 For an elaboration of a positive reading of contemporary developments in terms of international society, see Buzan, 'From International System to International Society', pp. 348–52.

40 Zacher, Mark W., 'The decaying pillars of the Westphalian temple: implications for international order and governance', in Rosenau, James N. and Czempiel, Ernst-Otto (eds), *Governance with Government: Order and Change in World Politics* (Cambridge, Cambridge University Press, 1992).

41 One of the strongest statements on this issue is contained in a talk given at Chatham House, 'Western values in a hostile world', 23 September 1980. Bull Papers, Bodleian Library, Oxford.

42 Williamson, John and Haggard, Stephan, 'The political conditions for economic reform', in Williamson, John and Haggard, S. (eds), *The Political Economy of Policy Reform* (Washington, International Institute for Economics, 1994), p. 530.

43 See, for example, Franck, Thomas, 'The emerging right to democratic governance', *American Journal of International Law*, **86**(1) (January 1992); and Farer, Tom J., 'Collectively defending democracy in a world of sovereign states: The western hemisphere's prospect', *Human Rights Quarterly*, **15** (1993).

44 Rawls, John, 'The law of peoples', in Shute, Stephen and Hurley, Susan (eds), *On Human Rights* (New York, Basic Books, 1993).

45 Bull, H., and Watson, A. (eds), *The Expansion of International Society* (Oxford, Clarendon Press, 1984) p. 430.

46 On this subject see Jackson, Robert H., *Quasi-states: Sovereignty, International Relations and the Third World* (Cambridge, Cambridge University Press, 1990).

47 Strange, Susan, 'The defective state', *Daedalus*, **124**(2) (Spring 1995), p. 57.

48 For a such a sceptical view see Wade, Robert, 'Globalization and its limits: the continuing importance of nations and regions', in Berger, Suzanne and Dore, Ronald (eds), *National Diversity and Global Capitalism* (Ithaca, NY, Cornell University Press, 1996).

49 Strange, 'The defective state', p. 72.

50 Review of *The Reason of States*, *Times Literary Supplement*, 28 March 1978.

51 See Harris, 'Order and justice', especially pp. 728–33.

52 See Brown, C., *International Relations Theory: New Normative Approaches* (Hemel Hempstead, Harvester Wheatsheaf, 1992).

53 Bull, H., review of Beitz, C., *Political Theory and International Relations*, Bull Papers.

54 Dunn, John, '*The Nation State and Human Community*'. Published in Italian as *Stato Nazionale e Communita Umana* (Milan, Anabasi, 1994). Not yet published in English.

55 Hampshire, S., 'Liberalism: the new twist', *New York Review of Books*, 12 August 1993, p. 43.

56 Bull, H., 'Has the sovereign states system a future?', p. 12.

3

Hedley Bull and the Idea of a Universal Moral Community: Fictional, Primordial or Imagined?

NICHOLAS J. WHEELER AND TIM DUNNE

One of Hedley Bull's favourite epigrams was that 'professors don't make good policymakers'.[1] This reification of the quality of detachment is one which contains within it the kernel of two important principles. The first is that the role of an intellectual is to be unrelentingly critical of *all* political principles. Bull was always suspicious of 'missionaries' who purported to be speaking and acting on behalf of universal values. The second concerns his recognition of the need for distance from the short-termism of foreign policy-making. At the same time, Bull had little time for those who failed to empathize with the concerns of state leaders, recognizing that, as he put it in his lectures on *Justice and International Relations*, 'terrible choices have sometimes to be made' between conflicting moral values.

Bull's understanding of the role of an academic/intellectual can be contrasted with his friend and intellectual sparring partner, Richard Falk, whom he came into contact with at Princeton in 1963. For Falk, the role of the academic was to act as an advocate for universal moral values such as peace, economic and social justice, ecological sustainability and human rights. The belief that critique can transform political practices leading to the development of a global community of humankind is what distinguishes Falk's conception of the role of an academic from that maintained by Bull. Underlying this disagreement is an even more profound, and in a sense prior question, as to whether the foundations exist on which to build a global community. Bull expressed considerable scepticism as to whether it was possible to ground ethical principles *a priori*, and took great pleasure in drenching exponents of the natural law tradition, notably Michael Donelan and E. B. F. Midgley. However, there is a curious ambivalence at the heart of Bull's moral philosophy concerning how far it relies on a minimal moral foundationalism. The problem arises because despite Bull's hostility towards attempts to ground ideas of common humanity, he nevertheless remains open to the possibility of reaching a global consensus on substantive moral values. This raises the central question of the chapter: is it possible to construct an ethical defence of common humanity which does not rest upon foundational claims to 'truth'?

Before excavating Hedley Bull's ethical foundations, it is necessary to reconstruct his dissatisfaction with the ethical relativism which he associated principally with E. H. Carr. In part one of this chapter we will elucidate why Bull believed that Carr's realism was morally bankrupt. Crucially, Bull argued that Carr's notion of morality was a crude form of instrumentalism whereby morality was merely a reflection of the will of the stronger. For Bull, this argument ignores the existence of common interests and common values which are for the good of the powerless as well as the powerful. Bull ends his critique of Carr by calling for a reorientation of international relations around 'the idea of international society'.[2] We will show how Bull believed himself to be fashioning a theory of international society which was not simply a convenient fiction serving to mask over the *real* interests of the satisfied powers.

The second part of the chapter will investigate the moral bases underpinning Bull's conception of the society of states. Bull defends the society of states as a vehicle for achieving the goal of 'world order' which he makes the ultimate test of any ethical position. By this, he means the achievement of the 'universal goals' of social life which he seems to posit as a necessary condition for the existence of order in all societies. Although his discussion of 'universal goals' in *The Anarchical Society* intimates the existence of minimal moral foundationalism, in other writings published contemporaneously, he critiqued the moral foundationalism of others. He singled out the work of Michael Donelan and E. B. F. Midgley for their presumption of a pre-existing global community of humankind derived from natural law principles.

Having demonstrated Bull's ambiguity with regard to his ethical foundationalism, the final part of the chapter considers how far Bull espoused a non-foundationalist ethical commitment to 'an imagined community of mankind'. In his discussions of human rights, Bull seems to place considerable emphasis on the potential of humankind to identify morally with each other on the basis of their shared sympathy and experiences.[3] This raises the intriguing question whether his preference for sentiments rather than foundations represents a form of 'pragmatism'[4] which underpins contemporary postmodern thinking in international relations. Nevertheless, having been drawn to the vision of an imagined global community in *Justice in International Relations*, Bull set clear limits to the growth of 'cosmopolitan moral awareness'. Pragmatic sympathy can only extend, for Bull, among states who inhabit an inter-cultural consensus; and it is this which he was fearful of writing against the background of ideological fragmentation in international society in the late 1970s. An example of Bull's scepticism about the achievement of a universal moral community is his trenchant critique of Richard Falk's advocacy of universal moral values. As with Bull's critique of Donelan and Midgley, we see how he picks up Carr's 'critical weapon' and turns it against universalists in order to expose the hollowness of their belief in an immanent global community.

Transcending Carr's view of ethical relativism

E. H. Carr advanced a devastating critique of ethical universalism in *The Twenty Years' Crisis*. Carr's master stroke was to relativize the universalist claims of statesmen in order to reveal the partial interests which were driving their arguments. By way of illustration, Carr pointed to Britain's historic defence of free trade, and the defence of the Versailles Treaty by Britain and France. Realism was therefore an instrument which enabled the theorist to reveal the reality behind the mask. Carr's insistence upon wielding the weapon of the 'relativity of thought' reflected his belief that there were no foundations upon which to formulate independently valid ethical practices. State leaders might sincerely espouse universal moral claims, but Carr asserts that they will always be partial because 'these supposedly absolute and universal principles were not principles at all, but the unconscious reflexions of national policy based on a particular interpretation of national interest at a particular time.'[5] Carr singled out natural law for criticism as one of the central streams of ethical universalism. This stream became a torrent during the inter-war period as natural law 'resumed its sway' and modern international law 'became more markedly utopian than at any previous time'.[6] He exposed natural law as an empty shell which – like utopianism in general – failed because of its 'inability to provide any absolute and disinterested standard for the conduct of international affairs'.[7]

In '*The Twenty Years' Crisis* thirty years on', Hedley Bull argues that Carr's work is an important exercise in criticism but is ultimately inadequate on prescriptive grounds. Bull challenges head-on 'the weapon of the relativity of thought'[8] which Carr believed to be the apotheosis of realist thought. Relativism, argues Bull, is inadequate because it denies 'all independent validity to moral argument'.[9] In order to reinforce his critique of Carr's moral relativism, Bull contests Carr's interpretation of the road to war. Bull is willing to accept that the interstate order constructed at Versailles served the interests primarily of Britain and France, and that the policies they pursued were intended to uphold *their* special circumstances. However, Bull departs from this realist analysis at the point at which Carr was prevented from making 'a moral case for resistance at Munich'.[10]

The essence of Bull's dismissal of Carr's moral relativism is the purported existence of some values (for example, order) which may be for 'the good of international society as a whole'.[11] This is the key point with which Bull concludes his critique of Carr's political realism:

> The idea of an international society - of common interests and common values perceived in common by modern states - is scarcely recognised in *The Twenty Years' Crisis*. In the course of demonstrating how appeals to an overriding international society subserve the special interests of the ruling group of powers, Carr jettisons the idea of international society itself. This is the idea with which a new analysis of the problem of international relations should now begin.[12]

The above passage underlines the depths of Bull's dissatisfaction with the normative void left by Carr's realism.[13] In place of Carr's political realism, Bull sought to construct an international theory which more closely reflected the practices of sovereign states. Bull asks the question how far the ideas of theorists of international society reflect the language of state leaders, and he concludes that 'the element of a society has always been present, and remains present, in the modern international system'.[14] According to Bull's famous definition, international society exists because states are 'conscious of certain common interests and common values' and believe themselves to be '*bound* by a common set of rules and institutions'.[15] In the paragraphs below, we will consider in more depth what Bull intended by the words 'common interests and common values'.

Bull's defence of international law is central to his vindication of the existence of international morality.[16] In response to the realist argument that states obey international law only when it is in their self-interest, Bull suggests that what is more surprising is that states 'so often judge it in their interests to conform to it'.[17] This narrow argument about the motives of states in conforming to international law is projected onto the broader canvas of international society as a whole. Given the recognition by states that they have rights and duties in their relations with one another, the case for international society against *realpolitik* is that states will adhere to the rules and norms of the society of states even when these conflict with their narrowly defined interests.[18] The argument which Bull is making - although at times somewhat implicitly - is that states should act (implying an element of agency) in a way which strengthens the normative principles of international society.[19]

Despite challenging Carr's ethical relativism, a number of Carr's realist sirens can be detected in Bull's work. Both were cognizant of the fact that in international politics conflicts of interest were, in Carr's words, 'real and inevitable'.[20] For this reason, Bull was keen to remind the liberal idealists that the dilemmas of statecraft require state leaders to agonize over 'terrible choices'.[21] In addition to recognizing the ubiquity of conflict, Carr and Bull both acknowledged that international politics was a complex site upon which the ritualistic clashes of power and morality, war and law, were played out. A third area of agreement between Carr and Bull concerned the centrality of the traditional practices of statecraft, such as the balance of power and war, to the management of international relations.

In the final analysis, Bull acknowledged Carr's skill in mobilizing the weapon of the 'relativity of thought' to critique the fictional world community of the 'utopians', and later Bull showed himself to be not averse to slaying contemporary universalists with this weapon.

Hedley Bull's rejection of natural law

Whilst Bull believed, in contrast to Carr, that there were shared moral beliefs in world politics, he nevertheless agreed with Carr that natural law provided spurious grounds upon which to guide moral actions. At the beginning of *The Anarchical Society* Bull outlines his conception of order and its relationship to natural law. Following his former Oxford tutor, H. L. A. Hart, Bull argued that there were certain minimal requirements which were preconditions for the existence of all societies: security against violence; respect for agreements; stability of possessions. He identified these as 'elementary, primary or universal goals of social life'.[22] What is important about Bull's discussion of the prior conditions for social life is his claim that in their absence 'we cannot speak of the existence of society'.[23] Although asserting certain 'universal goals', he questions how far these goals are 'mandatory' and the extent to which the rules underpinning them are 'self-evident to all men'.[24] Here Bull differentiates his position from natural law thinking and its assertion that there are 'principles, and by derivation, rules, which exist objectively'.[25] Thus, despite a superficial affinity between Bull's universal goals and minimal moral foundationalism, Bull seems to be refuting any essentialist or natural foundations for these goals.

The textual ambiguity evident in Bull's discussion of the ontological status of the 'universal goals' in *The Anarchical Society* is conspicuously absent in his discussion of 'really existing' natural law theorists. In a number of review essays in the late 1970s Bull was highly critical of writers sympathetic to the natural law tradition who assumed that a primordial community of humankind was 'already in place'. In this instance, he had in his 'sights' the natural law thinking of E. B. F. Midgley and Michael Donelan. In his critique of Midgley in 'Natural law and international relations', Bull counselled against the foundationalist premise of 'a fixed point of reference' from where 'all moral disagreements can in principle be settled'.[26] World politics, according to Bull, is an arena where individuals and groups 'are in conflict about the most basic moral ends'.[27] Bull also challenged the more 'empirical equivalent of natural law' evident in Michael Donelan's work. In his review of Donelan's edited collection *The Reason of States*, he offered a trenchant critique of the natural law principles which framed Donelan's understanding of the society of states:

> Michael Donelan writes that political theorists have assumed a world of separate states ... He proposes that instead we begin with the assumption of 'a primordial community of mankind', of which the world of separate states is but a particular arrangement. ... The trouble with this is that while individual human beings are primordial, and separate states a mere arrangement of them, the community of mankind is not primordial but is on the contrary a mere figment of the imagination.[28]

Michael Donelan's response, galvanized by his adversary's accusation that some of the essays in the volume were 'half-baked', accused Bull of being a 'positivist' for not regarding the global community as anything other than a means by which diverse cultures 'agree enough about expediency and power to run an orderly states-system'.[29] In the letters page of the following month's *Times Literary Supplement*, Bull clarified his position in relation to Donelan's: '[T]he issue, as it appears to me, is not whether "in *reason*" there exists a moral community of mankind, but whether one exists in *fact*.'[30] By the term 'in fact', Bull means whether the moral community exists as a shared practice among state leaders and the extent to which universal values permeate the wider consciousness of humankind.

What is interesting about Bull's exchanges with these two proponents of natural law thinking is that they both underestimate the extent of his moral universalism. E. B. F. Midgley accused Bull of being the slave of a 'liberal arts' modernism which prevented him from discovering 'what are the fundamental truths'.[31] Similarly, in the case of Donelan's 'empirical' natural law theory, it is surely a mistake to characterize Bull as someone who regarded states as 'moral islands'. The strongest response to Donelan's critique of Bull is his defence of the society of states as an instrument for delivering the moral value of 'world order'.

Bull defines 'world order' as 'those patterns or dispositions of human activity that sustain the elementary or primary goals of social life among mankind as a whole'.[32] He contrasts this with order among states (which he calls international order) and argues:

> Order among mankind as a whole is something wider than order among states; something more fundamental and primordial than it; and also, I should argue, something morally prior to it ... 'world order' is more fundamental and primordial than international order because the ultimate units of the great society of all mankind are not states (or nations, tribes, empires, classes or parties) but are individual human beings ... it is necessary at this point to state that if any value attaches to order in world politics, it is order among all

mankind which we must treat as being of primary value, not order within the society of states as such ...[33]

Therefore, *pace* Donelan, the underlying moral universalism in Bull's thinking concerns his insistence that individuals are the ultimate moral referent. International order is only to be valued to the extent which it delivers 'world order', which Bull makes the litmus test for the ethical claims of the society of states.[34]

The problem with Bull's discussion of 'world order' as a transcultural moral goal is twofold. In the first instance, Bull provides no discussion as to the content of these goals in *The Anarchical Society*, and only a few fragments in other writings. The closest Bull comes to elaborating upon the content of these goals is in his review essay on 'The universality of human rights' where he specifies 'arbitrary killing, torture and imprisonment' as part of the near universal consensus on what constitutes the 'universal goals'.[35] The difficulty is that whilst all states espouse these goals, how each state chooses to define and implement them depends upon its own particular culture and values. This raises the question whether it is possible in Bull's theory to reconcile cultural relativism with the *universal* consensus on the primary and elementary goals of social life which underpins his conception of 'world order'.

The second and related problem associated with Bull's treatment of 'universal goals' concerns the tension between making the individual the primary referent for 'world order' and the license that Bull issues to states to decide what is necessary to secure them. For example, Bull's position offers no basis for evaluating between, on the one hand, the demands for civil and political liberties made by Chinese 'dissidents' and on the other, the Chinese government's claim that any concessions would critically undermine social stability. Is 'security from violence' to be defined in terms of the rights of those citizens campaigning for political freedoms, or is it to be defined as the rights of the collective to uphold communal over individual values? And who is to decide? In short, the problem for Bull (and one which re-emerges later in our discussion of the limits of Bull's international imagination) is that individuals are the primary referent but states are the principal agents.

Whilst Bull was sympathetic to the part played by cultural preferences in implementing the 'universal goals' – which he later equated with 'basic human rights'[36] – he nevertheless can be criticized for not specifically excluding certain practices which are surely incompatible with the 'universal goals'. Genocide and mass murder threaten fundamentally the goal of individual security against violence and are therefore antithetical to an authentic notion of communal security and identity. Consequently, any society which practises massive and systematic violations of 'basic human rights' is failing to uphold world order which, as we noted earlier, Bull made the ultimate referent for global moral conduct.

Bull's claim that international order is only to be valued to the extent that it provides for world order has been developed and clarified by Robert H. Jackson. The morality of the society of states, argues Jackson, 'presupposes the intrinsic value of all states and accommodates their inward diversity'.[37] This opens into the question, never explicitly confronted by Bull, as to whether states which perform acts of serial 'human wrongs'[38] forfeit their right to protection from the norm of non-intervention. For critical theorists of the society of states such as R. J. Vincent, Andrew Linklater and Bhikhu Parekh, a commitment to 'basic human rights' must set limits to state sovereignty.

Although Bull consistently rejected natural law foundations, his later thinking brings out more clearly his commitment to universal ethics. The problem that Bull wrestled with in his writings on human rights was whether it might be possible to arrive at a consensus which went beyond the declaratory commitment of governments to the goals of 'basic human rights'. In particular, having argued that there are no in-built human rights, Bull explored how far a consensus could be reached on the content of 'basic human rights' through a global inter-cultural conversation.

The limits of Bull's international imagination

As the preceding sections have argued, Hedley Bull dismissed E. H. Carr's claim that the idea of universal ethics was a convenient fiction without at the same time espousing natural law principles as the basis for his conception of a universal moral order. How, then, did Bull defend his ethical commitments? By focusing on Bull's thinking about human rights, the final part of this chapter will suggest that he espoused a non-foundationalist universalist ethic which has similarities with some recent postmodern theorizing.

Hedley Bull's 1983 lectures on *Justice in International Relations* present more starkly than in any of his other works the acceptance of cosmopolitanism as a voice in the debate about what constitutes justice in world politics. Bull's reasons for writing the lectures can be traced to his fear that the consensus on common interests and common values which underpinned European international society had shrunk, as a consequence of its globalization in the second half of the twentieth century. He had concluded *The Anarchical Society* with the judgement that the long-term survival of the society of states depended upon 'the preservation and extension of a cosmopolitan culture',[39] and in his lectures seven years later, he developed the theme that this required western states to recognize as legitimate the moral aspirations of the peoples of the South for economic and social justice.

Making explicit what had been alluded to in *The Anarchical Society*, Bull argued that the moral value of the society of states had to be judged in terms of what it contributed to the achievement of individual justice because the 'question of justice concerns what is due not only to states and nations, but to all individual persons in an *imagined* community of mankind'.[40] Bull is using the term 'imagined community' in contrast to a primordial understanding exhibited by natural law thinkers, as the following passage on Bull's conception of human rights makes clear:

> In the sense of rights established by some *a priori* moral rule that can be shown to be objectively valid, there are no human rights. ... If our conceptions of human rights are rooted not, as the eighteenth century declarations proclaimed, in the nature of things but only in our attitudes and preferences this does not mean that our choice of them is capricious or arbitrary. The moral attitudes we take up are the authentic expression of the ways of life we lead, and reflect our own history and character.

Bull's understanding that human rights are not derived from 'the nature of things' but rather that humanity is historically and culturally constructed contrasts with other liberal rights theorists like Louis Henkin and R. J. Vincent who ground universal human rights in essentialist notions of human nature.

What is striking about Bull's philosophical reflections on human rights is their similarity with Richard Rorty's defence of human rights pragmatism. Rorty liberates the discourse of human rights from the question of epistemology; for postmoderns, we can never know right conduct from right reason. Instead of asking the question, what are human rights and how do we know whether they are universally valid, Rorty prefers to ask, '[W]hat can we make of ourselves?'[41] Therefore for Rorty, 'the human rights culture seems to owe nothing to increased moral knowledge, and everything to hearing sad and sentimental stories'.[42]

The significance of the parallel with Rorty rests upon their shared commitment to a global human rights culture in the absence of foundationalism. In place of an ahistorical reason, Bull and Rorty emphasize our potential for transcultural solidarities and see the progress of global human rights as contingent upon this. Rorty asks us to imagine ourselves in the 'shoes of the despised and oppressed' and think 'what it is like to be in her situation – to be far from home, among strangers'.[43] Similarly, Bull identified a 'growing cosmopolitan moral awareness', at least among the 'advanced countries', which was leading them increasingly to 'empathise with sections of humanity that are geographically or culturally distant from us'.[44] Bull thought that the 'mere existence of this moral concern with welfare on a world scale represents a major change in our sensibilities'.[45]

The next step for advocates of non-foundationalist ethics is to show how we might inculcate empathetic sensibilities beyond the liberal zone. Bull suggests that the emerging awareness in western societies of individual human rights reflects the West's cultural preferences, but that there are some cultural preferences for which the West has 'no reason to apologise'.[46] In contrast to moral relativists like E. H. Carr who see the face of power behind the veil of moral argument, Bull is open to the idea that through a legitimate inter-cultural conversation, respect for human rights 'can be nurtured in soils where it has no roots at present'.[47] Bull's conception of a cosmopolitan culture required the West to regard other views on human rights as 'equally legitimate topics of conversation'.[48] Bull had in mind here the demands of the post-colonial and communist states for economic and social rights, and argued that a redistribution of wealth was vital for the creation of a new global consensus. His presumption was that the West should seek to accommodate these demands by states outside of the liberal zone on the condition that they accepted 'some degree of commitment to the cause of individual human rights on a world scale'.[49]

These sentiments about an 'imagined community' in *Justice in International Relations* are checked by an abiding scepticism as to how far it could be realized in practice. 'These cosmopolitanist ideas', he reflected, 'can determine our attitudes and policies in international relations only to a limited extent.'[50] The problem here is that Bull identified states as the only agency for progressive social and political change, arguing that in the absence of world government, there was a need for 'particular states to seek as wide a consensus as possible, and on this basis to act as local agents of a world common good'.[51] However, Bull doubted that sovereign governments had the necessary political will since they were 'notoriously self-serving ... and rightly suspected when they purport to act on behalf of the international community as a whole'.[52] Despite his vision of a global human rights culture flourishing in non-western societies, Bull pointed to the lack of consensus that existed in practice about the meaning given to these rights by different cultures. He worried that particular states who set themselves up as judges of what constituted universal human rights threatened the ethics of co-existence upon which the society of states was constructed:

> The promotion of human rights on a world scale, in a context in which there is no consensus as to their meaning and the priorities among them, carries the danger that it will be subversive of coexistence among states, on which the whole fabric of world order in our time depends. ... The cosmopolitan society which is implied and presupposed in our talk of human rights exists only as an

> ideal, and we court great dangers if we allow ourselves to proceed as if it were a political and social framework already in place.[53]

Although Bull was doubtful that the society of states could be relied upon to deliver a consensus on universal human rights, the above passage indicates that he saw no alternative to constructing ethical practices through international society.

Bull's conception of states as potential cosmopolitan moral agents can be contrasted with Richard Falk's conviction that the states system is a fundamental barrier to progressive global reform. For Falk, it is illusory to believe that statist élites can develop the necessary cosmopolitanist outlook, despite the global problems that cry out for solution. Whilst he praised Bull for recognizing that a viable 'world order' depended upon a consensus that included 'voices of discontent',[54] he was nevertheless scornful of what he interpreted as Bull's belief that states could be relied upon to implement a redistribution of wealth based on principles of global justice. According to Falk, 'the future of "world order" is too important to leave to the wisdom and action of governments'.[55] The only realistic agents of global transformation are transnational social movements committed to universal ethics.

In response to Falk's anti-statism, Bull cited two related reasons for rejecting his normative prescriptions. The first is Falk's failure to take account of how far the demands of the southern states could actually be reconciled with the interests of the West. The second concerns the way in which he and his colleagues in the World Order Models Project based their prescriptions for reform on their own value preferences and that there was a certain 'presumption in their claim that they speak for "spaceship earth"'.[56] Not only was he scathing about the legitimacy with which world order advocates set themselves up as conduits for the values of common humanity, he was also profoundly sceptical of Falk's ideas of 'consciousness-raising', claiming that it was naive and utopian to expect 'persuasion and exhortation'[57] to change the world. Thus, whilst Bull was not persuaded that states could be trusted to act as agents of common humanity, he categorically rejected the idea that global civil society could deliver ethical universalism.

Despite their antithetical conceptions of moral agency, Falk and Bull espouse a similar form of non-foundationalist ethics. In his 1992 book, Falk outlines the postmodern ethics which underpin his commitment to a universal moral community:

> The promise of a postmodern world depends on human initiative as well as historical tendencies. The prefiguring of the future in our imagination and lives gives each of us the possibility and also a responsibility to act. ... To be

> postmodern we need to develop the practices and nurture the consciousness that simultaneously inhabits premodern, modern, and postmodern realms of actual and potential being.[58]

What is significant about Falk's writing is that he continues to identify a key role for global civil society in bringing about a universal moral community. Bull had talked about an 'imagined community' but relied on states to bring it about, whereas for Falk, humankind has a primary 'responsibility to act' for suffering humanity 'with whom we share the planet'.[59] Falk invests 'imagination' with an ethic of responsibility for caring about others, and believes that by bringing 'postmodern ethics and politics concretely to bear' on the plight of suffering humanity, it is possible to imagine a new world into existence. The power of imagination in Falk's vision can be seen in his claim that the failures of statism are 'overwhelmingly associated with artificial and constraining boundaries on imagination and community'.[60]

Conclusion

We have argued that Bull was an ethical universalist (albeit more explicitly in his later work) for the reason that the ultimate moral referent of his theory is the welfare of individual human beings. In this sense, Bull did not fall on Carr's sword of moral relativism which prevented Carr from articulating a theory of universal moral community. Not only did Carr believe that there were no primordial grounds for this, he was also remorselessly sceptical about the capacity for human agents to construct a 'disinterested standard' for universal moral conduct.

One of the most powerful arguments Bull marshals against Carr relates to his dismissal of the possibility of any independent grounds for moral judgement. However, a close reading of Bull's work indicates that he never confronts the tensions between his implied minimal moral foundationalism and his reluctance to ground morality in truth. Bull's view of the social world is that ideas and values are not primordial and consequently he warns against '[t]heories which impute a natural or objective quality to moral values obscure this fact'.[61] This explains Bull's hostility to natural law theorists who believe in a universal moral code which is 'built into us'.[62]

Bull's rejection of natural law and reason as secure grounds for moral conduct has an affinity with Rorty's philosophical pragmatism. Bull felt that growing 'cosmopolitan moral awareness' was a product of the nurturing of the sentiments. Here he looked to the construction of an 'imagined' world community through an inter-cultural dialogue with its promise of a deeper consensus on, among other things, universal human rights.

Falk's identification of the sentiment '[t]aking suffering seriously'[63] as the basis of a new global politics also echoes Rorty's postmodern ethics. Whilst all three theorists reject epistemological foundations, they diverge over how far the imagination of individuals, and in particular intellectuals, has a role to play in inculcating transcultural empathy. Rorty argues that 'manipulating' the 'sentiments' of 'generations of nice, tolerant, well-off, secure, other-respecting students ... in all parts of the world is just what is needed - indeed *all* that is needed - to achieve an enlightenment utopia'.[64] Falk shares this belief in the power of consciousness-raising, but would dissent from the idea that education for élites is *all* that is needed. He recognizes that education has an important role to play in expanding our moral sensibilities, but thinks that this must be part of a broader assault on the political and economic structures of statism.

Falk employs the power of imagination to trump statist values and structures. In contrast, Bull was sceptical that appeals to the imagination could overcome the entrenched conservatism of the society of states. To his critics, Bull's vision of an 'imagined community' of humankind was ultimately constrained by his statist conception of agency. Yet the strength of his position is that it is anchored in the realization that moral progress has to be negotiated in the world of states.

NOTES

1 Bull, Hedley, 'Kissinger: the primacy of geopolitics', *International Affairs*, **56**(3) (1980), p. 487.
2 Bull, Hedley, '*The Twenty Years' Crisis* thirty years on', *International Journal*, **24**(4) (1969), p. 638.
3 Bull, Hedley, 'Human rights and world politics', in Pettman, Ralph (ed.), *Moral Claims in World Affairs* (London, Croom Helm, 1979), p. 89.
4 We are using 'pragmatism' as a theory of knowledge which is distinct from rationalism and empiricism. The latter epistemologies are in agreement that 'scientific knowledge must rest on a foundation of certainty that can guarantee the truth of our most confident beliefs. For the pragmatist, a foundation of this kind can be nothing but a myth; we do not have it, cannot have it, and could not justify it if we did.' Aune, Bruce, *Rationalism, Empiricism and Pragmatism* (New York, Random House, 1970), p. 177. Following Aune, we are using the terms 'foundations' and 'foundationalism' to signify the idea that there are secure grounds in which to anchor ethical universalism. For a recent examination of epistemology and international relations see Smith, S., 'Positivists and beyond', in Smith, S., Booth, K. and Zalewski, M. (eds), *International Theory: Positivism and Beyond* (Cambridge, Cambridge University Press, 1996), p. 11-44.
5 Carr, E. H., *The Twenty Years' Crisis 1919–1939* (London, Macmillan, 1946), p. 87.
6 Ibid., p. 174.
7 Ibid., p. 88.
8 Ibid., p. 75.
9 Bull, '*The Twenty Years' Crisis* thirty years on', p. 629.

10 Ibid. In fairness to Carr, he admitted towards the end of *The Twenty Years' Crisis that an Anglo-American hegemony might be preferable to a Japanese or German hegemony. Carr, The Twenty Years' Crisis,* p. 236.

11 Bull, '*The Twenty Years' Crisis* thirty years on', p. 629.

12 Ibid., p. 638.

13 However, without engaging in an extended discussion of the interpretation of Carr's work, we would argue that Bull's reading is unbalanced for two reasons. First, he underestimates the importance of morality in *The Twenty Years' Crisis*, and Carr's prescription that political theory required both realism and utopianism, morality and power. Second, by focusing on only *The Twenty Years' Crisis*, Bull is not sufficiently sympathetic to the strong utopian undercurrent of Carr's other works in international relations. The utopian dimension of Carr's thought has been developed by Ken Booth in 'Security in anarchy: utopian realism in theory and practice', *International Affairs*, **67**(3) (1991), pp. 527-45; Linklater, Andrew, 'The transformation of political community: E. H. Carr, critical theory and international relations', *Review of International Studies*, **23**(3) (1997), pp. 321-38; and for a comprehensive collection on Carr's work in International Relations and elsewhere, see Cox, Michael (ed.) *E. H. Carr: A Critical Appraisal* (Basingstoke, Palgrave, 2000).

14 Bull, Hedley, *The Anarchical Society* (London, Macmillan, 1977), p. 41.

15 Ibid., p. 13. Emphasis added. Andrew Hurrell has argued that 'the subjective sense of being bound by a community was the cornerstone of his definition of international society'. Hurrell, Andrew, 'International society and the study of regimes: a reflective approach' in Rittberger, Volker (ed.), *Regime Theory and International Relations* (Oxford, Clarendon Press, 1993), p. 63.

16 This point is captured well by R. J. Vincent's epigram, *ubi societas ibi jus est*. Vincent, R. J., 'Order in international politics' in Miller, J. D. B. and Vincent, R. J. (eds), *Order and Violence: Hedley Bull and International Relations* (Oxford, Clarendon Press, 1990), p. 55.

17 Bull, *The Anarchical Society*, p. 140.

18 Andrew Linklater traces the genealogy of this argument back to Vattel, who contended that a responsible state is not 'legally obliged to act in ways that will jeopardise its survival or endanger its vital national interests, but it is beholden to other states to place the survival of order before the satisfaction of minimal national advantages'. Linklater, Andrew, 'What is a good international citizen?', in Keal, Paul (ed.), *Ethics and Foreign Policy* (Canberra, George Allen & Unwin, 1992), pp. 28-9.

19 Linklater, Andrew, *Beyond Realism and Marxism* (London, Macmillan, 1990), p. 14. For an insightful analysis of the overlap between Carr and Bull, see Falk, Richard, 'The critical realist tradition and the demystification of interstate power: E. H. Carr, Hedley Bull and Robert W. Cox', in Gill, S. and Mittelman, J. H. (eds), *Innovation and Transformation in International Studies* (Cambridge, Cambridge University Press, 1997), pp. 39-55.

20 Carr, *The Twenty Years' Crisis*, p. 60.

21 Bull, Hedley, Justice in International Relations: The 1983 Hagey Lectures', in Alderson, Kai, and Hurrell, Andrew (eds), *Hedley Bull on International Society* (London, Macmillan, 2000), p. 227.

22 Bull, *The Anarchical Sodety*, p. 6.

23 Ibid.
24 Ibid.
25 Bull, Hedley, 'Natural law and international relations', *British Journal of International Studies*, **5** (1979), p. 172.
26 Ibid., p. 180.
27 Ibid.
28 Bull, Hedley, review of Donelan, Michael (ed.), *The Reason of States*, *Times Literary Supplement*, 28 April 1978, p. 474.
29 Donelan, Michael, *Times Literary Supplement*, 12 May 1978. p. 528.
30 Bull, Hedley. *Times Literary Supplement*, 26 May 1978, p. 585. Emphasis added.
31 Midgley, E. B. F., 'Natural law and the "Anglo-Saxons" - some reflections in response to Hedley Bull', *British Journal of International Studies*, **5** (1979).
32 Bull, *The Anarchical Society*, p. 20.
33 Ibid., p. 26.
34 For Bull, it was possible to see these goals being achieved at the level of the state, at the level of international society, and at the level of world society. His principal concern in *The Anarchical Society* was to show how these goals were provided for by the society of states.
35 Bull, Hedley, 'The universality of human rights', *Millennium*, **8**(2) (1979), p. 157.
36 Ibid.
37 Jackson, Robert H., 'Martin Wight, international theory and the good life', *Millennium*, **19**(2) (1990); p. 267. Chris Brown also makes this point: 'If diversity entails that states have the right to mistreat their populations, then it is difficult to see why such diversity is to be valued.' Brown, Chris, *International Relations Theory: New Normative Approaches* (Hemel Hempstead, Harvester Wheatsheaf, 1992), p. 125.
38 Booth, Ken, 'Human rights and international relations', *International Affairs*, **71**(1) (1995), pp. 103-26.
39 Bull, The *Anarchical Society*, p. 317.
40 Bull, *Justice*, p. 221. Emphasis added.
41 Rorty, Richard, 'Human rights, rationality, and sentimentality', in Shute, Stephen and Hurley, Susan (eds), *On Human Rights* (London, HarperCollins, 1993), p. 115. For an interesting discussion of Rorty and his relevance to international relations theory, see Cochrane, Molly, 'The liberal ironist, ethics and international relations theory', *Millennium*, **25**(1) (1996), pp. 29-52.
42 Rorty, 'Human rights', pp. 118-19.
43 Ibid., pp. 127 and 133.
44 Bull, *Justice in International Relations*, p. 221.
45 Ibid.
46 Ibid., p. 244.
47 Bull, 'The universality of human rights', p. 158.
48 We think this phrase of Richard Shapcott's captures well Bull's openness to the cultural preferences of others. See Shapcott, Richard, 'Conversation and coexistence: Gadamar and the interpretation of international society', *Millennium*, **32**(1) (1994), pp. 81-2.
49 Bull, *Justice in International Relations*, p. 221-2.
50 Ibid., p. 221.

51 Ibid., p. 223.
52 Ibid.
53 Ibid., p. 221.
54 Falk, Richard, *The Promise of World Order* (London, Harvester Wheatsheaf, 1987), p. 270.
55 Ibid., p. 271. Falk's portrayal of Bull, written in 1979, as an apologist for the statism of the society of states should be set against Bull's doubts in the Hagey lectures about how far 'self-serving' states could be trusted to act as 'local agents of the world common good'. Bull, *Justice in International Relations*, p. 223.
56 Bull, *The Anarchical Society*, p. 305.
57 Ibid., p. 304.
58 Falk, Richard, *Explorations at the Edge of Time* (Philadelphia, Temple University Press, 1992), pp. 22-3.
59 Ibid., p. 22.
60 Ibid., p. 6.
61 Bull, 'Human rights and world politics', p. 89.
62 This is Michael Donelan's useful description of the Natural Law position. See Donelan, Michael, *Elements of International Political Theory* (Oxford, Clarendon Press, 1990), p. 7.
63 Falk, *Explorations*, p. 22.
64 Rorty, 'Human rights', p. 127.
65 Bull, Hedley, 'International law and international order', *International Organization*, **26**(3) (1972), p. 588.
66 Ibid.

4

International System, International Society and World Society: A Re-evaluation of the English School*

RICHARD LITTLE

It has been argued recently that a 'seminal distinction' underpinning the English School's thinking about international relations separates out the existence of an international society from an international system.[1] The distinction was initially made by Bull in *The Anarchical Society*. He argued that 'where states are in regular contact with one another and where in addition there is interaction between them, sufficient to make the behaviour of each a necessary element in the calculation of the other, then we may speak of them forming a system.'[2] Such a system, it is argued, can be distinguished from an international society which is seen to exist

> when a group of states, conscious of certain common interests and common values, form a society in the sense that they conceive of themselves to be bound by a common set of rules in their relations with one another, and share in the working of common institutions.[3]

In addition and related to this central distinction, Members of the English School (MES) also make reference to world society. Whereas states provide the basic units of analysis in an international system and an international society, individuals constitute the essential units of analysis in a world society. For the MES, therefore, world society presupposes a 'world common good' which identifies the 'common ends or values of the universal society of all mankind'.[4]

The MES have looked closely at the relationship between world society, international society and international system. Because the MES have not used this terminology consistently, however, it is not always immediately apparent just how central these three concepts are for the MES approach. Wight, for example, does not distinguish between the ideas of international society and international system and nor does he make reference to world

* This chapter has been written with financial assistance from the Economic and Social Research Council

society. Instead, he tends to conflate all three terms in the concept of a states-system. The Greek city states, for example, are identified as a states-system. In using this term, there is no doubt that Wight saw the Greek city states as forming an international system, in the sense that each city state took the behaviour of other city states into account when making their own calculations. But Wight also saw the Greek city states as an international society bound together by common rules, interests and institutions. Finally, Wight advanced the argument that the Greek city states, like all the states-systems which he examined, were held together by a common culture that was shared by the citizens of all the city states. The Greek city states, in other words, were underpinned by a world society and the Greeks sharply distinguished themselves from the barbarians who were excluded from this Greek world society.[5]

The distinctions drawn between world society, international system and international society may seem, on the face of it, to be relatively straightforward. But the work of the MES demonstrates that the relationship between the three concepts is complex and imperfectly understood. At the same time, their analysis suggests that the relationship between these three concepts has some profound implications for our understanding of how international relations has developed.

As the concepts have come under increasing scrutiny from analysts who are not part of the English School, however, the nature of these concepts and the relationship between them have become increasingly controversial.[6] The aim of this chapter is to re-evaluate these concepts in the light of these critiques. The assessments of three analysts, James, Buzan and Shaw, will be explored.[7] James argues, in the first place, that it is not possible to sustain a meaningful distinction between system and society. As used in international relations the terms can be considered synonymous, and the only question which needs to be answered, according to James, is which of the two terms is the more appropriate. Buzan, on the other hand, accepts that a useful distinction can be drawn between an international system and an international society, but he argues, first, that the MES have failed to identify a clear-cut boundary between system and society, second, that the MES have developed an inadequate explanation to account for the formation and evolution of an international society, and third, that a world society must come into existence before an international society can evolve beyond a given point.

Finally, Shaw, who is a sociologist, unlike James and Buzan who are both international relations (IR) theorists, argues that the distinction between system and society is suspect, but, more important, that the MES have given theoretical priority to a state-centric approach to international relations when developing their distinction and, in the process, they have undervalued the significance of world society and thereby inadvertently reinforced a now outdated Cold War ideology.

Although these three critics all agree that there are problems with the way the MES draw on the distinctions between world society, international society and international system, their assessments of the English School are clearly incompatible. In the final section of the chapter, therefore, an attempt will be made to reconcile these divergent assessments. It will be argued that none of these analysts appreciate the significance of an important but largely unstated methodological assumption made by the MES. The MES assume that it is not possible to understand international relations from a single perspective; competing perspectives are required. Once the significance of this assumption has been grasped, it becomes necessary to reassess the criticisms levelled at the English School. Although the criticisms are largely invalidated as a consequence, Buzan, in particular, is still seen to make an important theoretical contribution.

Critiques of the English School

1. DISSOLVING THE SYSTEM/SOCIETY DISTINCTION

Throughout the international relations literature there are ubiquitous references to the international system and international society, usually without any attempt to distinguish between the two concepts. The indiscriminate use of the terms is seen by one writer, sympathetic to the English School position, to have resulted in 'confusion rather than illumination'.[8] There have been two responses to this confusion. One, favoured by the MES, among others, is to draw a sharp distinction between the two terms. The other is to question the validity of the distinction and to treat the two terms as synonymous.[9] James has developed the most systematic critique of attempts to draw a meaningful distinction between the two terms. He focuses his attack on the MES who have self-consciously endeavoured to pull the two concepts apart. Three features, he suggests, have been used to identify an international society and distinguish it from an international system. James seeks to undermine the capacity of all three of these features to discriminate between a system and a society. First, and most importantly, he notes, whereas an international society is established on the basis of rule-governed behaviour, by the MES, the regularized patterns of behaviour which can be observed in an international system are developed and sustained in the absence of binding rules. James, however, denies that states can interact on a regularized basis in the absence of established rules. Rules, he insists, must underpin any kind of regularized contact. James then reinforces his position by demonstrating that both Bull and Watson have acknowledged the force of this argument. Bull, for example, admits that 'agreements' can be established within an international system.[10] Even more revealing, Watson has acknowledged that he fails to see how an international system as defined by Bull could operate without the assistance of some 'regulatory rules'.[11] Once it is accepted, James argues, that rules are just as necessary in an international system as in an international society, then one of the most significant features used by the English School to distinguish between the two loses all its force.

James then turns to a second feature which has been used by the MES to distinguish between international systems and societies. Bull and Watson have argued that diplomatic machinery is a defining feature of an international society because international systems can persist in the absence of such machinery. James attacks this position by arguing that diplomatic machinery is synonymous with communication. In other words, it is only possible for states to communicate with each other provided that some kind of diplomatic machinery, however primitive, is in place. Again, James turns to MES to make his point for him. Bull, for example, acknowledges that an international system cannot come into existence in the absence of communication between states. He, however, wishes to draw a distinction between the modes of communication which operate in an international system and the more sophisticated modes which operate within an international society where communication is mediated through the presence of a professional diplomat.[12] James denies that such a distinction is valid, because, he argues, communication between states can only take place through the medium of diplomacy.

He then turns to the claim made by MES that only in an international society is there an awareness of 'common interests and common values'. In the first place, James insists that it is necessary to differentiate between interests and values. It is simply not the case, he argues, that common values have ever underpinned international relations. Indeed, he suggests that common values are not a necessary feature of any society. All societies are characterized by diverse and competing values. It becomes perverse, therefore, to suggest that common values are a characteristic of an international society. On the other hand, he considers it equally perverse to suggest that the regularized patterns of interaction which MES associate with an international system could emerge in the absence of common interests. Once, again, therefore, James insists that common interests cannot be used as a distinguishing feature of an international society.

Having dismissed the features used by MES to distinguish an international system from an international society, James extends his argument by demolishing the claim made by the English School that the features which characterize international society have only emerged between states which share a common culture. James readily acknowledges, for example, that European states share a common culture, but he vigorously denies that the rules, common interests, and diplomatic machinery which developed between these states were in any sense a reflection or product of this culture. By the same token, he asserts, the adoption of these rules, interests and diplomatic machinery, by states outside of Europe cannot be equated with cultural imperialism.

James develops his case persuasively and his insistence that MES have failed to establish a clear-cut distinction between international society and international system appears, on the face of it, to be incontestable. His assessment of the role of culture, however, is much more problematic and seems to rest on a misrepresentation of the English School position. MES do not suggest that diplomatic machinery, rules and common interests are a reflection of European culture. On the contrary, they wish to assert that these features have been identified elsewhere, in different cultures. The point they make is that these features only emerge when states share a common culture, reflecting the existence of a world society. The globalization of the European international society has been associated with cultural imperialism, therefore, not because of the extension of the rules operating between the European states, or their conception of interests, or their diplomatic machinery, but because the Europeans insisted that countries operating outside of Europe had to acknowledge and adopt the cultural values propagated by Europe before they would be permitted to enter the European international society.

2. RE-ARTICULATING THE SYSTEM/SOCIETY RELATIONSHIP

In contrast to James who seeks to eliminate the international system/society distinction, Buzan considers that the boundary line separating the two concepts has not been articulated with sufficient clarity. He readily acknowledges the heuristic value of the distinction, but considers that the English School approach to the distinction is theoretically underdeveloped. When MES discuss the distinction, moreover, an unacknowledged tension in their theoretical framework becomes apparent. The important benefits to be gained from the historical insights generated by the English School approach are partially undermined because of the theoretical deficiencies.

In revealing these deficiencies, Buzan draws attention to the relevance of the idea of world society. The tension exists in the English School's theoretical framework, according to Buzan, because world society is related to international system and international society in two different ways, and MES have failed to acknowledge or reconcile these divergent approaches. Buzan draws attention, first, to a developmental approach which is hinted at by Bull. According to this approach, 'international society is a kind of way station on the historical road away from a raw and unmoderated anarchy and towards a world society'.[13] From this perspective then, an international society comes into existence to mitigate the effects of anarchy and to provide the framework within which a world society can come into existence. But this evolutionary pattern runs directly counter to Wight's assessment, given credence by all the MES, that an international society has only ever formed in the context of a culturally homogenous region, which Buzan identifies as an established world society. From Buzan's perspective, Wight's reference to common culture demonstrates that for MES 'the formation of an international society actually depends upon the prior existence of a world society'.[14]

The tension between these two approaches identified by Buzan is obviously problematic and he finds nothing within the writings of MES that helps to resolve it. In an attempt to relieve the tension, Buzan turns to the theoretical literature on society which has been developed in sociology and identifies two very different models formulated initially by Toennies. The first provides a civilizational or *gemeinschaft* assessment in which society is 'something organic and traditionally involving bonds of common sentiment, experience and identity'.[15] This is obviously the conception of society which MES are making reference to when they refer to a culturally homogenous world society. There is no ambivalence here.

The tension starts to become more evident when attention is drawn to the idea of an international society. On most occasions, there is little doubt that MES are thinking of international society in *gemeinschaft* terms. In other words, it is accepted that international society is underpinned by a world society which shares common norms and values. But Buzan also finds evidence in Bull of an attachment to the second model of society which is identified in functional or *gesellschaft* terms. From the perspective of this model, society is depicted as 'contractual and constructed rather than sentimental and traditional'.[16] Far from international society requiring the prior existence of the common culture embedded in world society, the formation of an international society is functional in form and is depicted as a 'rational long-term response to the existence of an increasingly dense and interactive system'.[17]

For Buzan, the tension between these two approaches and models of society has the effect of blurring the international system/society boundary. The failure of MES to articulate the two distinct conceptions of society which they draw upon results, according to Buzan, in theoretical confusion and this is most manifest when they attempt to draw a boundary between an international system and an international society. Like James, Buzan draws attention to the fact that MES acknowledge that the features which they use to identify an international society can be observed in an international system. Watson, for example, observes that 'regulatory rules and institutions of a system usually, and perhaps inexorably, develop to the point where the members become conscious of common values and the system becomes an international society'.[18] Unlike James, however, Buzan does not cite this admission as evidence that the system/society distinction needs to be dissolved. He sees the admission as evidence of theoretical confusion which needs to be sorted out and of a boundary which needs to be redefined by establishing a new and different benchmark.

The confusion is associated by Buzan with the failure to maintain a clear theoretical distinction between the two conceptions of society and, more particularly, to clarify the theoretical implications of the *gesellschaft* conception of society. Instead, despite drawing on some of the theoretical implications of the functional model, the focus by MES is on the *gemeinschaft* model and an historical explanation formulated initially by Wight to account for the emergence of an international society. Although Wight is not at all certain whether a world society or common culture is a necessary precondition for the establishment of an international society, he argues that the only examples of international society which history provides are associated, in practice, with an established world society.

The underlying and unstated assumption made by MES that an established world society provides the best basis for the creation of an international society and that an international society built upon world society foundations will be stronger and more secure than an international society built upon any kind of alternative foundations is accepted by Buzan. But he insists that it is possible, at least theoretically, to conceive of an international society established on functional foundations, without the prior existence of a world society. Furthermore, Buzan asserts that the neo-realists have provided the functional logic which can account for the emergence of an international society from an international system.

Starting from the assumption made by Waltz that as the power of political units increases and they establish the ability to interact, then an unintended consequence will be the formation of an international system. In such a system, the units will not only engage in trade, but they will also experience insecurity.[19] Because the security dilemma is an inherent feature of an anarchic system, Waltz acknowledges that each unit will have to take the behaviour of all the other units into their calculations. As Buzan notes, therefore, Waltz and Bull start from identical conceptions of the international system. Buzan considers that both subscribe to a 'mechanistic' conception of the international system. As Watson observes, in an international system, the systemic pressures 'act mechanically, in the sense that they operate outside of the will of the community concerned'.[20] But whereas Waltz, from Buzan's perspective, fails to move beyond the mechanistic or systemic approach, Bull formulates a definition of society which is 'self-conscious and in part self-regulatory'.[21] Buzan accepts, therefore, that Bull and other MES have developed a framework which extends beyond neo-realism because they are able to establish so clearly 'the principle that system and society are distinct'.[22]

What MES fail to do is to separate out the functional logic of neo-realism from the historical perspective which dominates the English School perspective. Drawing on this functional logic, Buzan argues that it is possible to show how an international system can develop into an international society without the underlying assistance of a world society. But before he can put the functional logic to work, Buzan must first establish a clearly identified boundary line which can distinguish system from society. In seeking to identify this benchmark, Buzan starts from the premise that international systems and societies developed initially on a localized basis, as subsystems of a global system. It becomes necessary, as a consequence, to distinguish boundaries between regional subsystems as well as identifying the benchmark which separates systems from societies. Postulating the existence of regional international systems and societies also raises further questions about what happens when a regional international society comes into contact with a regional international system. Buzan discusses this process in terms of uneven development.[23] In other words, if a regional international society engulfs a regional international system, then the societal links will be more mature and developed in the established international society than in the regional international system. Buzan concludes, therefore, that international society is a differentiated phenomenon and that there are gradations of international society. He argues that at the core of a society the societal links will be very dense and they will become progressively thinner and more attenuated towards the periphery of society.

Introducing the idea of uneven development, however, clearly complicates the task of identifying an unambiguous benchmark between society and system. The solution is to be found, according to Buzan, in the idea of shared identity. From this perspective, an international society emerges unambiguously when units 'not only recognize each other as being the same type of entity, but also are prepared to accord each other legally equal status on that basis'.[24] Once this benchmark has been reached, Buzan argues, then a transformation occurs in the nature of international relations. Whereas weaker parties could easily be brought into an imperial relationship in an international system, these same parties have a much greater chance of survival in an international society where all parties acknowledge each other's sovereign independence.

Having established the benchmark which separates system from society,

Buzan is then able to demonstrate that the benchmark can be reached on the basis of functional logic and without the prior existence of a world society. Following Waltz's lead, Buzan demonstrates that once an anarchic international system has come into existence, the struggle to survive will give rise to a balance of power which in turn promotes the reproduction of the system. But, according to Buzan, the balance of power cannot guarantee the reproduction of the system. He accepts that in a 'free-for-all' system governed by self-help principles it is perfectly possible to envisage one unit transforming anarchy into hierarchy through the establishment of a world empire. Such a development, MES suggest, could help to transmit common culture; and Buzan agrees. But he also insists that common culture can be transmitted by means of functional logic. Operating on the principle identified by Waltz as 'internal balancing',[25] political units constantly monitor developments inside other units embraced by the system, and will seek to emulate any successful practices emerging elsewhere in the system.

As a consequence, the units will become progressively more similar in structure and as the system persists, and interactions become more regularized, the need for rules to mediate and facilitate this interaction will evolve until eventually the units will be pressurized into mutual recognition. In discussing this process, Buzan acknowledges that MES also make reference to the same process when discussing the evolution of international society. Bull, for example, argues that international society emerges in the process of placing limits on the use of force, making provision for the security of contracts and arranging for the assignment of property rights.[26] But Buzan insists that it is only at the juncture when the units trade mutual recognition that the international system is transformed into an international society. At the same time as identifying this benchmark, moreover, it is also important to recognize that the benchmark can be reached by two quite different routes. There is a need to distinguish, as a consequence, between societies which rest on a common culture and those which are multicultural and have developed purely on a functional basis. Buzan is not simply making the point, however, that there are alternative processes involved in establishing an international society, he is also wishing to assert the theoretical point that international societies arising from common culture will possess an inherent advantage over international societies created on the basis of functional logic.

Buzan notes that Bull became increasingly pessimistic about the potential for progress in an anarchic society. But Buzan believes that by eliminating the areas of confusion embedded in the ES approach, grounds for optimism emerge. Buzan postulates that once an international society has come into existence, then international relations will proceed on a much more self-conscious basis. The major states, for example, will self-consciously endeavour to establish a balance of power as a policy goal. Moreover, Buzan also believes that the logic of his model indicates that a potentially infinite agenda will open up for international society. As the capabilities of states, and their interaction capacity, increase, so an incentive emerges for states to extend the scope for order. Functional logic dictates, moreover, that states will be pressurized into participating in this process because they risk falling behind the other states if they fail to become involved.

As an international society moves down this route, Buzan argues, it will become increasingly difficult to separate the evolution of international society from a parallel evolution in world society. The logic of his model indicates that a functionally generated international society will eventually start to take on board those features which provide an international society based on common culture with its inherent advantages. Just as the processes of emulation and socialization identified by Waltz propel states to develop as like-units in the journey from system to society, so the same logic will push states to develop similar cultural features. As a consequence, the point will come when the development of international society and world society will be inextricably intertwined. The evolution of international society and world society will proceed simultaneously on the basis of a common set of processes.

Like James, Buzan considers that MES have failed to discriminate effectively between an international system and an international society. But unlike James, he endeavours to show that the theoretical confusion displayed by the English School can be eliminated and the system/society distinction preserved. In the process, however, he has to work on a much broader canvas than the one used by MES and this enables him to identify an important and unrecognized link between the English School and the neo-realists. By highlighting the functional logic associated with neo-realism, Buzan is able to distinguish two quite separate approaches to the formation of an international society lodged within the English School approach. On the face of it, despite the common starting point, Buzan's innovations enable him to advance some considerable theoretical distance beyond the concluding position reached by MES. Reassessing MES in the light of Buzan's analysis, however, it will be suggested, in the final section, that if he had drawn more extensively on their work, he could have identified a route which would have allowed him to travel further and more easily.

3. TRANSCENDING INTERNATIONAL SOCIETY

Despite their differences, Buzan and James, along with MES, depict international society in positive terms. They see international society not only as a fruitful concept for understanding international relations but also a progressive force in world politics. As Buzan observes, promoting the concept of international society helps to construct a way of thinking about international relations that if widely adopted would have 'beneficial effects on the practice of how states relate to each other'.[27] In developing this argument, moreover, as shown in the previous section, Buzan also endeavours to show that beyond a certain point, international society can only progress if there is a concomitant evolution in world society. Shaw, operating from a sociological perspective, develops an almost diametrically opposed position, distancing himself from both James and Buzan, as well as MES. He asserts, in the first place, that world society, or what he prefers to call global society, has 'an ideological significance which is ultimately opposed to that of international society'.[28] His principal objective is to demonstrate that the English School, while acknowledging that world society has a moral priority over international society, develops a mode of analysis which gives international society ontological priority over world society. Recent events, Shaw asserts, have seriously challenged the significance which MES - as well as James and Buzan - ascribe to international society. At the heart of his analysis is the assertion that the theory of international society can be best understood as a 'central ideology of the international system in the Cold War period'.[29] With the Cold War at an end, it follows that the significance of the idea of international society is becoming increasingly redundant and that it is necessary to adopt an alternative framework in order to make sense of what is going on.

Unlike James and Buzan, however, Shaw avoids establishing a sharp dichotomy between system and society on the grounds that Bull, and indeed all MES, recognize that society is no more than an 'element' in the international system.[30] His analysis, therefore, also begins by focusing on the way in which the international system should be distinguished from international society. He starts from the premise that the concept of an international system is more fundamental and less problematic than international society, since it simply denotes a pattern of interaction between states. But even here alarm bells start ringing for Shaw because the concept thereby restricts analysis to an essentially state-centric approach. This initial difficulty associated with the English School approach is then compounded by the identification of international society as an 'element' of the international system. Shaw asserts that by establishing this indissoluble link with a state-centric framework 'the concept and terminology of international society only work providing that the insulation of international studies from theoretical discourse with other social sciences is maintained'.[31] This claim rests on the assumption that no where else in the social sciences does it make any sense to lock the concepts of state and society together as MES do. And Shaw believes that progress can only made if international relations are 'theoretically integrated in the mainstream of the social sciences'.[32] Once this attempt is made, a second problem with the English School approach is immediately exposed. Shaw argues that MES define society in terms of a consensus among its members and there is, as a consequence, a commitment to the functional view of society which Shaw considers to be widely discredited. Functionalists, it is argued, presuppose the normative coherence of society. Such a presupposition is now eschewed, according to Shaw, first because it fails to recognize that conflict is an inherent feature of any society, and second, because functionalists insist upon defining society in terms of one of its dimensions. The definition, in other words, forces the conclusion that the emergence of conflict, or the loss of consensus, denotes the elimination of society. Instead of being identified as a complex and multifaceted phenomenon, society is reduced to a set of functional relations.[33]

Shaw prefers to identify society in terms of human relationships involving 'mutual expectations and understandings with the possibility of mutually oriented actions'.[34] Only functionalists, he argues, require society to be defined in terms of 'consensus around a coherent value system'.[35] This line of argument, of course, brings us full circle back to the position adopted by James. But, unlike James, Shaw does not think that it is helpful to apply the concept of society to relations between states. He sees it as potentially confusing to talk of a society of states 'when most societies are understood to be composed of individual human beings'.[36] But even if the English School terminology is accepted, Shaw remains critical because MES consider international society to be 'self-sufficient, with no theoretically articulable relationship to the larger pattern of human relations'.[37]

Given the weight that Shaw places on this argument, it is surprising, at first sight, to find him accepting that states do in fact behave as though the international system and society represent a 'relatively discrete order of reality, distinct from, even as it interacts with, world politics, world economy, culture and society'.[38] But instead of taking this fact for granted, as MES do, Shaw insists that this 'self-evident separation of the international system and within it of international society, is however something which needs to be explained and critically examined'.[39] Shaw's explanation is that the study of international relations came of age during the course of the Cold War which, retrospectively, can be seen to be a highly unusual historical period. 'Uniquely in modern history outside wartime, the international unequivocally dominated society and domestic politics.'[40]

Only when the Cold War came to an end did it become clear, according to Shaw, how effectively the structure of the international system had managed to straitjacket domestic politics. In the aftermath of the Cold War, there was an explosion in domestic politics and the reverberations had dramatic consequences for international politics. Instead of international politics imposing constraints on domestic politics, the process was reversed and previously stable international structures have been ruptured by the impact of domestic politics. Shaw believes that this development has shattered the attempt by both neo-realists and MES to establish the study of international politics as an autonomous discipline. Although MES and the neo-realists diverge on many issues, they have both encouraged the development of an independent study of international relations. The move was sanctioned only because it took place during a very atypical phase of world history. Throughout the Cold War it was plausible for neo-realists to talk of an international system of states and for MES to talk of an international society as independent realms of activity. But, Shaw insists, events in the post-Cold War era are 'breaking up the insulated categories of international theory'.[41] Like Rosenau,[42] Shaw believes that we are moving into an era of 'post-international politics' and that it will become obvious that the 'self evident separation of the international system and within it of international society' was a peculiar product of the Cold War.[43]

From Shaw's perspective, the immediate aftermath of the Cold War represents a point of transition. He recognizes that English School advocates of international society may well be encouraged by the demise of global ideological fracture which threatened the coherence of international society. But Shaw sees as more pertinent the increasing violation of the non-intervention norm which lies at the heart of the international society perspective and he asserts that the resulting 'ad hoc modification to international practice' is undermining the 'theoretical perspective of international society'.[44] In developing this argument, Shaw does not wish to assert that the idea of international society lacks any theoretical utility. His aim is to attack the English School belief that international society has 'no theoretically articulable relationship to the larger pattern of human relationships' and to assert instead that international society is a sub-society or sub-culture of a wider global or world society.[45]

Contrary to Bull's assertion that there is not yet a world society in existence, Shaw insists that there is 'a global system of social relations in which all human beings are, to some extent, connected, and which covers the entire globe'.[46] These social relations can be identified in terms of 'global commodity production and exchange, through global culture and mass media, and through the increasing development of world politics'.[47] But Shaw accepts that in order to sustain this argument, it is necessary to rely on a weak conception of society. International society, by contrast, rests on a stronger conception of society, which is built on common values and a degree of consensus.

Once it is accepted that there is a useful theoretical distinction to be drawn between international society and world or global society then it becomes meaningful to investigate 'the transformation of relationships between the international and the global'.[48] But to take advantage of this possibility, it is necessary to engage in 'substantive theoretical reformulation'.[49] In particular, it is necessary to give ontological priority to global (world) society as evidenced in economic, cultural and institutional arenas. Shaw accepts that dominant institutions operate at the international level, but he insists that it is necessary to examine them in the broader context of world society. By the same token, Shaw accepts that the institutions which define international society have their own dynamic which deserves empirical investigation, but it remains the case that developments in international society must still be studied 'in the context of the entire picture of the development of world society which has theoretical priority'.[50]

From Shaw's perspective, then, the evolution of international society is only one feature of the overall process of globalization which describes the development of relations and institutions in world society. Shaw accepts that the processes associated with the development of international society have been important, but he also insists that they can only be understood when examined in the context of other processes which have encouraged the evolution of world society - in particular the processes associated with economic and cultural integration. From Shaw's perspective, the Cold War arrested the development of globalization. The evolution of international society was given priority over the processes associated with the formation of a global economy and a global culture which underpin the development of world society. Now that the Cold War has ended it has become more important than ever, Shaw argues, to ensure that the ideological implications of neo-realism and the English School are recognized. Such approaches are seen by Shaw to provide normative and theoretical priority to the state system. With the Cold War over, Shaw believes that the potential now exists for the emergence of a genuine sense of global responsibility within the framework provided by an embryonic global civil society. Evidence for this development is identified with the increasing desire within world society for humanitarian intervention. There is, Shaw argues, an evident struggle 'between the instincts of statesmen to maintain the principles of sovereignty and intervention, and the pressures from global civil society to transcend them'.[51] Shaw accepts that a fundamental and explicit shift in this direction is unlikely for a very long period of time. Nevertheless, these issues will form 'foci of contestation' and Shaw believes that theorists have an obligation to 'clarify' the relations between two sets of concepts: one associated with international society, and the other with world society and to acknowledge their associated ideological implications.[52]

Reconciling the differences

The three critics of the English School each express their case cogently and with conviction. Yet, in the final analysis, their views are mutually contradictory and it is necessary to investigate more closely the validity of their claims. The intention here, however, is not to adjudicate between the competing assessments, but rather to find a way of reconciling the differences so that our understanding of international relations as well as our appreciation of the English School can be enhanced. This task will be undertaken from two different angles. First, it will be suggested that in developing their critiques of the English School, the three critics have failed to take sufficient account of the methodological posture adopted by MES. When the approach is looked at more closely, it becomes clear that none of the three critics has correctly appreciated the methodological starting-point adopted by the English School. The criticisms made by James, Buzan and Shaw all need to be modified when the methodological posture adopted by MES has been taken into account.

Distinct from, but related to, this methodological position, are the ontological assumptions made by MES. Again, the three critics have not fully grasped the position adopted by MES. The arguments advanced by the critics, however, can be re-evaluated once these methodological and ontological assumptions have been clarified, and a more rounded assessment of the English School view of international relations can then be presented.

1. THE ENGLISH SCHOOL METHODOLOGY

On the face of it, MES have always been deeply suspicious of methodological discussions and very little has been done to clarify the position. Indeed, Bull went out of his way to ridicule the attempts being made, largely in the United States, to develop a more systematic approach to methodology in international relations theory.[53] Attention is also frequently drawn to Wight's claim about the absence of international theory and his characterization of the international system as a 'realm of recurrence and repetition'.[54] Yet a closer examination quickly demonstrates that MES adopted a much more sophisticated methodological position than is immediately apparent. Like many US analysts, they favoured a systems methodology, to compare and contrast how international relations have operated in different historical eras. As a result of their investigations, from an early stage, MES presupposed that international relations have evolved and changed over time and that contemporary international relations are in some important respects unique.

MES have worked on the methodological assumption that because activity in the international arena is complex and ambiguous it is necessary to examine the arena from divergent perspectives. These perspectives, to some extent, capture the competing forces at work within the international arena. Bull has identified the methodological implications which flow from the fact that the anarchic international system is also an international society and a transnational network of relations. He argues:

> Because international society is no more than one of the basic elements at work in modern international politics, and is always in competition with elements of a state of war and of transnational solidarity or conflict, it is always erroneous to interpret international events as if international society were the sole or the dominant element.[55]

The methodological injunction which flows from this position considers it a mistake to 'reify', as Bull puts it, the international system, international society, or world society. Instead, it is essential to accept that although it is possible to view the international arena as an international system, this must never be done at the expense of recognizing that the international arena is also an international society and a world society. When viewing international relations in terms of a system rather than a society, for example, different features of reality are brought into focus. Watson concludes, therefore, that the distinction between international systems and societies is useful 'not because it causes the complex reality of international relations to be simplified into this category or that, but because it allows that reality to be illuminated by considering it from a particular point of view'.[56]

None of the three critics acknowledge this methodological injunction and as a consequence they inadvertently misrepresent the English School position. In fact, this is hardly surprising since MES make so few attempts to explicate the nature and implications of their methodological position. It is, however, possible to translate this position into more conventional social science terminology, first, by depicting the international system as a structural mode of explanation and international society as an agency-based mode of explanation, and, second, by locating these different modes of explanation on different levels of analysis.

States, according to MES, are constrained by the anarchic structure of the international system. Analysing international relations from a systemic perspective, therefore, is seen to generate a mechanistic mode of explanation which is identical to the structural approach adopted by the neo-realists. Seen from this perspective, policies adopted by states are shaped by the structure of the international system. But MES also recognize that states can, to some extent, ameliorate the effects of the systemic structures, by forming the kind of institutions associated with international society. These institutions can act as a buffer against these systemic forces. During the

Cold War, for example, the United States and the Soviet Union found ways of slowing down the arms race by establishing arms control measures. The bipolar structure of the international system, while undoubtedly stimulating the arms race, did not completely determine policy. There was room for manoeuvre. And within this space, the two super powers could act as independent agents, co-operatively developing security regimes which helped to foster the development of an international society.

It is also possible, in the second place, to translate the English School methodology into the social science terminology associated with levels of analysis. The impact of the international system and international society can be seen to operate on different levels of analysis. But MES are also quick to point to the existence of world society operating on a third level of analysis. MES, moreover, are acutely aware that there are important links between these levels of analysis. International society, for example, is seen to be in some way causally linked to world society, although MES do not proceed very far in accounting for the nature of this link.

Despite their aversion to methodological discussion, therefore, the English School can, without much difficulty, be tapped into a long-established set of methodological concerns. By ignoring these methodological implications, the critics fail to recognize some of the important implications of the English School's position. For example, by attempting to dissolve the distinction between international systems and societies, James fails to see that the English School are drawing on divergent levels of analysis to provide different perspectives on a common reality. Buzan makes a similar error. By attempting to draw an ontological distinction between international system and society, Buzan fails to recognize that the distinction is established by MES primarily on methodological grounds.[57] And, by the same token, although Shaw recognizes that international system and society are describing a common reality, he seriously underestimates the significance that MES attach to world society, and fails to recognize that world society is seen to operate on a different but no less significant level of analysis.

Once it has been recognized that the critics have failed to take account of the methodological position adopted by the English School, it becomes possible to reassess their critiques. First, it can be suggested that because James fails to recognize that for MES, system and society are part of a common reality, his criticism falls to the ground. Bull, in particular, was willing to acknowledge that an international system cannot operate in the absence of an international society. For systemic forces to operate, they require an international society as a backdrop. The criticism developed by James, however, does apply to Buzan, who also fails to recognize that MES see international system and international society as providing different perspectives or levels of analysis. Buzan does not recognize that his ontological boundary separating system from society violates the methodological posture adopted by MES. Nevertheless, his analysis draws attention to an important distinction between *gemeinschaft* and *gesellschaft* societies which could usefully be accommodated by the English School. Finally, although Shaw underestimates the importance of world society in the English School framework, he does demonstrate that there are important ideological implications associated with the three perspectives which need to be taken into account. Levels of analysis raise more than methodological issues.

2. THE ENGLISH SCHOOL ONTOLOGY

The three critics all focus exclusively on the ontological implications of the distinctions drawn between international system, international society and world society. This focus of attention is eminently understandable, however, because MES also acknowledge that there are ontological as well as methodological implications to be drawn from these distinctions. The difficulties arise because the critics fail to examine the ontological implications in conjunction with the methodological implications. The consequences of this failure prove most interesting in the case of Buzan because of his desire to extend the framework provided by the English School.

Buzan's analysis is flawed from the English School perspective because he does not recognize that although system and society can be separated theoretically, they must be capable of mapping onto a common reality. By giving priority to an ontological distinction, Buzan eliminates this possibility. MES, by contrast, give priority to the methodological distinction and open up the possibility of comparing societal and systemic forces. But MES run into problems when attention is turned to the evolution of international society. Bull and Watson acknowledge that Europe could be examined from both a systemic and a societal perspective. But when they come to discuss the evolution of the European international society, it becomes very unclear how this expansion should be characterized. In very general terms, they appear to envisage the European society/system interacting and then absorbing other international society/systems. But the nature of the links between these states-systems is left unclarified.

Curiously, before Bull and Watson embarked on their study of the evolution of world society, Wight had already established a framework for describing this process. Whereas Bull and Watson portray the European international society steadily expanding through the centuries, Wight envisages a global states-system in operation throughout this period. But the international society aspect of this states-system is characterized in terms of a dual circle. The centre circle is made up of the European states which recognize each other as equals and is underpinned by a common culture. The states in the outer circle are related to the European states on the basis of rules, interests and institutions, but there is no common culture and the rules, interests and institutions take a different form to the ones that operate within Europe.[58]

Although this model is very Euro-centric in formulation and therefore provides a very incomplete picture of the world system, it can be considerably strengthened by attaching it to Buzan's analysis. The inner circle can be defined in *gemeinschaft* terms, while the outer circle can be defined in *gesellschaft* terms. It then becomes clear that the boundary established by Buzan to separate system from society - a manoeuvre which is methodologically flawed from the English School perspective - can be used to separate the *gemeinschaft* centre circle from *gesellschaft* outer circle.[59] Systemic relations can then be mapped onto this societal model.

Conclusion

This chapter has described three critiques of the English School. All three critiques share a common flaw. Each fails to take account of the methodology which underpins the approach adopted by MES. When this methodology is taken into account, the English School proves to be much more robust and resistant to criticism than any of the three critics recognize. Despite the failure to recognize the implications which flow from the methodological position adopted by MES, the critics nevertheless manage to throw an interesting light on their approach and Buzan's analysis can be incorporated into the approach to its considerable advantage.

The argument developed in this chapter hinges upon the assumption that the critics have failed to understand the implications which flow from the methodology which underpins the English School approach. If this is true, then two conclusions can be drawn from this analysis. First, the failure of MES to spell out the nature and implications of their methodological position has precipitated considerable and unnecessary confusion. Second, the confusion can be reduced by making clear that the methodology underpinning the English School approach is lodged much more centrally in the social science tradition than is often recognized.[60]

Notes

1 Watson, A., *The Evolution of International Society: A Comparative Historical Analysis* (London, Routledge, 1992), p. 4.

2 Bull, H., *The Anarchical Society: A Study of Order in World Politics* (London, Macmillan, 1977), p. 10.
3 Ibid., p. 13.
4 Ibid., p. 84.
5 See, in particular, Wight, M., *Systems of States* (Leicester, Leicester University Press, 1977).
6 The identification and early criticism of the 'English School' came from R. E. Jones. See 'The English School of international relations: a case for closure', *Review of International Studies*, 7(1) (1981), pp. 1-14.
7 James, A., 'System or society', *Review of International Studies*, **19**(3) (1993), p. 269; Buzan, B., 'From international system to international society: structural realism and regime theory meet the English School', *International Organization*, **47**(3) (1993), pp. 327-52; Shaw, M., 'Global society and global responsibility: the theoretical, historical and political limits of "International Society"', *Millennium*, **21**(3) (1992), pp. 421-34.
8 Zhang, Y., 'China's entry in international society: beyond the "Standard of Civilization"', *Review of International Studies*, **17**(1) (1991), pp. 3-16, especially pp. 3-4.
9 See, for example, Berridge, G., 'The political theory and institutional history of states systems', *British Journal of International Studies*, **6**(2) (1980), pp. 82-92.
10 Bull, *Anarchical Society*, p. 249.
11 Watson, A., 'Hedley Bull, states systems and international societies', *Review of International Studies*, **13**(2) (1987), pp. 147-53, especially p. 151.
12 Bull, *Anarchical Society*, p. 170.
13 Buzan, 'From international system', p. 338.
14 Ibid., p. 337.
15 Ibid., p. 333.
16 Ibid.
17 Ibid., p. 334.
18 Watson, 'Hedley Bull', p. 151.
19 Buzan draws on Waltz, K., *Theory of International Politics* (Reading, MA, Addison-Wesley, 1979).
20 Watson, *Evolution of International Society*, p. 311.
21 Buzan, 'From international system', p. 331.
22 Ibid.
23 Ibid., p. 345.
24 Ibid.
25 See the discussion in Waltz, *Theory of International Politics*.
26 Bull, *Anarchical Society*, pp. 4-5.
27 Buzan, 'From international system', p. 330.
28 Shaw, 'Global society and global responsibility', p. 433.
29 Ibid., p. 422.
30 Bull, *Anarchical Society*, pp. 41 and 319.
31 Shaw, 'Global society and global responsibility', p. 428.
32 Ibid.
33 Ibid., pp. 428-9.
34 Ibid., p. 428.
35 Ibid., p. 429.

36 Ibid.
37 Ibid.
38 Ibid., p. 424.
39 Ibid.
40 Ibid., p. 425.
41 Ibid., p. 426.
42 See Rosenau, J. N., *Turbulence in World Politics* (Hemel Hemstead and New York, Harvester Wheatsheaf, 1990).
43 Shaw, 'Global society and global responsibility', p. 424.
44 Ibid., p. 427.
45 Ibid., p. 429.
46 Ibid.
47 Ibid.
48 Ibid., p. 430.
49 Ibid.
50 Ibid.
51 Ibid., p. 432.
52 Ibid., p. 433.
53 See Bull, H., 'International theory: the case for a classical approach', in Knorr, K. and Rosenau, J. N. (eds), *Contending Approaches to International Politics* (Princeton, NJ, Princeton University Press, 1969).
54 Wight, M., 'Why is there no international theory?' in Butterfield, H. and Wight, M. (eds), *Diplomatic Investigations* (London, George Allen & Unwin, 1966).
55 Bull, *Anarchical Society*, p. 51.
56 Watson, 'Hedley Bull', p. 153.
57 Buzan can, of course, argue that Bull also made an ontological distinction between system and society. But the methodological distinction takes priority.
58 Wight, *Systems of States*, pp. 125–8.
59 The relationship between the inner and outer circles is discussed in more detail in Little, R., 'Neorealism and the English School: a methodological, ontological and theoretical reassessment', *European Journal of International Relations*, **1**(1) (1995), pp. 9–34.
60 This line of argument is more fully developed in Little, R., 'The English School's contribution to the study of International Relations', *European Journal of International Relations*, **6**(3) (2000), pp. 395-422.

5

Four Meanings of International Society: A Trans-Atlantic Dialogue

OLE WÆVER[1]

Introduction

In recent years, the debates on and of the so-called English School have again come to touch mainstream international relations, i.e. American theories. After a long period of American disregard of the English School (except for a few offhand references to *The Anarchical Society*[2]), the concept of 'international society' has gained new notice in particular in those circles either elaborating or critically engaging with 'constructivism'.[3] Also due to an increasing attention to international law and attempts to mate international law and international relations, the English tradition with its continuous inclusion of international law has come back into focus.[4] Possibly also the general 'pattern' of American(ized) international relations points to a new attention to the English School: the 1990s are witnessing a moderate move by the mainstream towards more 'philosophical' and historical reflections (which meets a demand from post-structuralists and constructivists - without of course going all the way to what was wanted by them). This opens up for the English School, viewed as a moderate, comprehensible, non-extreme approach, to re-import philosophical, ethical and historical reflection without actually having to read 'one's own' reflectivists.[5] From the eastern - mainly British - side of the Atlantic, American mainstream international relations and the English School have also been re-connected, often in attempts to show the superiority or at least respectability of the English School.[6]

The relationship between American mainstream international relations ('the discipline') and the English School is a curious story of sporadic contacts and periods of near isolation. If we use the standard picture of 'the discipline' (as defined by US developments) as going through a number of great debates, there was a strong English component to the first debate (realism vs. idealism) with Carr's *The Twenty Years' Crisis*[7] as the defining work, and although the second debate was largely about a new American trend, 'scientific' international relations, the debate as such was triggered and focused by an intervention from the British school.[8] In the third debate (realism vs. interdependence vs. marxism; the inter-paradigm debate), however, the English School played little role. Even the obvious business of comparing and connecting the triptych of the inter-paradigm debate with that of Martin Wight (Realism, Rationalism, Revolutionism) was not a big enterprise. (The slightly different choice of which positions to include is not terribly interesting, but the different status of the 'paradigms' or 'schools' - not which, but what are they - certainly deserves serious attention.[9])

Possibly, the lack of contact during this period had causes on both sides of the Atlantic. The American debate (which should here rather be read as 'the mainstream' because it can contain non-American, even British, contributors, as with the key-role of Banks in defining 'the inter-paradigm debate') did not find the 'English School' a very interesting position because the mainstream debate focused on what we would call today the 'ontological' questions - what the world is made up of (states, welfare seeking individuals, or classes - and therefore an emphasis on the reflections themselves, on the traditions, seemed an oddly indirect approach.[10] The English School, on its side, might have been less interventionist vis-à-vis mainstream debates during this period because it went through a rather less productive, less theory-inclined, introverted, and more repetitive phase;[11] more on this later when I sketch a series of 'generations' in the English School.

With the fourth debate of international relations - the 1980s to early 1990s' debate between rationalists and reflectivists - the English School gained renewed prominence, and the question has arisen: how to view the English School contributions in relation to American theoretical development. Have the Americans simply taken a long and tortuous road to rediscovering what the English School has said all along?[12] Is the English School an interesting *position* worth aiming for, although in its original English version imprecise and unscientific to an extent that makes it inferior to American international relations theory (in which case the best of all worlds will be when the Americans arrive scientifically to the English School position)?[13] Or are there important differences between the two but with a potential for fruitful synthesizing?[14] Or do they pursue converging interests with each having important lessons for the other at different points, but no possibility of actual merger (the principal conclusion of the examination that follows)?

The focus for this comparison will be the conceptions of ideational structures and their relationship to power and interests in American mainstream rationalism, American (mainstream?) constructivism, American post-structuralism and the English School respectively. What exactly is the nature of institutions/international society - where and what is it, how and why, and how much is there of it?

The lessons from this chapter can thus be taken in two different forms: as debate *about* the English School, its strengths and weaknesses vis-à-vis American international relations; or as debate *within* the English School, and here, in particular, clarifying different meanings of international society, and thereby - more constructively - different layers or parallel forms of international society as these are analysed/constructed in the different languages of 'society' involved in the literature of the English School, something which becomes clearer by comparison with the American literature. The former is a 'theory' question; for those less interested in 'the English School' and more in 'international society', the chapter can be read the second way.

The chapter is structured as follows. Section one outlines an interpretation of the phases and main debates of American international relations. From this platform, three main American positions are delineated: mainstream institutionalism, constructivism and post-structuralism. After a similar overview of the four phases of the English School, each of the three American positions are compared with the English School. To examine more closely the cardinal question of what exactly international society consists of, and thus where to place it in relation to the different conceptions of institutions in the different American theories, four American theorists - Kissinger, Morgenthau, Ashley and Keohane - are introduced in order to show by analogy some of the possible main positions one can take on how to relate international society and interests. Finally, some of the dichotomies shared by these positions are deconstructed, with pointers to a missing type of institution based on the work mainly of Richard Ashley. Here it can be seen that similar problems are present within the English School conception. At this point it has become possible to construct a more systematic typology of meanings of international society, and the article then concludes in terms both of the natures of international society and by arguments about the development of the discipline - on both sides of the Atlantic.

Disciplinary developments and parallel phases

THE DEVELOPMENT OF THE (AMERICAN) DISCIPLINE OF INTERNATIONAL RELATIONS

It has become a convention to tell the story of international relations in terms of greater and lesser debates, and rightly this discipline uses the image of battles to structure its self-conception more thoroughly than most other disciplines. It is useful to summarize these debates here because they offer us both a record with which to compare the phases of the English School in order to understand the periods of contact and isolation, and suggest which current positions to choose for the comparison with the English School.

The first and founding debate of the discipline was that of realists and idealists in the 1930s and 1940s, epitomized by Carr's *The Twenty Years' Crisis 1919–1939*[15] and Morgenthau's *Scientific Man vs Power Politics*,[16] not much of a debate actually, but constructed afterwards as one.[17] The second debate was more real as debate, but maybe for that reason less easily ritualized as uncontested history on which to build. In the second debate, 'modern', post-war American ideals of social *science* clashed with the traditional methods of diplomatic history, law and philosophy as manifested in all of the major realist works of the first debate, including the two mentioned above. The self-assured offensive of the 'scientists' had mostly appeared in the late 1950s to early 1960s, but the debate as debate appeared in the late 1960s,[18] and when it was thus defined as a debate it was largely over as such, ready to enter the records of the discipline as yet another self-defining moment.

The third debate - in Britain also known as the inter-paradigm debate - followed from a crisis of the realist world-view.[19] Trans-nationalism, interdependence and Marxist dependencia analysis emerged to paint different pictures of what international relations was all about.

The next chapter of the story is less undisputedly established as a numbered debate to be included in the succession, but most would agree that something like a major battle occurred again in the mid-1980s to mid-1990s - why not call it 'the fourth debate'?[20] Postmodernists and other 'critical theorists' challenged the discipline as to its philosophical basis, its view of language, knowledge, truth, science, politics and ethics. Not everybody would take positions at one of the extremes, but it was clearly felt that the axis that could generate the most heated debate was the one between what became known as 'rationalists versus reflectivists'.[21] The move towards this axis was interrelated with the rapprochement between neo-realists and neo-liberals who came to agree on a common model for 'social science'; almost a delayed victory for the scientific side of the second debate.

The 'official' formulation of the rationalist–reflectivist debate was interestingly done in terms of two approaches to international institutions. This is interesting for our current purpose, because it should make it easier to connect this debate to the question of what international society is and how the English School has conceived of it. According to Keohane, 'rationalistic theory can be used to explore the conditions under which cooperation takes place, and it seeks to explain why international institutions are constructed by states'.[22] Thus rationalist theories of institutions take actors with given interests as their starting-point and then study whether or when they choose to construct institutions. Reflectivists work the opposite way round. They mostly study more encompassing institutions (such as state sovereignty, self-help or power-balancing) and they argue that:

> institutions do not merely reflect the preferences and power of the units constituting them; the institutions themselves shape those preferences and that power. Institutions are therefore *constitutive* of actors as well as vice versa. It is not sufficient in this view to treat the preferences of individuals as given exogeneously; they are affected by institutional arrangements, by prevailing norms, and by historically contingent discourse among people seeking to pursue their purposes and solve their self-defined problems.[23]

Keohane's article has been much criticized by 'reflectivists' for the way it lumps people together, for the label and for the 'unfair' evaluation based on the terms of rationalists. His exposition of the 'two approaches' does, however, capture something important from the fourth debate: the question of whether theory is to start from given states (as choice-making individuals) and see what systemic patterns and specific arrangements can be explained from features of their set-up and possibly internal characteristics, or to study how these units are produced by something that can variably be called practices, discourses, institutions or structuration. This dimension will be absolutely central to the investigation in this article.

If the fourth debate is numbered and named at the time when it is fading off, as the others were, this means that we are now 'after the fourth debate', which probably is a useful designation for bringing out especially the emerging role of 'constructivism'. After the fourth debate, which was a very harsh battle between rationalists and mainly post-structuralist 'reflectivists' who mutually depicted the other as not only wrong but harmful and dangerous, a constructivist position has increasingly managed to establish itself somewhere in the middle ground between the two.[24] Some of the constructivists are very keen on distancing themselves from post-structuralism and emphasizing that although they do not share the rationalist research programme (in terms of choice theoretical ontology and 'micro-foundations'), they do share the aspiration for social scientific explanation and research programmes.[25]

Thus, the main positions with which to compare the English School at present are neo-liberal institutionalism (as the major 'rationalist' theory of institutions), constructivism and post-structuralism. Neo-realism could have been considered as well since it does have views on institutions,[26] but this contrast does not seem terribly interesting. Sophisticated neo-realism might be able to connect fruitfully to the English School and will be dealt with below, together with other rationalists.

FOUR PHASES OF THE ENGLISH SCHOOL

Before we proceed to the actual comparison of these positions, we should have an overview of the evolution of the English School in order to understand the way its relationship with American mainstream international relations has evolved. The English School has passed through four phases that do not correspond neatly to the four debates of the discipline.

1959–1966: Phase 1, struggling for a position on 'international relations' and developing a problematique of international society.
1966–1977: Phase 2, producing the main works: *The Anarchical Society* and *Systems of States*.
1977–1992: Phase 3, employing the approach; filling out holes, etc.
1992– Phase 4, renewed creativity; setting the English School position in play in relation to new challenges and theoretical innovations.

Phase 1 1959 marks the founding of the British Committee, and 1966 is the year of publication of *Diplomatic Investigations* as well as of Bull's 'International theory: the case for a classical approach'.[27] From Thompson's 1954 invitation to Butterfield to set up a British parallel to the American Rockefeller Committee (with Morgenthau, Niebuhr, Wolfers, Waltz and others), the British group that eventually formed first had to struggle to define their overall attitude to International Relations as well as to international relations, i.e. to the (idea of) a discipline as well as its object of study. Should international relations be viewed as a subject in its own right? On the one hand, there was a clear feeling that the Americans who were then starting to construct international relations seriously as a discipline were on to something,[28] but, on the other hand, as Butterfield noticed at a later point:

> For a long time after Martin [Wight]'s appointment as Reader in International Relations, he was not quite persuaded of the credentials of the subject as an academic study; in the same period I, too, was sceptical ... and in any case I would hold that there are certain subjects, including history ... that can best be taught, best studied perhaps, by people who don't believe in them too much.[29]

Furthermore, the committee had to figure out what to focus on as the most interesting question – and the answer became 'international society': 'The most fundamental question you can ask in international theory is, What is international society?'[30]

Phase 2 From 1966, the ideas of *Diplomatic Investigations* and of the never published results of the second collective committee project (on historic states-systems) were unfolded into two of the major works of the School, both appearing in 1977: Bull's *Anarchical Society*, foreshadowed by his chapters in *Diplomatic Investigations*, and Wight's posthumous *Systems of States* that explores further the theme of 'Western values' from *Diplomatic Investigations* by investigating the origins of the European states-system, but it also publishes Wight's main input into the second project. In its empirical sweep, this was executed by Watson,[31] while several of the theoretical problems of historic systems are still unexplored.

The works of Bull and Wight took diverging or maybe complementary roads. Wight (in line with the argument about sovereignty in 'Why is there no international theory?') explored *other* states-systems, including studies of the formative period of the European states-system (i.e. the border in time and space of the European system to other kinds of international society). Bull, in contrast, explored in greater detail one system: our European-turned-global states-system, its mechanisms, institutions and ethical dilemmas. Bull and Watson's *The Expansion of International Society*[32] is, in some sense, a touch point between the two, while Watson's *The Evolution*[33] clearly is in the Wightian vein.

Phase 3 After the publication in 1977 of these two main works, some of the empirical projects by the original figures continued,[34] and the work by others in preparing much of Wight's theoretical works for publication continued.[35] More visibly, a new 'generation' of English School writers had begun to appear on the scene[36] and even published collectively in ways that clearly contributed to the image of a school.[37a] They would use the terms and schemata of Wight and Bull, employ the approach, and in many ways fill out holes left by the founding works, read those classics that had been ignored, discuss new political dilemmas with the old reference points, and in general use the three R triptych to attack all new positions as being either barren realists ignoring international society or naive revolutionists risking the acquis or acquired knowledge of existing international society. Probably, it is no accident that it is in this period we get the 1981–1989 Jones–Grader–Wilson debate, the major existential self-reflections of the 'school'.[37b]

Phase 4 1992 saw some novel appearances: The *Millennium* Special Issue[38] and the Limerick workshop, on which the present volume is based. Several new names started to appear, and some of the known ones took up new issues, all pointing to a renewed creativity, a new willingness to engage with theoretical and philosophical issues and to reflect on the English School in relation to other approaches. In contrast to the preceding phase there was now a willingness to set English School insights and approaches at stake in relation to new challenges and theoretical innovations.

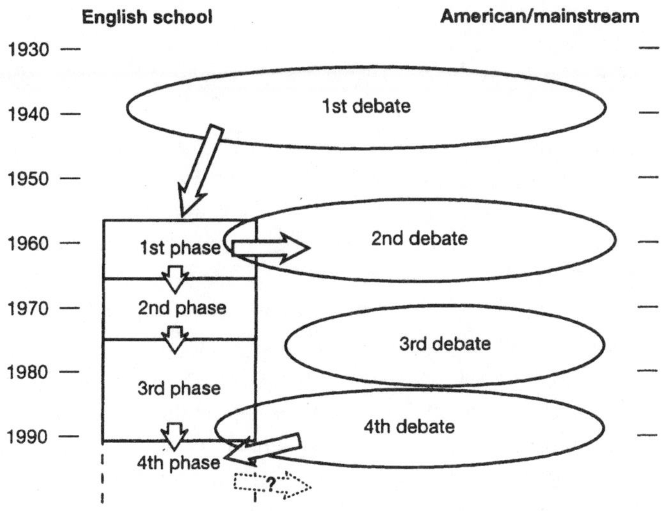

Figure 5.1 The evolution of international relations in Britain and the USA

How do these four phases correspond to the American debates and what interaction can be discerned? This has been summarized in Figure 5.1.

The feasibility of this comparison and interaction model could be questioned by the argument that this is not an external relationship: there have been many Britons doing mainstream international relations, and there are Americans studying international society. Yes, but clearly there is a distinct tradition, the English School, and 'whilst there are *islands* of international society thinking in North America, there is a *tradition* of international society thinking in Britain'.[39] Correspondingly, there have been English (School) interventions in the main arena - but the arena as such *is* American International Relations.[40] At times, however, the activities of the English School *were* either themselves central to the development of the discipline (notably Bull's intervention in the second debate) or closely connected to it. This is the whole point of Figure 5.1. Some of the disciplinary debates have had more English School connection than others and their circles therefore stretch further to the left in the figure.

The so-called first debate shaped the English School much more than it did American international relations. In American international relations, the realist/idealist debate soon became stereotyped and mainly relevant as a disciplinary instrument for charging all critique with 'idealism'.[41] Realism increasingly became a 'strawman', rarely found in real life, but important for the self-conceptions of other schools;[42] with the English School it stayed a serious issue. While struggling for a middle way, for something beyond realism, one did not ignore the warnings of the original realists. As perceptively noticed by Tim Dunne, the major figures were all realists ready to swing back a bit from the full realist reaction against idealism (Butterfield and Wight were clearly influenced by Carr).[43]

The second American debate is obviously the one with the most direct involvement from the English School, because Bull was one of the two main protagonists. In stark contrast is the absence of any English School role in the third debate. This has to be seen in relation to the tendencies of the third phase of the English School, which has been labelled here 'repetitive'. It is not that these third phase works are weak or uninteresting. Quite the contrary, they are often of high scholarly quality - impressive and convincing, exactly because they have the character of completing a picture. Almost as a kind of Kuhnian 'normal science' they have achieved the precision and cumulation of the closed world. When a set of categories, arguments and problems are solidly established and not questioned, it is possible to construct quite elaborate deliberations on this fixed foundation. Especially for our transatlantic problematique it is clear how little import or export of ideas takes place in this phase.

Regarding 'The English School of international relations', Roy E. Jones claimed in 1981 that 'repetition has set in and is likely to get worse as the years pass,' and 'pupils caught up in this sterile regime move inevitably from scholarship to scholasticism'.[44] The point might be overstated, but at least for a period there seemed to be some truth to the evaluation. For a period, the literature of the English School (i.e. the main 'theory' of international society) was locked into a pattern of repeated rejection of misguided exaggeration in one (realist) or other (revolutionist) direction and reiterated celebration of the golden mean.[45]

This, however, did not necessarily have to follow from some inner deficiencies of the conceptual apparatus or the methodologies (as claimed by Jones). It could be the case that since the school became institutionalized at a specific place, with a specific community it achieved specific social functions pushing it in the direction of repetition and reconfirmation rather than challenge and innovation. The programme as such could therefore still contain potentials if brought to meet other substrata in international relations such as for instance the equally parochial American writings on regimes and institutions, the often self-ghettoizing post-structuralists or finally 'real' historians and experts in international law.[46] Possibly, the problem with the English School was that it had actually become - *an English School.*[47]

The fourth phase seems to prove this. As argued by Tim Dunne,[48] the English School has shown theoretical progress, and in particular, as argued by Iver Neumann, this has happened exactly from the time when I pronounced that it would not.[49] Nicholas Wheeler and Tim Dunne talk about a new wing or a tradition of 'Critical International Society Studies' and there are various attempts to link reflection in and on the English School to most of the major theoretical debates elsewhere in the discipline. This, however, does not in itself mean that the English School has something to say that is not said better elsewhere. We need to explore more systematically how the English School corresponds to and/or differs from the major positions in the discipline at large. As argued in a previous section, this should at present mean American mainstream (neo-liberal) institutionalism, constructivism and post-structuralism.

COMPETITIVE COMPARISON

The English School vs. American mainstream institutionalists

This is the comparison most often made in the new literature on English and American international relations. To repeat the main points, it is argued that the subjects and interests of the two are closely connected; but the concepts of science and of institutions differ.[50] Buzan asserts that 'Regime theory and international society are part of the same tradition, but due to the peculiarities of academic discourse, they have become largely detached from one another'.[51]

First, Andrew Hurrell[52] and Tonny B. Knudsen[53] argue that the two have different concepts of science: it is well known that Wight and Bull saw the task of international relations as continuing reflection in a *tradition* of thinking and debate. Bull quotes Samuel Alexander's 'thinking is also research', and Wight's work on the 'three traditions' is very clear on addressing debates that are unresolvable, and rather to be re-enacted, rephrased and up-dated, not in order to achieve the impossible closure, but because they capture important dilemmas, ethical, practical and philosophical problems with which to grapple. This is in strong contrast to the preference by American rationalists for testable hypotheses and clear theory based on explicit micro-foundations.

Second, the international society literature and neo-liberal institutionalism have different answers to the question why norms and rules are actually followed. The neo-liberal institutionalists have a very specific argument: rational egoists (self-interested gain maximizers) can achieve co-operation – and thus realize potential gains – by setting up institutions that facilitate co-operation by some very specific mechanisms, all ultimately possible to classify as reduction of transaction costs: monitoring compliance and thus helping in overcoming the assurance problem, facilitating communication, and in various other ways affecting incentives so that gains can be realized which were already in the interest of actors to pursue, but where co-operation was not rational behaviour without institutions. This is a precise argument in being both explicit about what assumptions have to be made (no altruism necessary for instance) and what mechanisms carry the argument.

This 'American' argument is not foreign to 'English' international society argumentation. It is a *part* of the explanation for the emergence and evolution of international society - but not the whole story. As shown by Hurrell, these arguments have been used for centuries, but intermingled with a large number of other arguments about the emergence of co-operation. Therefore, 'the reformulation of the problem of co-operation within more rigorous rationalist models has brought clear benefits, above all in terms of giving greater precision to the functional benefits of norms, the concept of reciprocity, and the ways in which co-operation can develop between self-interested actors'.[54] The writers of the English School have also at this point been 'classical', i.e. their conception of international society is an often under-specified combination of these various factors.[55] Hurrell puts it like this:

> There have been many answers to this question [the reasons why states obey rules that are usually unenforced and mostly unenforceable]: power and coercion, self-interest and reciprocal benefits, institutionalized habit or inertia, the existence of a sense of community, procedural legitimacy of the process of rule creation, or the moral suasion that derives from a shared sense of justice. Previous explanations of co-operation have often tended to produce an aggregate list of these kinds of factors without providing any precise guide as to their interrelationship. This was one of the most common criticisms of Bull's work.[56]

American institutionalists are more precise about one of the arguments. The English School, furthermore, did not have only this argument and one other - they had a long, aggregate list. It is, therefore, a question whether Buzan is fair to the English School when he claims that *the* alternative to a rationalistic and functionalistic *Gesellschaft* explanation is (and can only be) a culturalistic *Gemeinschaft* one, where an international society grows organically from a shared culture. The methodological argument for a classical approach is not pure epistemology, it is a statement about ontology too: that the nature of international society is (or at least is closely connected to) reasoned debate and conceptual reflection, i.e. just as the study of international relations is seen as three traditions of conversation, so too the arrangements among units in the international system are in a continuous process of reasoning, not simply a *Gemeinschaft* reflection of a *feeling* of community, nor a Keohanian strategy for remedying sub-optimal realization of absolute gains. This kind of society cannot be fitted into a functional model like Buzan's where increasing interaction capacity 'pushes' states so closely together that they have to handle their interaction more consciously and therefore develop an international society. Because different 'systems' (or regions) will do this differently, according to the concepts they employ for this purpose, it might be said that there is a cultural dimension to this - it is like a *tradition*.[57] Neither is this the *Gemeinschaft* extreme, however, because it does not 'grow' from the cultural roots in a semi-automatic way, nor does it 'reflect' this culture in a way where only one form would be possible - like a tradition it is open to disagreements and changes but always in a way where one understands better by including a grasp of where it comes from (see Figure 5.2).

Thus there is an additional 'layer' of international society (in addition to *Gesellschaft à la* Keohane and Buzan and *Gemeinschaft* as attributed to Wight), one which consists of the mutual binding and self-binding that is established through the practice of argumentation among states, a practice which involves - not as an academic mistake, but as a political reality - a mix of arguments about prudence, ethics and legality. As argued convincingly by Hurrell, this is a problem for rationalist institutionalists because the individual rules (which they try to explain) are tied to the broader pattern of internal more-or-less legally formed rules. Often the general interest in international society is important in explaining compliance with specific rules, while the specific rules add up to a general system of international law that is constitutive of the structure of the states-system itself.[58] Because states come to believe they have a long-term interest in this international legal system, the rules achieve obligation and normativity in a way which becomes more law-like and where compliance is hard to calculate in terms of specific and calculable interests. This merges into the truly moral dimension of international society where a sense of obligation becomes a real factor. All this is placed between the rationalist and functionalist explanation and the cultural, *Gemeinschaft* logic.

This split of what at first seemed like a dichotomy will be central to the argument of later sections in this paper. It is clear that the Americans have one specific argument here that is *part* of the concept of international society, but what 'international society' contains *beyond* the rationalistic, American argument should not be wrapped into one cover term - it contains at least two distinct levels.

Finally, it should be noticed that 'rationalism' is not only neo-liberal institutionalism. Rationalism can validly be seen as a 'neo–neo synthesis' where neo-realists and neo-liberals meet on the basis of their rationalist concept of science (and common hostility towards post-structuralists), and thus rationalism is at least equally defined by neo-realism. Whereas most

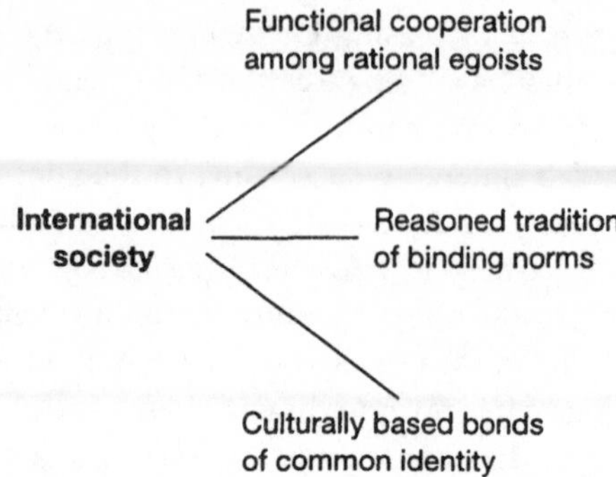

Figure 5.2 Engaging with rationalist institutionalism

English-American comparisons have focused on the neo-liberals, Barry Buzan and Richard Little have tried not only to create links from the English School to mainstream (neo-liberal) institutionalism, but also to its close kin: neo-realism. Most other authors use neo-realism only as a foil in their presentation of the merits of English School reflection, but Buzan has tried to argue that from the basis of neo-realism (or rather sophisticated improvements on it, called structural realism), one can explain the emergence of international society as a natural product of anarchy. The cultural (*Gemeinschaft*) version of the origins of international society is not useful for theory purposes (nor for our post-western, multicultural system) and therefore a functional theory has to be generated. The factor of interaction capacity[59] can explain why states under anarchy at a certain level of technological development are pushed towards mutual recognition of sovereignty which forms the basic, first step of international society. What Buzan does is to formulate an even more rationalistic theory of co-operation than that of Keohane. Behind the more specific 'regimes', he places the more general international society from which the regimes draw validity (this is similar to Hurrell's argument, here, however, less critically phrased in terms of incompatible epistemologies and, rather, as an improvement); and he then even goes on to add a causal factor behind this international society explaining *when* it becomes rational for states in an anarchy to construct international society. By thus linking system and society, neo-realism, neo-liberal institutionalism and the English School, Buzan has taken the zone of overlap between English School and American rationalist mainstream international relations to its fullest.

Recently, Richard Little[60] has refined this neo-realism/English School link further by taking up a number of the sophistications of the English School conception which will be explored further in the remaining parts of this article.

The English School vs. American (mainstream?) constructivists

The first of the American positions, neo-liberal institutionalism, has been used by English School advocates for showing differences that illustrate the specific merits of the English School. In contrast, the second American theory, constructivism, has not been criticized, and instead English School members have said 'yes, but we always said so'. Iver Neumann, Tim Dunne and others argue that there is a close correspondence between English School conceptions and recent American constructivism, and thus claim that American constructivists have reinvented an English wheel. There are two comments to make on this argument: first that it is more true than it ought to be, and, second, that it leaves a lot unexplained.

The main (but then also infinite) importance of the work of Wendt lies in his unfailing exposure of the role in mainstream explanations of exogenously given actors with constant identities and interests. Yes, states follow self-interest, but then we should be more interested not only in the making of 'interests' but even more in the origins of this 'self'. Behind every interest there is an identity. Wendt has shown how mainstream theories are much more deeply marked by this blind spot than one might notice at first. For instance, Waltz is on these terms not overly structuralist, as is usually thought; he is rather atomistic in his ontology, because the structure is explained from some already existing units, which have attributes such as being self-seeking before they enter any structure. Wendt in contrast wants almost all unit characteristics to be social, thus embedded in interaction and therefore malleable over time as units develop new patterns of interaction. And institutionalists like Keohane are, according to Wendt, making life unnecessarily difficult for themselves by adopting neo-realist assumptions about exogenously given interests, where their institutionalism would fly much more easily if process could reshape identities (as it actually did in their intellectual forefathers' neo-functionalist integration theory).[61] This very powerful argument about the weaknesses of existing theory and the need for a focus on identities and social constructions surprisingly leads on to Wendt's own theory being formulated in a rather narrow way where not only state-centrism is retained, but where construction is solely located at the systemic level. Somewhat surprisingly this system-level conception is based mainly on sociological and social-psychological theories at an individual level that are then transposed on to states (as individuals).

The main focus of Wendtian constructivism becomes the way central categories or structures of international relations are not objective laws but dependent on actors defining themselves this way; identities and collective cognitions are mutually constitutive, and what some others would call structures are intersubjectively constructed and thus amendable to rearticulation by those practices. Since Wendt mainly engages with discussions at the level of general theory, his main interests become the very general and overarching concepts that define the rules of the game: sovereignty, anarchy, self-interest; and the 'identities' that form the other side of such coins are therefore also very general ones, mostly 'What does it mean to be a state?'. This of course is a very important question, and a major gain to be aware that 'state' is not a constant category - even if the system continues to be state-based and state-centric it can change dramatically as the meaning of statehood is constantly rearticulated.

However, there has to be more to 'identities' than the generalized meaning of 'state'. Also the English School has focused mainly on such questions as what are the systemically given constraints for the individual units adopting this identity? What are the generally valid rules? In contrast we might laboriously approach things from below and from within, and investigate how the different actors construct their world; for instance, in Europe, how actors define themselves in terms of states and nations at the same time as involving the category of Europe - most likely involving it differently, but involving it nonetheless in the different constructions. Erik Ringmar has criticized Alexander Wendt's constructivism for being

> fundamentally one-sided: the problem of identity formation is constantly seen from the perspective of the system and never as a problem each state and each statesman has to grapple with. He can tell us why a certain identity is recognized, but not *what that identity is* ... His structural bias constantly sets limits to his investigation: just as the structure of the international system cannot make a state act, it cannot make someone have a particular identity. Just as the structure cannot explain historical changes, it cannot by itself explain changes in identities. What Wendt needs, but cannot provide with the help of the theoretical perspective he has made his, is an account of how states *interpret* the structures of international politics and how they *use* them in interaction with others.[62]

If constructivism works from within instead, it can for instance try to explain how a concept like 'Europe' is stabilized by its inner connections to other - perhaps more powerful - 'we-identities' such as states and nations. This demands that one is open to the fact that multiple we-identities overlap. There is no room for this in the agent/structure dualism of Wendt, where the state is the agent and the international system is the structure.[63] In this approach there is only one kind of 'unit we', with transformations in the (systemic) rules regulating the formation of such we-identities. Therefore, a concept like 'Europe' will either have to out-compete the nation-states (and become the new unit), or it has to be conceived of as collective rules among the units, not multi-layered units. In Europe, where the concept of Europe has gained an identity of its own, the nation/state identity has been transformed, and this not (or at least not only) in the Wendtian sense of how the meaning of statehood or nationhood (or sovereignty as such and identity as such) have changed, it is also a question of how the *different* state/nations in different ways have 'Europe' integrated into their we-identities.[64] Europe has thereby a political reality in its own right which is obscured by the dichotomic choice of state or system; it is in a half-way position which is invisible to the state-centric version of constructivism.

Constructivism *could* very well mean to study how each unit has to construct its own world. In the words of Erik Ringmar: 'A theory of the construction of identities and interests is radically incomplete as long as it views individuals and collective entities only from the perspective of the system.'[65] States are redefined not only 'as states' but also each in their own 'subjectivity'. This might be a more exacting approach, but in some sense more true to the basic constructivist premise that we cannot start from some world 'as it really is', but only from worlds as they are created. Any larger interpretations have to be seen as additional stories and worlds constructed by the theorist.

This 'radical constructivist' critique of mainstream constructivism actually hits at English School international society too, which operates only on outside-in constructions of meaning, not inside-out. Thus, English School advocates might find points of convergence with the 'really existing' American constructivism, but this is not the only possible form of constructivism, nor even the most obvious form to give it on the basis of its own critique of mainstream international relations.

Therefore, it is not enough to show that the English School has seen international society as constructed (i.e. stands up to the new constructivism), the question is *how*: how it is constructed (for itself), and how we see (how observers construct 'international society'). We have not settled so very much when Dunne argues:

> the English School has always stood four-square in the constructivist camp.... For the English School, the society of states is not a given. It has been constructed by states but is not reducible to them. As a structure, it contains the behaviour of states through institutions (or practices) which embody highly developed forms of intersubjective identity that rationalism cannot comprehend.[66]

Since constructivism can mean many different things, one further has to ask, who constructs what - and perhaps most importantly, how solidly is it constructed?

Here, Dunne[67] has given a clue by pointing to one important difference between Wendtian constructivism and the English School: the new American constructivism seems to portray the rules of international society as much more malleable and open to reformulation than the English School typically has. Ontologically, and in principle, these rules are in both cases socially constructed, not somehow pre-given, but even something socially constructed can be very hard to change. At this point, Wendt seems to be engaged in sending the same message as the post-structuralists, and for instance Coxian Critical Theory ('this is not given by nature, therefore it could be different'), whereas his sociological approach should logically also be open to formulations in terms of sedimented practice, structure or institutionalization.[68]

This can be further clarified with the help of a David Dessler argument (originally pushed in the opposite direction) about conscious decisions on rules vs. reproduction of structures.[69] This was an argument made because Waltz presents practices as influencing the eventual reproduction of rules *only* in terms of their micro-logics where the macro-effect totally escapes the actors. Dessler argues that there is *also* an element of acting on rules in terms of views on their reproduction, breach or reformulation, of making choices on the basis of preferences regarding the systemic outcome. This argument can be turned around in that Wendt and Co. often seem to present rules as *only* about the choices of identities, 'character planning' and mutual shaping.[70] In contrast, the English School is more inclined to see situations of 'necessity' and thus rules and situations that appear to actors very 'structural'.

According to Dessler, Waltz portrays 'structure as those conditions of action that are (1) spontaneous and unintended in origin, (2) irreducible to the attributes or actions of individual units, and (3) impervious to attempts to change them or escape their effects'.[71] In the transformational (scientific realist, agency-structure) conception, 'by contrast, structure is a medium of activity that in principle can be altered through that activity. Any given action will reproduce or transform some part of the social structure: the structural product itself may be intended or unintended.'[72] Since, however, there are obviously certain things - rules, patterns of distribution of resources, etc. - that are more strongly embedded in practices (viz. sovereignty) these have to be treated as 'deeper' layers. Therefore, attempts to transcend such rules will be met with much more resistance from the system, whereas other rules are much easier to modify or escape. Constructivist theory really has to develop such a layered structure of rules if it is to be able to encompass, and enlarge on, structural realism, but these rules have been difficult to deliver.[73] The result is that constructivist theory appears to say: 'everything can (in principle) be changed if just practice changes', which is true 'in principle' but not always equally relevant to the issue at hand.

It might seem at first that this contrast between transformational structure vs. 'realist' strong structure (necessity, brutal facts and tragic set-ups) should be traced back to another key distinction of constructivism, constitutive vs. regulatory rules, on which the English School, according to Dessler, is weak since they only deal with regulative rather than constitutive rules (which might explain their acceptance of hard structures; they do not see how the deeper patterns are also rules). This is, however, hardly a fair criticism; Wight and Bull certainly are aware that concepts like sovereignty and non-intervention are not only rules about what states are allowed to do or not do, they are constitutive of the very meaning of state, and different states-systems have different constitutive principles. The difference between the ontology of constructivists and the English School probably runs somewhere else: whether everything is 'rules' vs. the concept of rules used in a more narrow meaning. English School writers would only talk of rules when the regulation takes the form of 'international society logic', whereas the conception of the English School is that there are always three logics at play: the realist logic of the international system, the 'rationalist' (Grotian) of international society, and the revolutionist world society one.[74] Thus, 'rules' in the narrow sense are interacting with dynamics that are only 'rules' in a looser or wider sense of the word. This does not (as implied in much constructivist construction of their competitors) necessarily imply that one is thinking in terms of some kinds of primitive, material, hard, objective, rule-free world. It only presupposes that there are situational logics that escape the control of actors - most clearly represented by Herbert Butterfield's brilliant piece on 'the tragic element in politics',[75] where it is argued that when historians have gained distance from a conflict and stop reproducing the self-righteous conceptions of either side, it appears how much both sides were caught by the logic of the situation and their possibly benign intentions were trapped by the structure of the political constellation. This argument, which was simultaneously phrased as 'the security dilemma' by John Herz,[76] points to the factor that also Waltz in principle is interested in: the positional arrangement of the units as a *sui generis* social reality of its own, with causal 'emergent powers'.[77] The nature of this structural-realist argument is often obscured by being presented as ultimately pointing to the power of material capabilities, a material concept of structure. However, it can be retained as a level of causation in its own right without leaving the social and entering the material. Structure can be very structural, still social. This should in principle also be the view of constructivists who often lean heavily on scientific realism *à la* Bhaskar, but in practice this is down-played, probably because they are caught by the 'conflict formation' of international relations theory, where their task is to argue that 'things could be different' while realists argue that they could not.

Thus, in parallel to the previous section where we found an American theory cultivating one specific element of international society and thereby

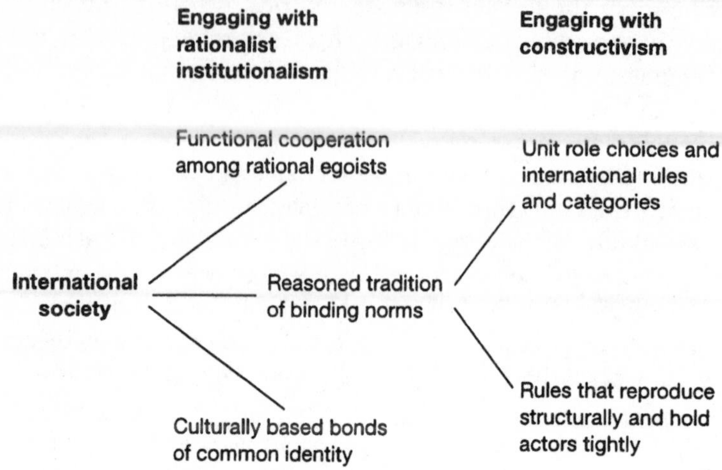

Figure 5.3 Two engagements with Americans

had the English School conception subdivided into first two, then three layers, we have here seen American constructivists cultivating a distinctive kind of institutionalization whereby the English School can become conscious of one more split in its original international society conception.

The English School vs. American post-structuralism

Post-structuralists have generally taken a positive attitude to the English School.[78] Partly, this is an instance of the general tactics of post-structuralists mobilizing classical realism against neo-realism[79] and to some extent also classical liberalist themes like ethics against neo-liberal institutionalism,[80] but also it has to do with the attitude of the English School, its textual orientation, with much energy put into the constant rereading and reinterpretation of classics, the nature of Wight's trialogue as an ongoing undecidable debate, and various other expressions of a like-minded scepticism towards safe and final answers.

Der Derian is expressly positive, and often presents himself as having roots in the English School as well as post-structuralism. Having had Bull as supervisor, his dissertation and first book, *On Diplomacy*,[81] was presented as a radicalization of the English School. His 1995 reader begins with Wight's 'Why is there no international theory?', concentrates on English School writings and contemporary critical positions - feminist, constructivist and post-structuralist - and the collection is prefaced by Adam Watson. In Der Derian's own formulation:

> This collection does something new with something old, by reinvestigating realism through a dialogue between classical international theory and critical theoretical challenges to it. It signals the arrival if not yet the acceptance of a broader range of plural realisms for a newly multipolar, multicultural International Relations. However, were I to rank the reasons, the primary purpose of this collection is to honor ancestors and mentors. ... [It] offers tribute to the 'English' school of realism ... However, one of the more valuable things I learned from Bull was not to allow excessive debt to inhibit new and possibly risky undertakings. Hence the strategy to couple classical with critical investigations, in order to call into question the natural hegemony of traditional realism[82]

A further 'reason to pair international theory and critical investigations' is 'their joint recognition that there is no natural center to international relations'.[83]

For most of the other post-structuralists, there are some specific elements in English School writings that have been of special interest: Wight's 'Why?' article and Bull's argument about domestic analogy.[84] Post-structuralists have put much emphasis on the bifurcation of political thinking into domestic and international, where each has been balanced by having the other as a mirror image.[85] The complex relationship between domestic and international political thought is thus close to the heart of post-structuralists, and this is exactly what the domestic analogy argument is about.

Already in his pieces in *Diplomatic Investigations*, Wight argued that international theory has to stand on its own feet in reflecting on the unique features of international relations. This of course relates to the basic argument for the importance of international society and the Grotian middle way. Both realists and revolutionists are likely to employ the domestic analogy: realists in saying order and society can *only* be what it is domestically, and if it is not like that, it is not order at all - international relations is pure anarchy; revolutionists in striving for a transferral of domestic principles to the international realm. The Grotian 'rationalists' claim that there is an international society as a kind of society different from the domestic, but nevertheless making a difference to the pure power games of anarchy. International society is thus a key argument for assuming that there is a *sui generis*, unique social reality at the international level to be studied in a language of its own.

The domestic analogy in its narrow sense is the specific question of whether international order should be constructed by emulating domestic models. Not only 'idealist' advocates of reform use this analogy, realists also conceive of possible improvement along these lines.[86] Realists further use the domestic analogy in a second form as an argument for the impossibility of reform: order and peace can only mean what it does domestically, and since this is impossible internationally, no reform is possible.[87]

Richard Ashley, in his most persistent engagement with Bull and the domestic analogy,[88] argued that Bull unduly accepted the domestic image as valid for domestic society (and only invalid when transferred from its literal to its figurative sense, as analogy), that a strict boundary between domestic and international was implicit in the argument; and that Bull ironically contributed to a strengthening of the domestic analogy by reinforcing the image of domestic society as literal, primary and unproblematic, and international affairs as fragile, unsettled and ambiguous. In a more recent article,[89] he has made his disagreement with Bull more clear and, to simplify a little further, one could put it like this: Ashley takes the domestic analogy much more seriously than Bull does. To Ashley, it is real, important and efficient - it is a central component of the discourses that have structured and continue to structure our political spaces. Bull, in contrast, presents the domestic analogy first of all as an element in intellectual debates over international relations theory, i.e. it is a mistake, a mistake made by theorists and practitioners alike, but presented as something to be criticized in the sense of trying to arrive at a better, more accurate language for describing international relations. In Ashley's analysis, the domestic analogy is rather to be critiqued in the sense of being correct by being effective - the world is structured like this, but partly because this discursive figure is in operation.

This usage of the 'domestic analogy', beyond what was imagined by Bull, will be taken up in a later section for the possible insights to be gained by engaging more with the work of Ashley and reimporting some of this into the English School thinking about international society.

Rob Walker ends an article[90] by struggling with his usual dilemma: what kind of practice could follow from his demonstration that the modernist, sovereignty-based discursive structures are capable of handling (almost co-opting) most of the 'radical' challenges because these challenges reproduce the very categories of sovereign modernity (such as domestic analogy)? Some kind of 'post-structuralist practice' is not easy to imagine (although elsewhere he tries to do this in terms of new social movements), and he then points to the English School and 'international society' as a practice not truly transformative, but the best within the reach of current practice - the place to connect an imaginable praxis to a promising perspective, something that at least holds the potential of helping to bring about something more far-reaching at a later stage.

In the case of post-structuralism, it is not so clear how the concept of institutions/international society should be located in relation to the two previous American theories as well as the English School. The articles that explicitly compare post-structuralism and the English School have not focused on their concepts of institutions as much as on their concepts of science and especially their attitudes to the domestic analogy. It is, therefore, not possible to complete the image (the one that has evolved through Figures 5.2 and 5.3) on the basis of the surveys of theoretical debates. A comparison with rationalism generated Figure 5.2 and with constructivism led to Figure 5.3, but only after more careful analysis can post-structuralism lead us on to Figure 5.4 and ultimately Figures 5.5 and 5.6. We need to go into more substantial arguments about institutions from different 'American' and 'English' writers in order to get to the fine nuances of the post-structuralist position on institutions in relation to those drawn up in Figure 5.3.

Conclusion to comparisons

It is easy enough to say that the English School has various advantages, if one compares it to 'the mainstream' in the usual way, i.e. build a straw man neo-realism or concentrates on only one dimension of the difference between Keohanian institutionalism and English School international society. But if one takes the full range of contemporary American international relations, there are insights and sophistications that are not self-evidently handled by the English School. Today, 'after the fourth debate', much thinking is still structured by the set-up of the fourth debate: rationalism versus reflectivism; institutions are products of rational choices by pre-given actors or (meta-)institutions produce subjects as well as objects. This axis of debate is worth considering vis-à-vis international society.

So far we have found, in comparison with the rationalists, that the international society of the English School could be subdivided into three layers, and through the discussion with constructivists, one of them was subdivided bringing us to four. By including also post-structuralists, we achieved a sense that something is still missing. Are there one or two more layers to be inserted into our emerging typology?

Towards grammar – and back to Manning?

There is no need to continue 'second-debate' attacks on the English School for not being 'precise' or 'scientific' enough. There are reasons for the deviation from rigorous precision. English School procedures correspond to their conception(s) of the ontology of the object: if international society is largely a reasoned tradition of intersubjective commitments, the study hereof should be interested in ethical and political arguments, changing concepts of political order and of the various traditions of thought in the field. American debates have, however, not stayed with the second debate, and especially the fourth debate, between rationalists and reflectivists, points to an important axis which also runs through the English School (partly as disagreement among different English School authors, partly as an ambiguity of expression). Thus, we will try to use this axis as a tool for getting closer to actual English School debates than the more 'external' comparisons of the first part of this chapter. Special emphasis will, however, be given to the input of Richard Ashley in order to overcome the hurdle experienced at the end of the last section: how to formulate the contribution of post-structuralism in terms of a refinement of English School conceptions of international society - how to add a third column of the evolving figure, and thereby a more comprehensive typology of meanings of international society.

BUT WHAT *IS* INTERNATIONAL SOCIETY?

> Communication may take place, envoys may be exchanged and agreements entered into without there being a sense of common interests or values that gives such exchange substance and a prospect of permanence, without any sense that there are rules which lay down how the interaction should proceed, and without the attempt of the parties concerned to co-operate in institutions in whose survival they have a stake.[91]

Bull here points to the critical question, exactly 'how much' is necessary in order to justify use of the term *international society*? Answering this question is the task of the 'definitions' given (and often quoted), where probably the most famous are:

> By an international society we mean a group of states (or, more generally, a group of independent political communities) which not merely form a system, in the sense that the behavior of each is a necessary factor in the calculations of the others, but also have established by dialogue and consent common rules and institutions for the conduct of their relations, and recognize their common interest in maintaining these arrangements.[92]

> This is the idea of international society: the notion that states and rulers of states are bound by rules and form a society or community with one another, of however rudimentary a kind.[93]

> A *society of states* (or international society) exists when a group of states, conscious of certain common interests and common values, form a society in the sense that they conceive themselves to be bound by a common set of rules in their relations with one another, and share in the working of common institutions.[94]

> Those which make a conscious social contract by instituting rules and machinery to make their relations more orderly and predictable and to further certain shared principles and values.[95]

> International society ... is the habitual intercourse of independent communities, beginning in the Christendom of Western Europe and gradually extending throughout the world. It is manifest in the diplomatic system; in the

> conscious maintenance of the balance of power to preserve the independence of the member communities; in the regular operations of international law whose binding force is accepted over a wide though politically unimportant range of subjects; in economic, social and technical interdependence and the functional international institutions established latterly to regulate it. All these presuppose an international social consciousness, a world wide community sentiment.[96]

Common interests and values, common rules and institutions.[97]

International society involves values, rules and institutions and these are common in the strong sense that the main actors have an acknowledged interest in maintaining these as such, i.e. a certain political and moral unity. Hedley Bull writes about Martin Wight's approach to *Systems of States*:[98]

> by contrast with those studies of states-systems which view them as determined purely by mechanical factors such as the number of states in the system, their relative size, the political configuration in which they stand, the state of military technology, he places emphasis on the norms and values that animate the system, and the institutions in which they are expressed. A states-system, in Wight's view, presupposes a common culture.[99]

Also Bull and Watson in the Introduction to *The Expansion of International Society*, note that:

> It was never the case, before Europe unified the globe, that relations between states or rulers that were members of different regional international systems could be conducted on the same moral and legal basis as relations within the same system, for this basis was provided in part by principles that were culturally particular and exclusive: the unity of Christendom, the community of the faithful in Islam, the conception of the Chinese empire as the Middle Kingdom.

Does an international society presuppose a common culture, or can it exist without one? This is *not* an ambiguity of the school, it is a conscious tension which animates the analysis and even one which is attributed to the real world as a real problem: can the international society that was originally established through the expansion of the European society continue after the decline of cultural homogeneity?[100]

So this is not the axis of theoretical uncertainty, it is a research topic. How then *do* we define the width of deliberation and indecision of the concept as such? The School's own disagreements, or you might say acknowledged axes of variation, are three. The three discussions - or spectrums - that have been most explicitly articulated within the school are: (1) pluralist vs. solidarist conceptions of international society; (2) practical vs. purposive associations: and (3) regulatory rules beyond international societies ('the Ottoman problem').

Pluralist vs. solidarist conceptions of international society

With pluralism, states are the principal barriers of rights and duties in international law, and states agree only on some minimum standards such as mutual recognition of sovereignty and non-intervention. They have diverging concepts of justice, their joint wish for order brings about some basic rules. The solidarist conception takes a stronger view on the enforcement of international law. Since individuals are the ultimate members of international society, there can be a right and duty to humanitarian intervention which the pluralists would be reluctant to concede.[101] Involved in the idea of 'international society' we find the recognition that states have 'legal duties', and that these are enforceable.[102] The use of force is legitimized by international society although the link has been in an often changing relationship to the moral and legal order.[103] The international society perspective, therefore, opens up a tension on this question. This, however, could be seen as a fruitful set-up for addressing interesting questions, as most clearly shown in the discussions of Wheeler and others on humanitarian intervention.

Practical vs. purposive associations

This is a slightly different way to state something not completely unrelated to the previous axis.[104] Nardin distinguishes between purposive association (Oakeshott's 'civil' association), where states co-operate to promote shared purposes such as trade or mutual defence; and practical associations (Oakeshott's enterprise associations) defined by common rules.[105] Nardin makes the distinction first of all to show how the latter type is the only one that can carry obligations as such; in the former type, the authority of rules will always be conditional on a consequentialist argument about benefits, whereas the association defined by norms can place rules and obligations as binding *as such*. Chris Brown[106] has emphasized (in line with the previous work of Nardin[107]) how the alleged strength of the practical/civil association is its compatibility with pluralism, in contrast to the purposive/enterprise association which demands a uniformity of members that is neither attainable nor attractive. The critiques of this argument usually focus on the 'neutrality' and universality that has to be imputed to the basic norms of international society, like sovereignty, non-intervention and the European form of state. Mostly, the argument focuses on the way these 'neutral' or 'universal' categories are biased and privilege specific interests and historical experiences. In a somewhat different take, Brown points out that this minimalist pluralism in practice finds it hard to be as pluralist as it should be according to its own proclaimed procedures, and actually requires some forms of intolerance in order to prevent certain behaviours and even certain kinds of units. Thus, it seems impossible to establish the one extreme of this dichotomy as a solution, but the argument did point to two very different logics that somehow seem in practice to end up pointing to each other, where the theorist would want to cultivate them separately.

As with the first distinction, Nardin points to the link between international society as a complete, abstract system of states-as-states on the one hand, and the various activities that they actually engage in and the multiple actors and individuals who try to do politics towards each other and the state. Although, the states-system can usefully be conceived in its own terms, it will in practice always get entangled with politics at other levels. This is what Bull's classical statements place under the heading 'international society' versus 'world society'. Politics and morality conducted in terms of people as people creates a completely different dynamic than that of the states-system - a dynamic that both threatens the orderliness of the society of states and simultaneously promises to deliver a more solid, cultural and political underpinning for international society.[108] The first two discussions can therefore be placed on the axis 'international society–world society', and thus they are within the grasp of the conception as such.

The Ottoman problem

This refers to the following:

> While families of states (to use a biological metaphor) like Hellas and the European *grande république* developed complex inter-state societies within the framework of a culture, some more purely regulatory machinery, on what we might call Tell el Amarna lines, is also necessary for the operation, the orderliness, of a system that extends beyond a single culture. The most striking example is the arrangements between the *grande république* and the Ottoman Empire.[109]

The Ottomans were not part of the European international society and did not want to adopt its rules and institutions. They were, however, powerful enough to be taken into account by all major powers in the European system (notably in the seventeenth and eighteenth centuries). And forms for engagement *were* found, in this case by drawing on the Ottoman concept of capitulations which were soon given a new twist (and later on turned into a powerful instrument for the Europeans in dealing with non-members of their international society). The Ottomans 'and the European powers they dealt with did "conceive themselves to be bound by a common set of rules in their relations" and "shared in the working of common institutions".'[110] Thus, something *like* an international society has to develop beyond the real one.[111] As recently argued by Richard Little, Wight's answer to this problem probably was to think in terms of concentric circles of society-ness: an inner and an outer circle, a tighter and a looser society.

This, like the Nardin discussion, raises the question of some kind of minimal or 'neutral' base line of rules. In the words of Wight:

> How can we describe this cultural community? Does it consist essentially in common morality and a common code, leading to agreed rules about warfare, hostages, diplomatic immunity, the right of assylum and so on? Does it require common assumptions of a deeper kind, religious or ideological? Is there wide variation between the common code of one states-system and of another? Or do they all belong to the great pool or practices and platitudes, supposedly common to the human race, where men seek for Natural Law?[112]

Are there *some* rules that are just 'the necessary rules' to which cultural and political particularism is added? Such an idea would seem to tie in with the Buzan argument about a culture-free, functional logic for the emergence of international society. However, the Ottoman argument can also be read as saying something very different: there are always rules, even where there is not a real society. To constructivists it can be no surprise that rules are involved even in the most barren 'systems' which were alleged to be mechanic. There can be no system without society, because there can be no social action without rules, they would say.[113] However, to the extent that there is a clear idea in the English School conception of 'how much' is needed for an international society to exist, it is still possible to follow Watson's line, and say 'no international system as defined by Bull has operated without some regulatory rules and institutions, and it is hard to see how one could; but that is not enough to call it a society'.[114] It is therefore too easy to use the constructivist dictum about the inevitable involvement of rules to collapse the system/society distinction: there could be important differences of degree. But the constructivist argument should be a warning against assuming that the proto-society formed among culturally diverse powers is purely regulatory and that the rules take *one* specific, natural and neutral form; rules always involve a degree of contrivance, they always have to be invented and imagined and thus they will necessarily differ and usually also take an imprint from the cultural environment(s) within which they are created. Furthermore, the distinction between regulatory rules and constitutive rules is problematic, and regulative rules will always end up becoming more or less constitutive as well. Whatever 'practical' arrangement is formed among a group of powers, will therefore also tend to become part (maybe a small part, but part nevertheless) of the identity of these units. The 'Ottoman' question about regulatory rules beyond the 'real' international society is by way of this intervention shown to deal with largely overlapping concerns to the two other debates.

Are these three discussions then the really significant ones, or are they rather the ritualized debates one has to take as English School member, thereby precluding more worrying tensions? Is this the 'problematization' that defines these as the important questions to address, and thereby defines attempts to ask other questions as not serious?[115] A more inconvenient question could be posed about what exactly this international society is made up of, and how it is held together. As beliefs, conventions, commitments, or something else? This could seem to be close to especially the second - practical/purposive (and thereby also the first: pluralist/solidarist) - debate. However, it makes a significant difference how the question is put.

By asking the classical English School way the reflection comes to run along the axis 'How much moral standing should the state have vis-à-vis individuals and humankind?' which becomes a rehearsal of classical realist/cosmopolitan themes and ultimately stays within the logic of sovereignty. Not state sovereignty, but the basic modern idea of the sovereign self as source of truth and will. From this modern basis, sovereignty ultimately has to rest somewhere. Realists place it in the state, 'idealists' in the individual, and the more sophisticated approaches such as the English School are undecided and oscillate between the two.[116] There is no way to mediate these demands, only to keep playing them against each other, because the basic concept of knowledge and authority demands that answers take the form of pointing out a locus of sovereignty. Without seeing how this is a kind of domestic analogy in another register (not world government, i.e. repeating the nation-state as organizational form, but authority, knowledge and identity as the meaning of politics), the English School distributes its main debates along this classical-modern axis.

With a perspective that transfers less of the state-like demand on the discourse on international society, it is possible to ask other questions about its nature. First of all: what kind of social practice are we talking about? More on this in what follows. In between the standard debates and the unwelcome ones are two that have been articulated but not much discussed: one is that of specifying a boundary to define when there is enough society to say an international society is in existence, and second, the question whether international society is a sufficiently coherent phenomenon, whether there is enough one-ness that it can take on its own role and carry the burden placed upon it in English School explanations[117] - or whether it is more of an indistinct cover term for phenomena with variable attributes.

On the boundary issue, Barry Buzan has claimed to possess the solution. Mutual recognition of sovereignty is the boundary between system and society, because then the units acknowledge each other as like units and thereby as in some sense 'identical', whereby a society comes into being. This argument is unsatisfactory for two reasons, one logical and the other historical. The 'identity' argument mixes up two senses of 'identity': of the different units seeing each other as being 'similar', and whether they conceive of the whole they form as possessing an individuality that gives them an identity in their togetherness. In the second meaning, one can very well share an identity with someone which one definitely does not think of as the same kind of unit, cf. most obviously a male–female couple (but also the whole Durkheimian argument about the relationship between society and division of labour). From an historical perspective, Buzan's argument is unacceptable because it only covers one type of system, that of state sovereignty, which precludes international society in asymmetrical systems and, for instance, rules out an international society after sovereignty, for instance in an emerging neo-medieval European order. In reply to this Buzan would have to rely on exactly the kind of path-dependent argument he wanted to avoid in his article: he would have to say that the international society of Europe got *established* under sovereignty and then could be *carried over* into a post-sovereign order. This loses both his own functional theory with its links to regime theory and neo-realism, and even more ironically he loses the ability to use the English School on world historical variation and thereby betrays his own grand project with Richard Little,[118] a problem Little has also hinted at.[119]

Another possible answer could be to follow Little's line and stress that international system, international society and world society are different dimensions of reality, simultaneously operating without a mediating, joint language. Then international society would not be an either/or question, but would be a matter of degrees; all three are always there, only their mix varies. This would seem consistent with much of the logic of the English School, but on the other hand it has been a stable assumption of the School that one could somehow talk of an international society as existing in some places and times and not in others. A suggestion for an answer to this puzzle will have to wait until the end of the article.

The second problem is that of oneness. How are all these cases linked? Something is shared, but what exactly? Values, norms, culture, language, concepts, principles, rules of the game or something like that are seen as crucial for the workings of international relations. The arguments in the examples, however, differ: values are something different from perceptions, and they in turn are certainly not identical to rules of the game, etc. English School writers seem often to assume that all such ideational matters are closely related, but the nature, location and attributes of values, norms, principles, and so forth are very different. The argument of international society obviously is that some kind of 'society' exists, therefore the units relate to each other differently than they would otherwise have done.[120]

These distinctive effects (this 'otherwise') can, however, be seen manifested at very different levels, in rather dissimilar ways, and international society seems a very dispersed, scattered and multilayered phenomenon. The conceptual and theoretical questions about distinctions and connections, about how these *different* phenomena relate, have not been very enthusiastically analysed in the literature. Often the concept of international society has actually prevented this further reflection by enabling a vague aggregate reference to this whole cluster of phenomena which, in its totality, seems very powerful and able to explain much, while exploration of the relationship between say culture, norms and diplomatic language is obscured by the fact that there are no longer differences between them; they are all just international society. Much parallel development has been seen in the last ten years in the enthusiastic acceptance in many areas of 'culture' or 'identity' as explaining everything.

In the remaining part of this article, we will try to draw on sociology and semiotics in an attempt to examine the question: Exactly what/where is international society? Is it in the norms, rules, values or institutions? Of whom? It is not of the population at large (which would be world society), but is it then of the state as such, of its decision makers, or of a larger élite? In what way does international society matter? Are we talking about beliefs that are in the deepest sense shared, or about conventions that are followed because this is deemed rational? Does the shared language make it possible to *understand* others, or just to create a form of politics based on the assumption that we have something we call understanding?[121] What is the relationship between 'self-grown' norms emerging out of a culture at large[122] and the political struggle over the valorization and definition of key concepts?

TWO AMERICAN INSTITUTIONALISTS (KEOHANE AND MORGENTHAU) AND TWO AMERICAN DECONSTRUCTIVISTS (KISSINGER AND ASHLEY)

The two tasks still to be performed by this chapter if it is to deliver what has been promised are to find out more precisely what post-structuralism has to say to international society and thereby complete the figure developed in the first section, and to clarify the coherence (or lack thereof) in the concept of international society. The procedure for this final stretch will be to present some well-known American arguments and show how they represent different strands of what to the English School is international society. By showing how they take clearer attitudes to the question of what and where the society is, they further question how viable it is to keep all this lumped together in an undifferentiated pool of norms, values, culture, institutions and common interests. This discussion of authors outside the English

School is intended to show how seemingly minor differences account for qualitative differences among theories, in the end focusing on radically distinct phenomena and processes. The main insight of the debate is, however, the way the categories of the American positions not only at the expressive level have something to say to the English School; more interestingly they can be deconstructed - or maybe even self-deconstruct - in a way which less voluntarily speaks to the English School about a missing category, the one that we were also missing in the first section. After this, a few semiotic and sociological considerations will be added, and a research agenda defined.

A common language of states can emerge more narrowly as the construction of a *specific* set of 'rules of the game' for managing a political constellation or a regional system (regimes and Kissinger). The Wight-Bull society is a *general* phenomenon - not linked very closely to instrumental policies towards specific actors or situations. This differs from the study of specific 'regimes' or the attempts to construct basic systems of management of a regional security order: 'a legitimate order'.[123] This latter approach should seem more trivial, but we will soon see how it reveals some surprising sophistication.

In Kissinger's study, *A World Restored*, the main point is to show the importance of the existence or non-existence of a *legitimate order* for the form international politics is taking: *if* a legitimate order exists (i.e. if there is a certain shared set of norms, a shared concept of legitimacy) diplomacy can unfold, so to say, in this language; if there is no legitimate order, politics essentially follow the logic of war, it is pure manoeuvre, an attempt to install certain rules. Hence, the importance of the question whether the order is accepted by all major powers, or in contrast a major power is *revolutionary* in the sense of contesting the order, and thereby turning politics into a struggle *over* the order instead of a struggle *inside* this order.

In the introduction, Kissinger points out that a legitimate order has nothing to do with 'justice' in any substantial sense - only the question of shared understandings of legitimacy. And in the conclusion it is made clear that the existence of a legitimate order, although it can be said to be in 'everyone's interest, since it precludes major war, it is nevertheless always a partly manipulated affair, where a certain state (or social agent in it) has succeeded in establishing the principles that fit to its domestic order - and it has had sufficient suggestive force to make these principles work as a frame for international politics.

Morgenthau and many other classical realists saw the balance of power and other elements of international politics as *not* automatic but dependent on a shared language. Without the common culture of diplomats (i.e. with the democratization of foreign policy!), international politics lost its flexibility, its finesse and its chances of creative management by diplomats. It has tended since then to degenerate into war and war-like policies (the Cold War). Ideologies and/or nationalisms stand in the way of the only reliable peace strategy: hard work by diplomats sharing a certain language and culture. This is to a large extent the grand story of *Politics among Nations*.[124]

The logic here is close to that of the more culturalist figures among the English School – or maybe more to the view nowadays sometimes attributed to them. Butterfield, Wight and Watson have emphasized strongly that international societies have always grown up within shared cultures. Butterfield even made the strong claim, quoted by Watson,[125] that:

> the international systems so far studied ... do not seem to have been produced by the process of bringing together units which have hitherto been quite separate. The effective forces making for some sort of combination may be the elements of an antecedent common culture, but ... the startling fact is the importance of an earlier stage of political hegemony – a political hegemony which may even have been responsible for the spread of the common culture.[126]

And Wight was speculating even more provocatively in *Power Politics* about the question whether Europe should be seen as a system of sovereign equality threatened from time to time by would-be hegemons (as the European self-perception prefers it) or as a succession of drives for domination interrupted by periods of greater decentralization (an interpretation which the historical record equally allows for). Here, international societies are clearly not seen as rationalistic arrangements among separate states, but as an organizing format competing with the state, and an organic whole which precedes and competes with the states. According to Watson, the pendulum rarely is at the extreme of either tight empire or really equal and independent sovereigns. In this perspective, an international society seems to grow out of a societal, cultural basis in the region. It is not constructed by the states: it is there before them and they live off the same cultural ground as the international society which not only helps them to work together but also competes with them in the form of furnishing a basis for hegemonic attempts.

Regime theory and other liberal institutionalisms can be seen as the 'opposite' institutionalism to Morgenthau's. His 'institutions' (of shared language) are either present or not, but for 'deep' reasons. Subsequently, politics becomes concerned with setting up institutions in the more narrow sense (League of Nations, UN, etc.), which generally fails in relation to the lofty aims; but the important institution is the overarching one of a shared diplomatic culture, and *it* is not seen as contrived but a product of larger historical forces. Keohane, in contrast, conceives of institution-making in a way which manages to combine voluntarism and functionalism:[127]

institutions basically come about because they are functional, because they help to bring about co-operation which improves the gains of the relevant actors. This co-operation, however, is not possible to realize with the given structure of incentives, and therefore actors have to engage in a conscious effort of self- and partner-transformation through the instrument of manipulating the variables influencing the choice of co-operation or defection: institution-making is a central form of this, for the reasons outlined in the 'rationalist' section above. The situation contains possible gains that would be in the interest of all, but the institution and the ensuing co-operation only comes about through actors seeing this tragic set-up and escaping it.

We can thus see already quite different approaches:

- Morgenthau is interested in broad historical factors which determine the existence or erosion of a common framework (or shared 'culture').
- Kissinger views as an aspect of politics the convergence on codes and the continued competition about fine-tuning these codes and principles.
- Keohane and the regime theorists have studied especially the 'practical', instrumental interests which call forth regimes and institutions as means to realize policy co-ordination which is hindered by a kind of 'market failure'. The regimes reduce transaction costs, risk and information deficits.

All refer, to some extent, to norms, rules and institutions – 'international society'. But whereas Morgenthau sees the most basic elements of this as a language prior to political action, and Kissinger sees it as a language of politics inside power politics but also changing it, the neo-liberals have a more utilitarian and rational perspective on the emergence of, and possible institutionalization of, a shared 'language'. The international society literature has so far not made its own position clear on these levels. Obviously, it operates on all three, but would then need to specify when it is where as well as whether or how these levels interact.

Moreover, the inter-American contrasting can take us further. In relation to the seemingly neat and exhaustive Morgenthau/Keohane split, Kissinger cuts across with a conception of 'institutions' as both the condition for 'diplomacy' *and* a matter of political creation. A legitimate order is in the interest of peace and stability, and yet any legitimate order is always a particular order and articulated from the perspective of a specific actor. Reflectivists like Ashley in a sense are between Morgenthau and Kissinger. The reflectivists study 'conventions' or 'doxa' which are less conscious than Kissinger's principles and more political than Morgenthau's culture. They are seen as power relations, as in Kissinger, and as seemingly self-grown, as in Morgenthau.

Richard K. Ashley, in commenting on a Rosenau distinction between governance I and governance II (law-like, non-politicized patterns and regularities versus purposely developed patterns reflecting the intervention of human will and politicized attempts to achieve compliance), makes the point that the really important 'governance' is in-between. This 'governance III' as he calls it is 'taken to constitute the objective, necessary, autonomous, and even natural lawful conditions of conduct', it is taken to be beyond politics.[128] But these structures are actually products of politics, effects of practice. Furthermore:

> one must be ready to put in question the assumption, implicit in governance II, that the principal effect of knowledgable conduct is to render matters of governance explicit, subject to conscious deliberation, and open to politicized debate among the recognized subjects of global life ... [K]nowledgable practice also works to constitute a normalized mode of political subjectivity whose practical dispositions tend, on balance, to generate certain structures, to discipline resistances and silence competing practices; to exclude the question of the political content of those structures from serious debate; and thereby to secure the recognition of those structures, not as the historical and contingent relations they are, but as necessary, objective, and self-evident limits and conditions of politics in collective life. This is the possibility, in other words, that knowledgable practice is *productive* and that what it produces, among other things, is the recognizable structuring of subjectivity and objectivity on a global scale.[129]

'Laws' and 'structures' are products of social practice and even of purposeful actions but they are in many important cases not seen as within the reach of social and political control. The purposive actions are not self-consciously aimed at setting up these structures, but they nevertheless create or reproduce them. These structures involve the patterns of possible meaning which define what is, what is possible and what is not (objectivity), and who is and who is what (subjectivity). The categories defining the basic social universe do not fall from nowhere, they are the product of practice, but not necessarily practice openly or even self-consciously aimed at this result. Nor is it practice that is only by coincidence producing this result – there will typically be some degree of Giddens-like self-monitoring creating a trial-and-error convergence towards practices that serve specific interests or fit into larger structures.[130] The Type I/Type II dichotomy conceals that much political structuring takes the form of being non-questioned, de-politicized, taken-for-granted.

Therefore, something is lost when employing a number of popular dichotomies in social theory – also found in the international relations (and international society) literature[131] – like *Gemeinschaft/Gesellschaft*, between shared beliefs and co-operation based on rational expectations. *Gemeinschaft* appears as something 'innocent', (international) society in this sense is our larger family. *Gesellschaft* on the contrary appears as a question of power, of utility and calculation, but at least openly so. What is really interesting is that which operates in-between. The dichotomy could (and should) be further split up, but we can start by inserting a 'third', which is enough to show there is no neat dichotomy.[132]

Too easily, a correlation can appear where political is only that which is politicized, and the non-politicized accordingly is not a problem of human choice. A lot of important politics is not openly put as ideal, rational discourse on 'how we want to do things', it is involved in pre-structuring, defining and foreclosing the fields of possibility and imagination. Of course, this argument comes close to leftist ideals of emancipation and *Ideologiekritik*: the hidden structures and repressed possibilities are to be brought out. But for post-structuralists, the interest is on the invisible as such, not by dragging something secret out in the open, but by exposing the mechanisms that produce this blindness: e.g. the example used by Laclau and Mouffe,[133] during the Cold War democracy and socialism were constructed as a dichotomy by the dominant socialists as well as the western establishment, and thereby 'democratic socialism' was made an oxymoron. The point here is not to bring out that which was not visible, because it does not exist except where it can be articulated. Instead, it is possible to show *why* 'democratic socialism' sounded like a contradiction in terms, and how this was not a conclusion reached by logical reflection but a product of the way the terms socialism and democracy were defined - via each other. In line with the Foucaultian dictum that power is not repressive but productive, one studies not the poor marginalized realities and truths in order to restore them to their 'natural' size, but focuses on the mechanisms - visible and concrete - which structure what can possibly be meaningful and thereby show that these repressed dimensions are absent for good reasons, not because they are inherently weak or irrelevant but due to the way regimes of truth operate.

All this is rather different from power struggles of the usual 'regime' type where the self-interest of each actor leads it to attempt to give the rules a twist which serves its interests best while still realizing the possible joint or rather parallel gains of all actors. Ashley's is rather a meta-politics executed not from a self-conscious subject pursuing its given interests, but preceding this subject as one of the conditions for its formation.

Therefore, this kind of study will locate itself between the subjective and the objective. We study neither 'what politicians *really* think', nor 'objective reality'.[134a] A possible object of study is then *discourses*, as they do have structures, they have their own inherent logic. Subjects are then seen as the arena for conflicting discourses, not the origin of discourse; the perspective is turned around in contrast to the 'normal' way of seeing the relationship between subject and discourse, author and text.

This perspective attempts to trace the unstable constellations of 'society' and 'subjects' - both as products of conflicting strategies and practices, discourses and power. 'Power produces; it produces reality; it produces domains of objects and rituals of truth' (Foucault). Foucault wants to escape the image of *power* as 'limitation' or 'repression' (i.e. purely 'negative'), implying somehow that order, justice and normality is power-free. He wants to show instead that all social relations are power relations, and the view where some relations become 'power-free' is a specific form of exercising power. Therefore, it is so important for Ashley to avoid the conventional image, where some relations and 'cultures' are *outside* the field of power, are 'natural' or 'self-grown'.

In this specific Ashley article another main source of inspiration comes from the work of Pierre Bourdieu (from whom Ashley often quotes a phrase about 'the conductorless orchestration of collective action and improvisations', meaning something similar to the above presented arguments of Foucault). From Bourdieu, Ashley borrows the concept of *doxa*. Knowledge can be divided into three forms: orthodoxy, heterodoxy and doxa. The first two are relatively self-evident, doxa the taken-for-granted knowledge. *Orthodoxy* is voiced in answer to *heterodoxy*, while *doxa* is not articulated at all. The first two are politicized, one from a privileged position, the other contesting it. Both are in a desperate search for some ultimate ground, which is always undermined by the presence of the opponent (since there is also an opposing view, neither can be self-evident). Self-evidence is achieved only by *doxa*, which is self-evident yet ambiguous knowledge. Here, practices are modelled, transferred and learned as *practical competence*; arguments are not formally rationalized, and are never legitimized. Rather, knowledge is lived, not proclaimed.[134b]

In an international relations context, the concept of *doxa* makes it possible to grasp certain mechanisms upholding the most basic principles of 'international society' - and what is often taken to be the pre-society, immutable 'systemic' forces. The basic principle constituting this structuring of political space (and time) is the sovereign state. The organizing idea of state sovereignty was a powerful solution to the dilemmas posed by the waning medieval order,[135] and consisted of the dual (mutually constitutive) principles of the fragmentation of global political life into autonomous units, and their internal centralization, holding a monopoly of power and authority over a specific territory. This split meant, in the words of R. B. J. Walker, 'an exceptionally elegant resolution of the apparent contradiction between centralization and fragmentation, or phrased in more philosophical language, between universality and particularity. ... The principle of state sovereignty emerged in early-modern Europe as a replacement for the principle of hierarchical subordination',[136] which gradually gave way to the secular, territorial state, to the principle of spatial exclusion. Universal principles are then applicable within, not without; difference on the other hand is concentrated outside, and international relations is seen as essentially lacking 'community' and, therefore, it can only with difficulty be analysed as *politics*. International politics as a special sphere is constituted as a mirror image of domestic affairs. This contrast is not simply a coincidental after-the-fact difference, but is the way the two fields are constituted. Our idea of the international is basically built on an idea of what it is *not*: domestic politics (not rule of laws, not centralized). 'The principle of state sovereignty is easily mistaken for a bloodless and abstract legal concept, far removed from the immediate demands of policy and politics. But this is in itself an effect of concrete political practices.'[137]

Socially recognized systemic conditions establish the self-evident limits of politics, and thereby make up the conditions of meaningful social practice. Ashley focuses especially on how this kind of practice is able to produce the appearance of continuity and direction. Somehow the many practices are *oriented* and energies *concerted*, and we talk of the 'meaning' or 'pattern' - or 'order'? - of international politics. Thereby, it becomes possible to interpret international politics. This is why Ashley talks of 'a problematic of imposing international purpose'. These practices constitute individual subjects able to administer the complexities and tensions in disparate locales, whereby they generate collective structures that they take to be objective. There is no single source of power, meaning or order, but all these local practices produce the *effect* of a seemingly coherent and meaningful system.

The problem of imposing international governance involves an irony, an essential tension, because it is 'the *political making of the extra-political*, the *historical making of the timeless*, the *specific and arbitrary making of the universal and the necessary*. It is a problem of transforming a potentially *vocal* clash of competing interpretations into a *silently* affirmed collective truth.'[138] Moving in this paradox is yet another instance of working out a conception that 'does not reduce practice to a dichotomy of deliberate choice versus habitual or traditional routine, does not resort to an ahistorical partitioning of consciousness and subconsciousness'.[139] In routinized behaviour structures of power and meaning are reproduced, and subtle actions and innovations alter routines without these necessarily being articulated as the object of open politicization.

This Foucault–Bordieu–Ashley argument should lead us to be cautious about accepting the widespread dichotomy of 'self-grown', natural societies (*Gemeinschaft*) and the instrumental or contractual setting-up of institutions (*Gesellschaft*). Ashley's perspective is actually not that far from Kissinger's, who also moves in the grey zone of not too open politicization, co-ordination games, and not least the struggle for defining the terms for 'co-ordination'.

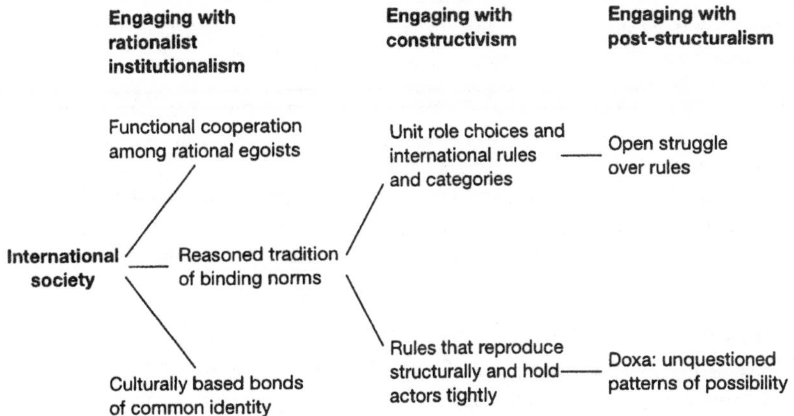

Figure 5.4 The English School's third American rendezvous

He even points to the above-mentioned irony especially for a *conservative* who (like Metternich) wants to establish an order as 'natural' and pre-political, but succeeds so much as to fail - the system is labelled the Metternich system, and is thereby seen *not* as self-evident, but as a specific one (of which he would allegedly prefer not to be credited).[140]

This layer of international society is about the *rules* governing that which appears necessary, and decides that which is thought to be possible (but contested, i.e. political) or impossible. Therefore, it is about the *structures* of meaning, not single ideas. At any specific time and place there are patterns in the conceptual universe that enable the creation of some specific objects and subjects and it is these patterns or structures that organize knowledge systematically. Our interest is therefore turned towards the inner structure and especially the 'deeper' codes of these knowledge patterns: the logic that structures what can be meaningfully said. It is therefore time to look again at 'The structure of international society'.[141]

INTERNATIONAL SOCIETY: THE GRAMMAR OF DIALOGUE AMONG STATES

C. A. W. Manning's seminar 'The structure of international society' is reflected in his book *The Nature of International Society* from 1962. There, Manning argues that the world of 'diplomatics' is a specific reality with its own 'structure': 'There is, in a given situation, an inherent logic.'[142] There is an 'international way of life'.[143] To understand this, one has to learn how to think in the world of diplomatic ideas.[144] This world is basically a mental construct, but it is this construct that makes the social cosmos 'a going concern'.[145] While the tangible reality consists of the activities of individual people, it is in some sense *real* that states *do* act and behave.[146] Through the concept of 'role', Manning argues that when de Gaulle speaks:

> not merely does he speak as in the name of France. France herself, he at least would seem to believe, is speaking through him. For in the realm of diplomatics it is not merely men, even in the international relations roles as statesmen, that behave. There is a sense in which there occurs also the behavior of countries, that is, of states. Such behaving is not, like that even of the rolesman, real behaviour. Rather it is behaviour by imputation, notional behaviour, and notionally the behaviour of states.[147]

The task of international relations as 'meta-diplomatics'[148] is to grasp the inherent logic of this game: the structure of international society. This is a world made largely of words, words that are therefore very real. Were the words to change, this social cosmos would disappear or change radically. But so long as these words are in place, the social cosmos continues to function - and this of course means that we are not talking about separate, free-floating words, but a *system* of concepts.

> [Will the anthropologist] not, on the contrary, approach the life-in-community of his French Canadians, or his Tibetans, as a single reality, to be holistically apprehended if it is duly to be understood? And once having decided that the ordinary cultural group may indeed so constitute an intelligible unit for study, need we doubt that this could be equally true of what is also in effect, if not literally, a cultural group - the plurality of states, coexisting as they do in a society so distinctively theirs? The habitat, the folklore, the mores, the very givenness of this group: all these are points for reflective investigations, as facets as a single theme.[149]

International relations, therefore, aims at 'a connoisseurship of the folkways of the international family. International relations as an academic subject examines the international way of life.'[150] It is a kind of anthropology, or rather social cosmology,[151] which with both names implies an approach trying to capture the totality and its constitutive rules. The question then is whether this socially constructed diplomatic world contains significant rules that actually have an independent causal role, or whether analysis in terms of power and interest could not tell us all we want to know?[152] Obviously, power and interests are strongly involved in diplomatics, but we can get a hint of how to conceive of this sphere from a surprising direction: Carl von Clausewitz.

Clausewitz, building on his well-known conception that on the one hand politics should always be the task-setter for war and on the other hand *in war* politics should not interfere unduly in preventing the soldier from acting rationally, suggests the following: 'Is not War merely another kind of writing and language for political thoughts? It has certainly a grammar of its own, but its logic is not peculiar to itself.'[153] Does diplomacy have a grammar too, or does it directly reflect the logic of the political struggle, that logic which is, in the case of war, translated through a specific grammar? While conflict is conflict, the instruments chosen imply specific grammars: war has one and diplomacy another; cf. Aron's classic remark about the diplomat and the soldier being the personae of international relations.

Although the 'original' impulses may in some indefinite sense come from elsewhere, the action of international relations always has to be expressed in one of the languages available: war or diplomacy. (And one might add, 'revolutionist', transnational and cosmopolitan action as a third option, world society - with a language of human rights and individual moral responsibility.) If one assumes that these languages are completely flexible - anything you want to 'say', you can find an expression for - they could possibly be without any independent force, and all explanation would be drawn from basic power drives. If, however, it is assumed that the languages do constrain, shape and define, then their grammars will have effects.

For instance, a principle like state sovereignty is neither an empirical designation nor an edict on limits of accepted behaviour, so that one can in a simple sense check empirical events against this description. Sovereignty is rather an underlying organizing principle, a structure only visible through its effects, and thus only to be 'seen' to the extent that the analyst shows, that the visible events can be understood as effects of this particular 'generative grammar'.[154]

> Indeed, it is difficult to believe that anyone ever asserted the 'states-centric' view of international politics that is today so knowingly rejected by those who seek to emphasize the role of 'the new international actors'. What was widely asserted about European international relations from the time of Vattel in the mid-eighteenth century until the end of the First World War was the *legal fiction* of a political universe that consisted of states alone, the doctrine that only states had rights and duties in international law.[155]

This 'legal fiction' has been and still is very real. There are exceptions and deviations, but this is exactly what they are: exceptions and deviations from a norm, and hard to make sense of in any other way. Even more difficult would it be to grasp the sovereignty-structured processes from the exceptions. Indeed, if one tried, counter-factually, to establish the workings of the system without this fiction, one would probably have great difficulties and thus realize that this idea is one of the building blocks of our system, it is present in the reasoning behind much action and is, thus, a *Realabstraktion* ('real abstraction') as we used to say in the Marxist debates of the 1970s about the concept of exchange value. The concept exists because it is practised constantly by so many actors and their action could never have been the same without this concept.[156]

Manning's orientation towards understanding the role of words and ideas as they are practised in the artificial but real world of diplomatics has not been much continued even within the recent revival of attempts to comprehend the structure of the international system in constructivist terms. Much of this has been more social-psychological than semiotic and focused on roles, scripts and identity formation. Ruggie has been more structuralist in postulating a 'generative grammar' and singled out 'sovereignty' as an organizing principle distinguishing the modern period from what came before, and what could follow.[157] A structuralist reading of Walker[158] could lead to similar insights, while mainstream constructivism[159] seems more interested in 'rules' and 'norms' in a vaguer and especially in a less densely connected sense - that there are numerous 'rules' floating around which states (and other actors) are both constituted by and acting upon.[160] But to see these as forming a system, some as being deeper than others, and thus international society having a grammar, has not been much developed beyond the pioneering but perplexing work of Manning.

One way to give it more precision, and to benefit from theories developed since Manning, could be to lean on Luhmanian autopoiesis, and see the international system as a self-organizing system with its central code differentiating and stabilizing the system. Each system crystallizes as a specific sphere on the basis of a certain code. In autopoiesis, one analyses for instance 'how the law thinks'.[161] Law has its own rationality (and rationale), regulated by the binary code 'legal'/'illegal' - not that this is all there is to law, but it is the way the law has to think in order to be law.[162] A system closes in on itself around its own inner logic and relates to the world through specific structural couplings.[163] The perspective of self-referential systems could be applied to international relations too.[164] Luhmann's stress on the importance of *codes* (central organizing principles) is close to the original ideas of Waltz stressing *anarchy*, *sovereignty* and *polarity* as distinct criteria which do not change gradually but in revolutionary ways. Ruggie,[165] Dessler,[166] Buzan et al.[167] and others have argued that the Waltzian structure can be retained as one of the best attempts to formulate the deep rules or generative grammar of the modern states-system, with the major modification that his ontology is wrong. They argue that deep rules are not eternal, necessary structures that can be deduced from the international condition as such. Rather, the structure is a contingent, social product, but powerful and structural nevertheless. In particular, the second tier should be seen as involving an act of conceptual innovation ('sovereignty') and, thus, be seen as a socially constructed, but terribly strong, self-reinforcing and self-referential system.

This entails that each system has its own unique trajectory, which, of course, ties in nicely with Martin Wight's work on *systems of states* where it is pointed out how the logic of international relations is not the same in all systems. This is different from the main interest of those focusing on the *general*, systemic pressures like Buzan and, to some extent, Manning. Watson asks: 'Do the code of conduct and the institutions of each system reflect the distinct values and religion of its common culture, or are the agreed rules essentially regulatory, conditioned by the same empirical pressures in all systems?'[168] This is not only the question (functionalist vs. culturalist explanation) of the importance of shared culture for the emergence of an international society. Not only is an international society dependent on cultural nearness,[169] there is also a particular logic to each international society. The rules and principles of a system like the European or, say, the Persian or Chinese does depend on culturally specific factors, and are therefore different. However, this specific International Society should not in any uni-linear manner be reduced to this culture as if the modern states system *had* to develop in a specific way because of its Christian origins (which would be to take all autonomy out of the international sphere once again). Rather, it can be said that these specific cultural factors offer the original fragments that are then amplified in the process they trigger (cf. chaos theory, fractals, etc.): the international society takes on a process of its own, it organizes itself in the process of stabilizing and shutting itself off from other systems, and, thereby, the codes become primarily a product of the system itself. Although the system would have been different had the triggering fragment been different, the fragment as such does not determine the system.

The self-referential nature of international society is clearly expressed by Manning.[170] Under the subheading 'Whence the Circularity of the Circle?' he says:

> What gives to International Law its binding force is what gives it its very existence - namely the thinking, that is, the conceiving, which makes it so. Men, in order to play law, need to conceive law and conceive it *as* law, to conceive it as binding. For law, *as* law, is binding.[171]

Not only law has this character, more generally, diplomatics 'as a going concern' include dogmas that are necessary for this game and not possible to argue in any ultimate way, beyond this on-going game.

More implicitly, self-referentiality is found in Butterfield's brilliant pieces on 'balance of power'[172] and 'raison d'état'.[173] Constantly, he is careful in not saying the 'balance of power' appears because states do some balancing, but points out the difference it makes when the concept as such is formulated. In relation to 'raison d'état', he proposes:

> neither to curse it nor to honour it, but, as with everything else that ever emerged in the past, just marvel at its existence - marvel indeed that anything should ever have existed at all. Then perhaps (just to please the utilitarians), I

will try to say something about the role it has had in the development of modern Europe.[174]

And the concept is certainly given a significant power in itself - concepts are seen as making a difference (as, e.g., when Butterfield counter-factually shows how Renaissance Italy, who did not know the modern concept of balance of power, did its balancing differently than they would have done with the concept). And these concepts are part of the self-referential conceptual worlds of different ages. (The balance of power 'seems to come from the modern world's reflections on its own experience'.[175]) Therefore, it is so important to avoid the many easy anachronisms and instead be alert to 'the subtly different meanings' a word has had at different times.

Another dimension of such self-referential systems thinking is represented in the English School by Wight's chapter on 'international legitimacy'[176] and Mayall's work on nationalism and international society.[177] By focusing on the basic principle of legitimacy in a system, 'the collective judgment of international society about rightful membership of the family of nations; how sovereignty may be transferred; and how state succession is to be regulated, when large states break up into smaller, or several states combine into one',[178] they clearly transcend the realm of disconnected and separate 'rules' in relation to a specific 'law' (is it followed? who wants it? etc.) and get to principles and codes that form a *system*. Most fundamental for the system is to regulate the criteria of membership, of what to include in the system, and this was what Wight discussed in terms of 'international legitimacy'. Then we can ask questions like what happens to other principles and norms when the basis of legitimacy shifts from dynastic to popular, because each period has had a relatively clear basic principle. And if the post-Cold War period is peculiarly bereft of such a principle, this might explain something of the confusions over Yugoslavia and some post-Soviet cases.[179] To study how and when these codes shift, one must first delineate epochs and then find the conceptual system of each epoch.[180] In a different context - the history of international law - Wilhelm G. Grewe has carried out an excellent analysis of how international law is an integrated system with a fair degree of internal coherence, which moves through periods of relative stability around a set of core concepts and ideas, and periods of change to a new code.[181] Since the tradition of 'international society' is strongly influenced by international law (especially when international law is at its most philosophical), it should be possible to integrate work like Grewe's into the study of international society.

The importance of this lies in the need to explicate *structures* of international society, in order for the concept to carry any explanatory burdens, and especially if the Ashley-Kissinger-Manning layer is to be developed into something analytically useful.

A taxonomy, an illustration and lessons for theory and discipline

A RESTATED TYPOLOGY

The examination so far has produced four layers of international society:

1. rationalist atomism (institution-building for rational egoists to realize potential co-operation gains);
2. constructivist voluntarism (open struggle over formative rules and principal norms);
3. materialistic necessity (hard rules to which the single unit has to bow); and
4. culturalistic holism (co-operation conditioned by shared civilization or culture).

Obviously, there is a danger that the four slide off in different ontological spheres and thereby they do not become categories to use simultaneously, but different or incompatible 'perspectives'. In this final section, I will therefore reformulate the four on a joint and consistent ontological basis. For this purpose, mainly, I will be using the third row, the post-structuralist engagement. (Some might find it ironic to use post-structuralism to reintegrate and to systematize, but if this makes the following controversial both to post-structuralists and their opponents - fine.)

Rationalist functionalism, the American approach, should be given credit for explaining how co-operation is possible *without* assumptions of altruism or collective commitment. English School theorists and more strongly constructivists and post-structuralists might argue that this is not one layer of international society - it is a mistake! They might question the minimalist, purely rational-egoistic co-operation, and argue instead that co-operative arrangements are always constructed; identities always have to be articulated so as to make co-operation possible, and that it is never abstract, pre-social units that meet. But there is a value to the Keohanian argument. Often in international relations, and also in the English School, it is assumed that when/if co-operation occurs, there must be some element of shared culture/identity involved which implies the logical link: *if* units were rational egoists, *then* co-operation would be impossible. Therefore, the American, rationalist argument is important as a kind of ideal type or purely logical border case, not as an empirical possibility. In this way, it first of all serves to deconstruct a dichotomy with chains of equivalence saying: shared community-cooperation-domestic plus benign international vs. atomism-conflict-international. (Keohane, the deconstructivist!?)

Finally, the rationalist analysis should include the additional step of

Buzan's argument about systemic pressure, about the need for international society arising out of increasing dynamic density/interaction capacity.

Layers two and three have already been established on a post-structuralist basis in what I have said earlier: number two as open struggle over rules and norms, and three as the grammar of possible meanings and actions.

The final layer to rethink is then the culturalism of Wight, to some extent Watson, and, in other ways, Morgenthau. Both within the English School and in the disagreement among the Americans, Morgenthau, Keohane and Kissinger, an argument over culturalism has been present. The issue is whether that which binds the actors is totally strategic and/or consciously constructed between them and, conversely, in what sense it is truly shared; how 'deep' is it 'common', so to say? Is there a sense in which some actors *are* closer, and, therefore, more easily form an international society? In arguments about international society or legitimate order it is implied that the actors with this 'code' (or language) in place are able to *understand* each other and *understand* the situation identically. Within a culture, one can have a degree of understanding not possible across cultures.

This assumption contains the standard common sensical image of understanding and communication with the unity and continuity of a process,[182] whereby some 'intention' is carried out and some 'message' carried over to someone else. This relates to a kind of common sense view of 'communication' 'as a vehicle, a means of transport or transitional medium of a *meaning*, and moreover a *unified* meaning'.[183] Against this, the post-structuralist stresses how the signifiers (in communication terms, the 'medium') are uncontrollable, always adding too much or too little and not simply representing the signified (the 'message'). The signifiers have a high degree of autonomy, and their play then overflows the allegedly primary signified. There is an 'essential drift' in writing, a force which breaks the controlling context – signs can always travel on, be quoted, take on new meanings, be repeated, and yet, in repetition, never hold exactly the same meaning.[184] Therefore, 'communication' cannot be captured by the image of transport of unified meaning. If this was the only possible meaning of 'communication', it would never take place. Not even when we talk to ourselves.

'Understanding' does take place;[185] the point is what this means. Maybe it only means that one enters a specific language game, and not that something identical is held in the minds of two parties? 'Understanding' might be a relatively recognizable social phenomenon with certain conventions regulating it, without a specific communication or information process having actually taken place in the sense of the *ideal* of understanding. 'The nature of hermeneutic knowledge is not hermeneutic.'[186]

Whereas much radical semiotics and post-structuralism, in the 1970s and early 1980s, seemed to say that communication and understanding were impossible (popular 'postmodernism'), it is obviously a fact that we go on communicating all the time, and we act as if we 'understand' what has been said. The Danish semiotician Per Aage Brandt has pointed out that we need to conceptualize this 'understanding effect' as a social process without making substantial assumptions of any identity between what is 'sent' and what is 'received'. A social phenomenon 'understanding' does occur. And in the same sense, actors operate in international politics on sometimes converging concepts and a shared language - which has decisive political effects. In Yuri Lotman's words we are talking about a 'semiosphere', the shared space of cultural codes which one can pass in and out of but with specific effects.[187] The point, however, is that it is unsustainable to think of 'incommensurability' between worlds because this presupposes, as its opposite, complete commensurability, a space of totally transparent communication occurs according to the ideal transport model. This romantic ideal has to be denied both when presented in the form of nationalism, as a culturalist theory of international society (or clashing civilizations), or for that matter as a theory of incommensurable paradigms in international relations.[188]

Without making substantive assumptions about language or values being

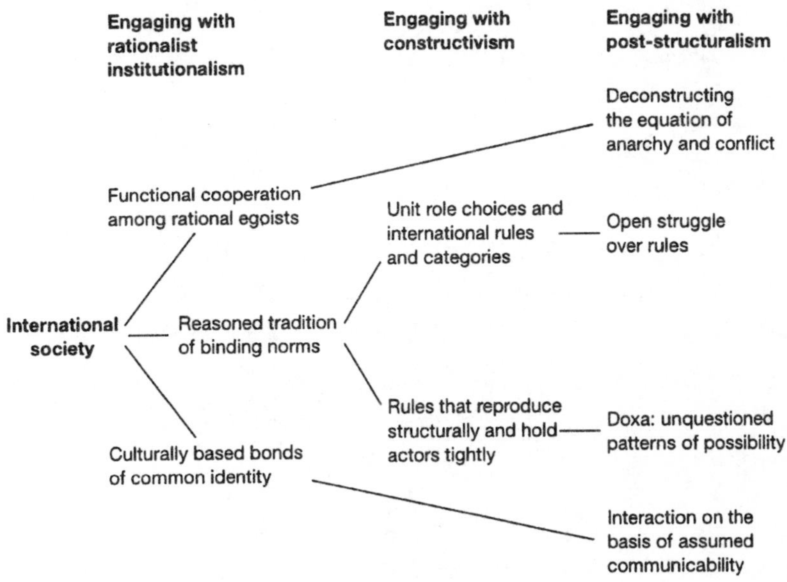

Figure 5.5 Post-structuralist reformulation

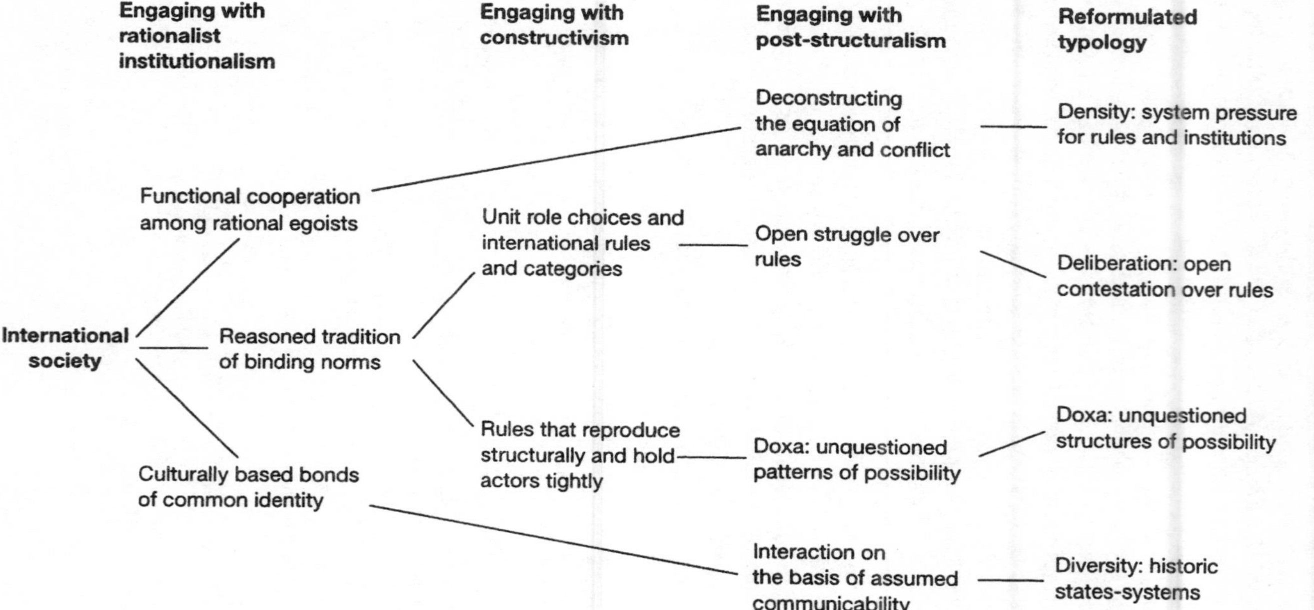

Figure 5.6 Four layers of international society

'shared' or 'the same', it is important to study when, why and how actors enter into a semiosphere where participants play games *as if* (or on the social assumption that) they 'agree' on principles and 'share' values.

What this fourth level is about is thus the construction of distance and of assumed communicability,[189] which points to the fact that international systems and societies have (explicitly or implicitly) been constructed as limited, i.e. as multiple. This points further to the important lesson for international relations that these systems have operated according to different sets of rules, and therefore we end up with this fourth layer as the study of historic states-systems.

These are four different layers of international society, because they are four questions which it is possible for the same person/perspective to ask in the same situation.

FOUR PARALLEL QUESTIONS

If, for instance, one was to study European security after the fall of the Berlin Wall, the four would point towards the following questions.

First, the utilitarian perspective of setting up the necessary and rational institutions for co-operation and co-ordination. European politics has been densely packed with arguments along these lines: discussions on 'European architecture', integration, stability, 'European peace order' (especially in Germany), all-European institutions, European order, and various other projects for joint, rational planning for the institutional setting of the new Europe. The perspective is present in numerous policy articles on e.g. the future of NATO – either prescriptively (why NATO is still necessary) or prognostically (will NATO survive?) – and maybe most systematically in work like Keohane, Nye and Hoffmann that investigate both the future of the institutions and the role played *by* institutions in shaping state policies. This perspective has been present also in debates within the rationalist affinity between neo-realism and neo-liberal institutionalism as most clearly seen in the two Mearsheimer debates.[190] The debate here is whether changes of structural conditions (polarity) modify incentive structures so that the construction or continuation of institutions becomes irrational and, therefore, impossible.

Second, the constructivist layer points to a transformation of the game with the end of the Cold War. Europe after 1989 will not necessarily repeat power balancing, and will not be conflictual just because it is multipolar (vide Mearsheimer). In a process of units transforming themselves (their identity) as they transform the regional (or the international) system, we arrive at a political process that can no longer be captured by the classical conception (whether that is referred to as 'realism' or 'sovereignty'). States have transformed the meaning of sovereignty towards an 'international state' where identity is no longer purely self-oriented but partly invested in the wider system.[191] There are a number of liberal transformationalist ideas exploring such development: complex interdependence, democracies that do not fight each other, or where behaviour has changed because the system is now made up of liberal states (Moravcsik, Slaughter-Burley) or trading states (Rosecrance). A less transformationalist idea involves integration as a game compatible with realist power reasoning but still involving a conscious strategy of game transformation.[192] Here at the second level, the issue is how states redefine themselves and the meaning of statehood, and thereby end repeated patterns of behaviour expected by neo-realists to continue. Structures that *could* operate as presumably given limits become politicized and the object of conscious choice; actors struggle over who to be and what game to play, and in the case of present-day Europe they often do so on the political assumption that the two questions are mutually constitutive.

Third, at the grammar level, we have had attempts to understand the changing status of the concept of self-determination, the question of whether legitimacy ultimately rests with state or nation, and an emerging norm of democracy as the source of legitimacy. In contrast to the relatively clear UN system of *states* actually having self-determination and national self-determination being played down, the post-Cold War system has exhibited a certain ambiguity without clearly overcoming the old principles.[193] The principles that are at stake here are among the deepest; those relating to international legitimacy because they define who are members of international society - does legitimacy arise out of some kind of national self-determination, from actual state control, or from some 'standards' defined internationally? All other principles and norms come second to this question about who we are talking about and who are to follow (or not) these rules. It is therefore a quite dramatic change if something happens to the principles of international legitimacy. It is at least a change of the epoch-defining scale on the Grewe list (1494, 1648, 1815, 1919, 1945, 1989). An even more dramatic claim does however appear as well.

Fourth, the basic organizing principle for international politics in Europe might be changing. A case can be made for seeing the emerging political structures as 'neo-medieval'[194] in that in Western Europe neither the states, nor the EU will be 'sovereign'. (Here, one would need a longer theoretical argument clarifying why the liberal disposal of the concept of 'sovereignty' was premature because the code of the self organizing international system has remained organized by the logic of territorial sovereignty.) In Western Europe we witness the return of overlapping authorities as in the Middle Ages, but also a historically unique situation where the *territorial state* dies before the *nations*; thus the talk of 'end of the nation state' is slightly misleading. The national idea is alive and well but the basic *political* organizing principle - twice as old as the national idea - of sovereignty, exclusivity and territoriality is giving way to new patterns. The metaphor of new Middle Ages is thus not meant literally, but mainly as a liberating exercise, freeing our theoretical reflection from the constraints of the system of sovereign statehood. We do not know what will be the logic of the post-sovereign system in Europe, and there is not much reason to believe it will be very similar to the Middle Ages, but nor will it necessarily be much like the modern system, so in order to free our imagination that we might be able to figure out the organizing principle of a 'postmodern' international system, we might go from the modern via the premodern.

The fourth level is here activated as a metaphor in reflections on the deepest layers of level three grammar. Not only the medieval system has appeared in this role, lately also empires have been tested as a possible metaphor for 'post-wall' Europe, with the EU centred order paralleling either the Roman Empire or probably more appropriately ancient and Chinese imperial systems of 'radial' power.[195] Thus, the fourth question - historical states-systems - which one should not expect to find at play in any direct sense with an examination of contemporary Europe, does after all appear in two indirect ways. One is in terms of reflections on the end of the age of western dominance.[196] The global system gets increasingly regionalized without any culture being dominant. This is not a change *in* Europe, but a major change *for* Europe.

Secondly, the new challenges to sovereignty have meant a questioning of the basic modern European principle and, thereby, of any simple continuity. It has, therefore, generated attempts to draw on other systems as analogies to capture the emerging forms of practice.

Layers three and four point to the possibility that the inner logic of the codes of international society might be in for a major reorganization. This is not very closely linked to the strategies of individual actors or national projects - it is more a process with its own inner logic operating at the international level (*How the international system thinks*), and thus distinct from agendas of layers one and two.

ENGLISH LESSONS

Finally, if all this is on our agenda - and so widely dispersed - what have we gained by using the term 'international society'? Is there any coherence, any value in this label? Yes, there are at least three gains:

- It is a signpost in the debates in international relations and a symbol of a continued effort to keep open a vital thinking space, which closes when international relations comes to be seen as made up of the realist/radical dichotomy.

- International society is generally an approach more open to history, culture and law than American mainstream theory and it is thereby a precondition for most of the agendas suggested here.
- It specifically suggests an emphasis on diplomatic codes, on the *logic* in *language* to be studied in *politics*: and the important differences of the four agendas notwithstanding, they all deal with something as classical and old-fashioned as diplomatic language, codes, political discourse - diplomatics. Something that used to be central to the discipline (or originally was *all* of the discipline), but with the gradual widening of international relations, this was not just relativized by more getting on board, it was actually lost out of sight, and the English School is the most powerful tradition to include diplomatics within a wider perspective.

The main negative lesson is that international society is not one tight 'thing'. As long as 'international society' is mainly a perspective to adopt, this is no problem. Then it means the shifts in our vocabulary generated by the provocative introduction of this tertium, shifts that open up for various studies that do not talk much of international society as such but could not have been conducted had not the basic 'international society' move been made.[197] If, however, explanatory burdens are placed on 'international society' as such, it soon becomes clear that it is not conceptually coherent enough to perform this task. In this respect much of the English School has a too 'thing'-like concept of international society.[198]

Does that mean that the boundary question (when does an international system qualify as international society?) is the wrong question? And that international society is not a thing but a perspective? No, it is possible to say still that international society is marked by specific features (although we have to run through four criteria) and therefore there are situations with and situations without international society. If there should be a real boundary, it must demand that it is possible to find four formulations that are really the same at four layers, i.e. dependent on which of the four modes of asking questions is adopted. At the first, it is when co-operation moves from specific to diffuse reciprocity;[199] at the second when identities are redefined so that the collective identity come either to carry direct loyalty (the classical cosmopolitanism discussion) or (probably more importantly) the discourse theoretical because the collective identity becomes central *within* the self-definition of the primary units (states);[200] the third entails a grammar that defines statehood (or some other unit) by mutual recognition or some equally specific principle,[201] so that there are strong and clear international principles that make unit legitimacy dependent on specific performance;[202] and, fourth, to be a clearly singular states-system with strong individuality.

All four refer to the step when a community beyond the units (but not taking on unitness or actor quality itself) attains an independent political reality beyond the instrumental will of the units.

The merits of the English School presented in this chapter suggest that it will be important to avoid an Americanization of the English School. It is, of course, nice that it has been rediscovered in America, but this - combined with the lure of the leading land of international relations - can easily lead to a reformulation of the English School where the parts are upgraded that most easily fit into or correspond to American theory, and, in particular, there is the temptation to get the wanted coherence by focusing on that which is closest to American mainstream rationalism, which seems to mean almost exclusively Bull, and a reading of him as would-be regime theorist. Some of the most important English School insights are, however, found in the work of Wight, Butterfield and even Manning. Their style of writing is much more alien to contemporary international relations and it will, therefore, take harder work to keep these strands alive - but, as suggested by the present reformulation, it should be worth it.

AMERICAN LESSONS - DE-DISCIPLINING THE DISCIPLINE?

The pattern 'after the fourth debate' explains not necessarily the revitalization of the English School, but at least the new openness of American international relations to it. It also should warn us about a possible price to be paid for re-entering the stage in this way. A trend of the mid-1990s in contrast to the mid- and late-1980s is constructivists out-manoeuvring post-structuralists as the main alternative to the rationalists and, thereby, shifting from philosophy to 'social science'. This raises interesting discussions, but the danger of this American 'after the fourth debate' move is that constructivism completely screens off post-structuralism, and, as it has been shown above, this would mean to lose important dimensions of a reinvigorated English School. Returning to Figure 5.1, the question-carrying arrow at the end about a possible English School contribution to the general evolution of the discipline on the main (American) arena could therefore be that of preventing a full execution of the 'after the fourth debate' move (constructivists replacing post-structuralists as the main alternative). As often noticed, socially and sociologically, the British international relations community is more inclusive than the American, and it is less dogmatically defined as 'social *science*' and open to more philosophy, more history, and more law. Therefore - paradoxically? - it might be able to keep some of the post-structuralist impulses alive when they are cleaned out elsewhere, keep them maybe under another name, any other name, but still get Americans to read and think about such issues through the respectable English School, when the dreaded pomos are finally out-manoeuvred in their 'original' 1980s appearance.

Notes

1 An earlier version of this chapter ('International society: the grammar of dialogue among states?') was presented at the workshop on 'The Nature of International Society Reconsidered', European Consortium for Political Research, University of Limerick, 30 March to 4 April, 1992. I would like to thank all participants and the editor in particular for helpful comments. My (then) colleagues Pierre Lemaitre, Lene Hansen, Knud Erik Jørgensen, Morten Kelstrup and Barry Buzan commented on an even earlier draft of which probably nothing is left in the present version.

2 Bull, Hedley (1977) *The Anarchical Society: A Study of Order in World Politics* (London, Macmillan).

3 Wendt, Alexander and Duvall, Raymond (1989) 'Institutions and international power', in Czempiel, Ernst-Otto and Rosenau, James (eds), *Global Changes and Theoretical Challenges: Approaches to World Politics for the 1990s* (Lexington, MA, Lexington), pp. 51-74; David, Dessler (1989) 'What's at stake in the agent-structure debate?', *International Organization*, **43**(3), pp. 441-73; Wendt, A. E. (1992) 'Anarchy is what states make of it', in *International Organization*, **46**(2), pp. 391-425; Keohane, R. O. (1988) 'International institutions: two approaches' (1984 ISA Presidential Address), *International Studies Quarterly*, **32**(4); Krasner, S. D. (1994) 'International political economy: abiding discord', in *Review of International Political Economy*, **1**(1), pp. 13-19; Krasner, S. D. (1995/96) 'Compromising Westphalia', *International Security*, **20**(3), pp. 115-51.

4 Slaughter-Burley, A.-M. (1993) 'International law and international relations theory: a dual agenda', *The American Journal of International Law*, **87**(205), pp. 205-39; Onuf, N. G. (1989) *World of Our Making: Rules and Rule in Social Theory and International Relations* (Columbia, University of South Carolina Press); Wind, M. (1977) 'Onuf – the rules of anarchy', in Neumann, I. B. and Wæver, O. (eds), *The Future of International Relations: Masters in the Making?* (London, Routledge), pp. 236-68; Keal, P. (1994) 'Dual agenda or American agenda? International relations theory and the sociology of international law', paper prepared for the annual conference of BISA, York, 19-21 December.

5 Wæver, Ole (1997) 'Figures of international thought: introducing persons instead of paradigms?', in Neumann, L. B. and Wæver, O. (eds), *The Future of International Relations: Masters in the Making?* (London, Routledge), pp. 1-37.

6 Evans, T. and Wilson, P. (1992) 'Regime theory and the English School of international relations: a comparison', *Millennium: Journal of International Relations*, **21**(3), pp. 329-52; Buzan, B. (1993) 'From international system to international society: structural realism and regime theory meet the English School', *International Organization*, **47**(3), pp. 327-52; Hurrell, A. (1993) 'International society and the study of regimes: a reflective approach', in Rittberger, V. (ed.), *Regime Theory and International Relations* (Oxford, Clarendon Press), pp. 49-72; Knudsen, T. B. (1994) *Det Nye Europa: Orden eller Kaos?* MA Thesis, University of Aarhus; Dunne, T. (1995) 'International

society: theoretical promises fulfilled?', *Cooperation and Conflict*, **30**(2), pp. 125-54; Dunne, T. (1995) 'The social construction of international society', *European Journal of International Relations*, **1**(3), pp. 367-90; Lose, L. G. (1995) *Conceptualizing International Order: International Society, Regime Theory and Sociological Approaches*, MA dissertation, University of Warwick.

7 Carr, E. H. (1939) *The Twenty Years' Crisis 1919-1939* (London, Macmillan).

8 Bull, H. (1966) 'International theory: the case for a classical approach', *World Politics*, **18**(3), pp. 361-77.

9 Wæver, O. (in preparation) *The Politics of International Structure.*

10 Wæver, O. (1996) 'The rise and fall of the inter-paradigm debate', in Smith, S., Booth, K. and Zalewski, M. (eds), *International Theory: Positivism and Beyond* (Cambridge, Cambridge University Press), pp. 149-85.

11 Jones, R. E. (1981) 'The English School of international relations: a case for closure', *Review of International Studies*, **7**(1), pp. 1-12; Wæver, O. (1992) 'International society: theoretical promises unfulfilled?', *Cooperation and Conflict*, **27**(1), pp. 147-78.

12 Dunne (1995) 'International society'; Dunne (1995) 'Social construction'.

13 Wendt, A. E. (1994) 'Collective identity formation and the international state', *American Political Science Review*, **88**(2), pp. 384-96; Keohane, R. O. (1992) Book review of Wight, *International Theory*, *American Political Science Review*, **86**(4), p. 1112; and possibly Buzan (1993) and Wæver (1992) 'International society'.

14 Knudsen (1994); Lose (1995).

15 Carr (1939).

16 Morgenthau, H. J. (1946) *Scientific Man vs. Power Politics* (Chicago, University of Chicago Press).

17 cf. Wæver, O. (1992) *Introduktion til studiet af international politik* (Copenhagen, Forlaget Politiske Studier), chs 1-3; Wæver, O. (1997), pp. 9-10.

18 Bull, Hedley (1966) 'International theory'; Kaplan, M. (1966) 'The great debate: traditionalism vs. science in international relations' *World Politics*, **19**(1), pp. 1-21; Knorr, K. and Rosenau, J. N. (1969) *Contending Approaches to International Politics* (Princeton, NJ, Princeton University Press).

19 Guzzini, S. (1998) *Realism in International Relations and International Political Economy: The Continuing Story of a Death Foretold* (London, Routledge).

20 Wæver, O. (1992) *Introduktion*; Wæver, O. (1996) 'Rise and fall'.

21 Keohane, R. O. (1989) *International Institutions and State Power* (Boulder, CO, Westview).

22 Keohane (1988), p. 160.

23 Ibid., p. 161.

24 Onuf, N. G. (1989) *World of Our Making: Rules and Rule in Social Theory and International Relations* (Columbia, SC, University of South Carolina Press); Wendt (1994); Ringmar, E. (1997) 'Alexander Wendt - a social scientist struggling with history', in Neumann and Wæver (eds), *The Future of International Relations: Masters in the Making?*; Wind, M. (1977) 'Onuf - the rules of anarchy', in Neumann and Wæver (eds) (1997), pp. 236-68.

25 Katzenstein, P. J. (ed.) (1996) *The Culture of National Security: Identity and Norms in World Politics* (New York, Columbia University Press); Adler, E. and Barnett, M. (1996) 'Governing anarchy: a research agenda for the study of security communities', *Ethics and International Affairs*, **10**.

26 Mearsheimer, J. L. (1995) 'The false promise of international institutions', *International Security*, **19**(3) (Winter 1994/95), pp. 5–49.
27 Butterfield, H. and Wight, M. (eds) (1966) *Diplomatic Investigations: Essays in the Theory of International Politics* (London, George Allen & Unwin); Bull (1966) 'International theory'.
28 cf. Dunne, T. (1991) 'The genesis and history of the English School of international relations' in Neumann, I. B. (ed.), *The 'English School' of International Relations: A Conference Report* (Oslo, NUPI Report 179, April), pp. 1–17.
29 Butterfield, H. (1975) 'Raison d'état', Martin Wight Memorial Lecture, University of Sussex, p. 5.
30 Wight, M. (1987) 'An anatomy of international thought', *Review of International Studies*, **13** p. 222. This statement has a dual meaning: to reflect on the *nature* of international society or to reflect on what international society *consists of* more precisely at a specific time. The latter means to engage in attempts to rationalize the concepts and arguments around which international politics move at a certain time, to engage in the political, moral and legal debates of the time; to do this not (primarily) in the sense of trying to solve (or just 'deal with') these eternal questions (as one could read Bull's principled arguments about the nature of the 'classical approach') but to study these concepts, logics and ordering principles in their historical and intellectual context, partly with the view of grappling with our own condition.
31 Watson, A. (1992) *The Evolution of International Society: A Comparative Historical Analysis* (London, Routledge).
32 Bull, H. and Watson, A. (eds) (1984) *The Expansion of International Society* (Oxford, Clarendon Press).
33 Watson (1992).
34 Bull and Watson (1984); Watson (1992).
35 Wight., M. (1986) *Power Politics*, 2nd edn (Harmonsworth, Penguin Books for RIIA); Wight, G. and Porter, B. (eds) (1991) *International Theory: The Three Traditions* (London, Leicester University Press for the RIIA).
36 Clark, I. (1989) *The Hierarchy of States: Reform and Resistance in the International Order*, 2nd edn (Cambridge, BISA/Cambridge University Press; 1st edn 1980); Donelan, M. (1990) *Elements of International Political Theory* (Oxford, Clarendon Press); Jackson, R. H. (1990) *Quasi-States: Sovereignty, International Relations and the Third World* (Cambridge, Cambridge University Press); James, A. (1980) 'Diplomacy and international society', *International Relations*, **6**(6); James, A. (1986) *Sovereign Statehood: The Basis of International Society* (London, George Allen & Unwin); James, A. (1989) 'The realism of realism: the state and the study of international relations', *Review of International Studies*, **1**(3), pp. 215–30; James, A. (1991) 'Sovereignty in Eastern Europe', *Millennium: Journal of International Studies*, **20**(1); James, A. (1992) 'The equality of states: contemporary manifestations of an ancient doctrine', *Review of International Studies*, **18**(4), pp. 377–92; Mayall, J. (1990) *Nationalism and International Society* (Cambridge, BISA/Cambridge University Press); Mayall, J. (1991) 'Non-intervention, self-determination and the "New World Order"', *International Affairs*, **67**(3), pp. 421–30; Miller, A. J. (1983) 'The role of deviance in world international society', *Millennium: Journal of International Studies*, **12**(3), pp. 244–59; Miller, J. D. B. and Vincent, R. J. (eds) (1990) *Order and Violence: Hedley*

Bull and International Relations (Oxford, Clarendon Press); Roberts, A. (1991) 'A new age in international relations?', *International Affairs*, **67**(3), pp. 509–26; Vincent, R. J. (1974) *Nonintervention and International Order* (Princeton, NJ, Princeton University Press); Vincent, R. J. (1984) 'Edmund Burke and the theory of international relations', *Review of International Studies*, **10**(3), pp. 205–18; Vincent, R. J. (1986) *Human Rights and International Relations* (Cambridge, Cambridge University Press and RIIA); Vincent, R. J. 'Order in international politics', in Miller, J. D. B. and Vincent, R. J. (eds) (1990) *Order and Violence: Hedley Bull and International Relations* (Oxford, Clarendon Press), pp. 38–64; Wright, P. M. (1984) 'Central but ambiguous: states and international theory' *Review of International Studies*, **10**, pp. 233–7; even in strangely inverted form: Linklater, A. (1982) *Men and Citizens in the Theory of International Relations* (London, Macmillan; 2nd edn, London, Macmillan, 1990); and maybe the most original work, but still within the set-up: Suganami, H. (1989) *The Domestic Analogy and World Order Proposals* (Cambridge, Cambridge University Press).

37[a] See Donelan, M. (ed.) (1978) *The Reason of State: A Study in International Political Theory* (London, George Allen & Unwin); Mayall, J. (ed.) (1982) *The Community of States: A Study in International Political Theory* (London, George Allen & Unwin); Navari, C. (ed.) (1991) *The Condition of States: A Study in International Political Theory* (Milton Keynes, Open University Press).

37[b] Jones, R. E. (1981) 'The English school of international relations: a case for closure', *Review of International Studies*, **7**(1), pp. 1–12; Grader, S. (1988) 'The English school of international relations: evidence and evaluation', *Review of International Studies*, **14**(1), pp. 29–44; Wilson, P. (1989) 'The English school of international relations: a reply to Sheila Grader', *Review of International Studies*, **15**(1), pp. 49–58.

38 'Beyond international society', **21**(3), 1992 – published in enlarged edition as Fawn and Larkins (eds) (1996) *International Society after the Cold War* (London, Macmillan). Not only other international relations perspectives entered, but also debates such as liberalism/communitarianism were related to the question of international society. Brown, C. (1992) *International Relations Theory: New Normative Approaches* (Hemel Hempstead, Harvester Wheatsheaf); Rengger, N. J. (1992) 'A city which sustains all things? Communitarianism and international society', *Millennium: Journal of International Studies*, **21**(3), pp. 353–69.

39 Dunne (1991), p. 2; Dunne (1995) 'International society', p. 127.

40 cf. Hoffman, S. (1977) 'An American social science: international relations', *Dædalus*, **106**(3), pp. 41-60; Smith, S. (1992) 'The forty years detour: the resurgence of normative theory in international relations', *Millennium: Journal of International Studies*, **21**(3), pp. 489-506; Krippendorf, E. (1987), 'The dominance of American approaches in international relations', *Millennium: Journal of International Studies*, **16**, pp. 207-14.

41 Walker, R. B. J. (1993) *Inside/Outside: International Relations as Political Theory* (Cambridge, Cambridge University Press).

42 Elshtain, J. B. (1993) 'Act V: bringing it all back home, again', in Rosenau, J. N. *Global Voices – Dialogues in International Relations* (Boulder, CO., Westview Press), pp. 97–116; Wæver, O. (1997) 'Figures of international thought: introducing persons instead of paradigms', in Neumann and Wæver (eds),

Future of International Relations, pp. 1–37.

43 Dunne (1994), p. 2; Dunne (1995) 'International society', p. 130.

44 Jones (1981), pp. 1, 12.

45 Wæver (1992) 'International society'.

46 cf. Bull, H., Kingsbury, B. and Roberts, A. (eds) (1990) *Hugo Grotius and International Relations* (Oxford, Clarendon Press); Wæver (1992) 'International society'.

47 It has often been pointed out that in relation to the 'founding fathers' the name 'English' school is awkward; if we talk about Manning, Wight and Bull, we are talking about a South African, an Englishman and an Australian. However, as a 'school' it has become largely England-based, centred around LSE, Oxford and Cambridge. Recently, however, the Welsh dimension has made the English label problematic again.

48 Dunne (1995) 'International society'; against Wæver (1992) 'International society'.

49 Neumann, I. B. (1996) 'Collective identity formation: self and other in international relations', *European Journal of International Relations*, **2**(2), pp. 139–74.

50 Hurrell furthermore points to the rejection of international law as a specific feature of American institutionalism. This happened probably for the discipline's internal and almost tactical reason that a distance to international law was necessary to avoid affiliation with the classical liberal problematique of enforcement as the product of a legalistic approach with rules far removed from power realities. Hurrell (1993).

51 Buzan, B. (1993) 'From international system to international society: structural realism and regime theory meet the English School', *International Organization* **47**(3), pp. 327–52.

52 Hurrell (1993).

53 Knudsen (1994).

54 Hurrell (1993), pp. 71–2.

55 Wæver (1992) 'International society'.

56 Hurrell (1993), p. 55.

57 cf. Wight, M. (1966) 'Western values in international theory?', in Butterfield and Wight, *Diplomatic Investigations*, pp. 89–131; that technological and other material factors alone cannot produce – but possibly trigger – systemic transformations and thereby precipitate orders is argued also by John Ruggie, who stresses that there is always an element of discursive construction, always a philosophical and conceptual job to do, e.g. in inventing a concept like sovereignty. See Ruggie, J. G. (1983) 'Continuity and transformation in the world polity: toward a neo-realist synthesis', *World Politics*, **35**, pp. 261–85; Ruggie, J. G. (1989) 'International structure and international transformation: space, time and method', in Czempiel, E. O. and Rosenau, J. N. (eds) *Global Changes and Theoretical Challenges: Approaches to World Politics for the 1990s* (Lexington, MA, Lexington), pp. 21–36.

58 Hurrell (1993), p. 59.

59 Buzan, B., Little, R. and Jones, C. (1993) *The Logic of Anarchy: Neorealism to Structural Realism* (New York, Columbia); cf. also dynamic density in Ruggie (1983).

60 Little, R. (1995) 'Neorealism and the English School: a methodological, ontological and theoretical reassessment', *European Journal of International Relations*, **1**(1), pp. 9–34.

61 cf. Wæver, O. (1995) 'Identity, integration and security: solving the sovereignty puzzle in EU studies', *Journal of International Affairs*, **48**(2), pp. 389-431.
62 Ringmar, E. (1997), p. 283.
63 cf. Wæver, O. (1994) 'Resisting the temptation of post foreign policy analysis', in Carlsnaes, W. and Smith, S. (eds) *European Foreign Policy: The EC and Changing Perspectives in Europe* (London, European Consortium Political Research/Sage), pp. 238-73; Neumann, I. B. (1996) 'Collective identity formation: self and other in international relations', *European Journal of International Relations*, **2**(2), pp. 139-74.
64 Wæver, O. (1990) 'Three competing Europes: German, French, Russian', *International Affairs*, **66**(3), pp. 477-93; Wæver (1995); Wæver, O., Holm, U. and Larsen, H. (in preparation) *The Struggle for 'Europe': French and German Concepts of State, Nation and European Union.*
65 Ringmar (1997), p. 285.
66 Dunne (1995) 'International society', p. 146.
67 Dunne (1995) 'Social construction'.
68 cf. Wæver (1994), pp. 266-8; Buzan, B. and Wæver, O. (1997) 'Slippery? contradictory? sociologically untenable? The Copenhagen School replies', *Review of International Studies*, **23**(2) (March), pp. 143-52.
69 Dessler (1989).
70 See, however, Wendt (1992), where he discusses why anarchy is reproduced.
71 Dessler (1989), p. 450.
72 Ibid., p. 461.
73 Wendt and Duvall (1989); Dessler (1989).
74 cf. Little (1995).
75 Butterfield, H. (1951) *History and Human Relations* (London, Collins), ch. 1.
76 Herz, J. H. (1950) 'Idealist internationalism and the security dilemma', *World Politics*, **2**(2), pp. 157-80.
77 cf. Bhaskar, R. (1979) *The Possibility of Naturalism: A Philosophical Critique of the Contemporary Human Sciences* (Brighton, Harvester Wheatsheaf).
78 There are exceptions: cf., e.g. George, J. (1994) *Discourses of Global Politics: A Critical (Re)Introduction to International Relations* (Boulder, CO, Lynne Rienner).
79 Ashley, R. K. (1981) 'Political realism and human interests', *International Studies Quarterly*, **25**(2), pp. 204-36; Ashley, R. K. (1984) 'The poverty of neorealism', *International Organisation*, **38**(2), pp. 2225-61, reprinted in Keohane, R. O. (1986) *Neorealism and its Critics* (New York, Columbia University Press).
80 Wæver (1996) 'Rise and fall'.
81 Der Derian, J. (1987) *On Diplomacy: A Genealogy of Western Estrangement* (Oxford, Basil Blackwell).
82 Der Derian, J. (1995) 'Introduction: critical investigations', in *International Theory: Critical Investigations* (London, Macmillan), pp. 1-10.
83 Ibid., p. 4.
84 Wight, M. (1960/1966) 'Why is there no international theory?', *International Relations* **11**(1), reprinted in Butterfield and Wight (eds), *Diplomatic Investigations*, pp. 17-34; Bull, (1977) *Anarchical Society*, ix and pp. 46-51. The argument about 'domestic analogy' is not particular to Bull, but widely shared among more or less realist writers, including Carr and Morgenthau, and the term can even be found in Manning (1936) (see Suganami (1989), p. 11), but in current usage, arguments about the 'domestic analogy' usually take Bull's

analysis in *The Anarchical Society* as reference point.

85 This is most clearly put by Ashley, R. K. (1987) 'The geopolitics of geopolitical space: toward a critical social theory of international politics', *Alternatives*, **12**(4), pp. 403–34; and Walker (1993).

86 Morgenthau for instance; cf. Suganami (1989).

87 cf. Ashley, R. K. (1987); Walker (1993).

88 Ashley, R. K. (forthcoming) *Statecraft as Mancraft* (manuscript of 1989).

89 Ashley, R. K. (1995) 'The powers of anarchy: theory, sovereignty and the domestication of global life', in Der Derian, J. (ed.) *International Theory: Critical Investigations* (London, Macmillan), pp. 94–128.

90 Walker, R. B. J. (1990) 'Security, sovereignty, and the challenge of world politics', *Alternatives*, **15**(1), pp. 3–28.

91 Bull (1977) *Anarchical Society*, p. 15.

92 Bull and Watson (1984), p. 1.

93 Bull in Bull, Kingsbury and Roberts (eds) (1990), p. 71.

94 Bull (1977) *Anarchical Society*, p. 13.

95 Watson, A. (1987) 'Hedley Bull, state systems and international studies', *Review of International Studies*, **13**(2), p. 147.

96 Wight (1966), pp. 96f.

97 Hoffmann, S. (1990) 'International society', in Miller and Vincent (eds), *Order and Violence*, pp. 13–37, p. 22, allegedly quoting or paraphrasing Bull.

98 In the preface to Wight, M. (1977) *Systems of States* (Leicester, Leicester University Press), p. 17.

99 For the contrast between mechanics and beliefs in international relations, see also Wight (1978), p. 81.

100 Notably Bull and Watson (1984).

101 Bull, H., 'The Grotian conception in international society', in Butterfield and Wight (eds) (1966), *Diplomatic Investigations*, pp. 51–73; Vincent (1974); Vincent (1986a) *Human Rights*; Vincent (1990); Wheeler, N. J. (1992) 'Pluralist or solidarist conceptions of international society: Bull and Vincent on humanitarian intervention', *Millennium: Journal of International Studies*, **21**(3), pp. 463–87; Wheeler, N. J. (1993) 'Human rights and security: beyond non-intervention', in Rees, Wynn (ed.) *International Politics in Europe: The New Agenda* (London, Routledge); Wheeler, N. J. (1996) 'Guardian angel or global gangster: a review of the ethical claims of international society', *Political Studies*, **44**(1), pp. 123–35; Wheeler, N. J. and Dunne, T. (1996) 'Hedley Bull's pluralism of the intellect and solidarism of the will', *International Affairs*, **72**(1), pp. 91–107; Neumann, I. B. (1997) 'John Vincent and the English School of international relations', in Neumann and Wæver (eds) (1997), pp. 38–65.

102 Kingsbury, B. and Roberts, A. (1990) 'Introduction: Grotian thought and international relations', in Bull, Kingsbury and Roberts (eds) (1990), pp. 8f; Bull, H. (1990) 'The importance of Grotius in the study of international relations', in Bull, Kingsbury and Roberts (eds) (1990), pp. 87ff.

103 Wight (1966), pp. 107f.

104 Nardin, T. (1983) *Law, Morality and the Relations of States* (Princeton, NJ, Princeton University Press); Nardin, T. (1992) 'International ethics and international law', *Review of International Studies*, **18**(1), pp. 19–30; Oakeshott, M. (1990 [1975]) *On Human Conduct* (Oxford, Clarendon Paperbacks); Oakeshott,

M. (1991 [1962]) *Rationalism in Politics and Other Essays*, new and expanded edition (Indianapolis, IN, Liberty Press); Brown, C. (1988) 'The modern requirement? Reflections on normative international theory in a post-western world', *Millennium: Journal of International Studies*, **17**(2), pp. 339-48; Brown, C. (1992) *International Relations Theory: New Normative Approaches* (Hemel Hempstead, Harvester Wheatsheaf); Brown, C. (1995) 'International theory and international society: the viability of the middle way?', *Review of International Studies*, **21**(2), pp. 183-96; Brown, C. (1996) 'Back to normal? Some reflections on sovereignty and self-determination after the Cold War', *Global Society*, **10**(1), pp. 11-23.

105 Nardin (1992), pp. 19f.

106 Brown (1995).

107 Nardin (1983).

108 Buzan, B. (1992) *The Evolution of International Society*, paper for the annual workshops of European Consortium for Political Research, Limerick, April; Buzan (1993).

109 Watson, A. (1990) 'Systems of states', *Review of International Studies*, **16**(2), p. 101.

110 Watson (1987), p. 148.

111 Wight (1972); Watson (1987); Watson (1990); Neumann, I. B. and Welsh, J. M. (1991) 'The Other in European self-definition: an addendum to the literature on international society', *Review of International Studies*, **17**(4), pp. 327-48; Little (1995).

112 Wight (1977), p. 34.

113 cf. also James (1993).

114 Watson (1987), p. 151.

115 cf. Ashley (1995).

116 Hjermind, C. and Jensen, L. D. (1996) 'Den etiske betydning af nye skillelinier efter den kolde krig', exam paper, Institute of Political Science, University of Copenhagen.

The English School is keen to point out how the domestic analogy produces the paradox of a dichotomy. However, its own argument consists of two dichotomies. Actually, the famous triad of theories is generated by a dual dichotomy. First, the domestic analogy (which takes the sovereign state as one's model for thinking about international relations) leaves two options: yes, the international can replicate domestic state-making (Kantian revolutionism), or no, it cannot and we are left to the recurrence of power balancing and anarchy defined as the absence of government (Machiavellian realism). The only alternative to the domestic analogy is the English School way of taking the international sphere seriously on its own terms, and not comparing it to domestic politics. This, however, means starting from the real, existing, evolving international society as it has been developed by the states of first, the European system, and then the global (Grotian rationalism).

In contrast to the two options left by the domestic analogy, this third way liberates international thinking from the domestic analogy but certainly not from inside/outside, nor from the centrality of the sovereign state. Thus, when one's thinking about international relations is not shaped by the sovereign state as a metaphor or model, it is built on the sovereign state concretely. cf. Wæver, O. (1996) 'Governance and emancipation: the order/justice dilemma again – or worse?', paper presented at the annual conference of International Studies Association, San Diego, 16–20 April 1996.

117 cf. also Rengger (1992).

118 Buzan, B. and Little, R. (1994) 'The idea of international system: theory meets history', *International Political Science Review*, **15**(3), pp. 231–55; Buzan, B. and Little, R. (1996) 'Reconceptualising anarchy: structural realism meets world history', *European Journal of International Relations*, **2**(4), pp. 403–38.

119 Little (1995), pp. 14, 18, 29ff.

120 'Powers will continue to seek security without reference to justice, and to pursue their vital interests irrespective of common interests, but in the fraction that they may be deflected lies the difference between the jungle and the traditions of Europe.' Wight, M. (1979), in Bull, H. and Holbraad, C. (eds), *Power Politics* (Harmondsworth, Penguin; first published 1946 as 'Looking forward' pamphlet, London, RIIA).

121 Brandt, P. A. (1988) 'Det semiotiske grundforhold', in Dinesen, A.-M. and Jørgensen, K. G. (eds), *Subjektivitet og Intersubjektivitet* (Aalborg, Arbejdspapirer fra NSU no. 28), pp. 7–15.

122 Wight (1977).

123 Kissinger, H. A. (1977 [1957]) *A World Restored: Castlereagh, Metternich and the Restoration of Peace 1812–1822* (Boston, Houghton Mifflin Company).

124 See also Craig, G. A. and George, A. L. (1983) *Force and Statecraft: Diplomatic Problems of Our Times* (Oxford and New York, Oxford University Press), pp. 57–72, for a more elaborate argument about the 'diplomatic revolution' where public opinion started to intrude systematically into foreign policy.

125 Watson (1992), p. 5.

126 Butterfield, H. (1965) 'The historic states-systems', unpublished paper prepared for the British Committee on the Theory of International Politics.

The quote then continues: 'Granted that a states system is already in existence, it may not be difficult to add to it new units which were once outside it – even units that are of a quite alien culture. ... It looks as though (in the conditions of the past at least) a states system can only be achieved in a tremendous conscious effort of reassembly after a political hegemony has broken down.' A twist which we will return to below (but for the sake of fairness towards Butterfield, this has to be listed here).

127 cf. Suhr, M. (1997) 'Keohane: a contemporary classic', in Neumann and Wæver (eds) (1997).

128 Ashley (1989), p. 253.

129 Ibid., pp. 253f.

130 The main inspiration here is from Michel Foucault, who claims that 'Power relations are both intentional and non-subjective', Foucault, M. (1978 [1976]) *The History of Sexuality, Volume 1. An Introduction* (New York, Random House), p. 94. Locally there are often explicit tactics, but the way the local exercise of power is connected and ends up forming comprehensive systems makes it hard to point out any 'headquarters' responsible for the overall strategy. And yet, the overall power structures in society are rooted in the local power – and *vice versa* (Foucault, M. (1970 [1969]) *The Archaeology of Knowledge* (New York, Pantheon Books), pp. 99–102. 'Great anonymous, almost unspoken strategies ... coordinate the loquacious tactics' (Foucault 1978 [1976], p. 95). Thus we have

to study 'strategies without a knowing strategist' and therefore organize not around 'perceptions' or other concepts aiming at what subjects really think, but study structures of meaning, i.e. discourse.

131 For instance, Buzan (1992), (1993); Manning, C. A. W. (1962) *The Nature of International Society* (London, G. Bells and Sons Ltd), pp. 176f.

132 Actually, Manning too rejects the dichotomy and argues that international society is a *tertium quid*: a quasi-*Gemeinschaft*: (1962), p. 177. It is quasi not in the sense of 'not yet', but 'strictly and in its essence a quasi-, and not a true, *Gemeinschaft*.'

133 Laclau, E. and Mouffe, C. (1982) 'Recasting Marxism: hegemony and new political movements', interview by Plotke, D., *Socialist Review*, pp. 91–113.

134[a] Wæver, O. (1989) 'Beyond the "beyond" of critical international theory', paper for the BISA/ISA Conference, London, March–April, also as *Working Paper* 1989/1 of the Centre for Peace and Conflict Research, Copenhagen, pp. 9–11 and 73f; Wæver, O. (1990) 'The language of foreign policy (a review essay on Carlsnaes)', *Journal of Peace Research*, **27**(3), pp. 335–48.

134[b] Bourdieu, P. (1977) *Outline of a Theory of Practice* (Cambridge, Cambridge University Press), esp. pp. 159–71.

135 Walker, R. B. J. (1989) 'History and structure in the theory of international relations', *Millennium: Journal of International Studies*, **18**(2), pp. 163–83; Ruggie (1983).

136 Walker, (1990).

137 Ibid., p. 20.

138 Ashley (1989), p. 259.

139 Ibid., p. 255.

140 Kissinger (1977 [1957]), pp. 9, 196f, 324.

141 Manning (1962).

142 Manning, C. A. W. (1957) 'Varieties of worldly wisdom', *World Politics*, **9**(2), p. 156.

143 Ibid., p. 158; Manning (1962), p. 211.

144 Manning (1962), p. 5.

145 Ibid., p. 6.

146 Ibid., p. 6; Manning (1957), p. 151.

147 Manning (1962), p. 6.

148 Ibid., p. x.

149 Manning (1957), p. 154.

150 Ibid., p. 158.

151 Manning (1962), p. 77.

152 cf. Krasner, S. D. (1993) 'Westphalia and all that', in Goldstein, J. and Keohane, R. O. (eds) *Ideas and Foreign Policy: Beliefs, Institutions and Political Change* (Ithaca, NY, Cornell University Press), pp. 235–64; Krasner (1994); Krasner (1995/1996).

153 Clausewitz, Carl von (1982 [1832]) *On War* (Harmondsworth, Penguin), p. 402.

154 Ruggie (1983); Wæver, O. (1991) 'Territory, authority and identity: the late 20th century emergence of neo-medieval political structures', paper presented at the first general conference of EUPRA, European Peace Research Association, Florence, November; Wæver, O. (1995) 'Identity, integration and security'; Wæver, O. (in preparation) *The Politics of International Structure*.

155 Bull, H. (1970) 'The state's positive role in world affairs', *Dædalus*, **108**(4), p. 112.

156 Sohn-Rethel, A. (1970) *Geistige und körperliche Arbeit*, (Frankfurt am Main, Suhrkamp).

157 Ruggie (1983); and, to a lesser degree, Ruggie, J. G. (1993) 'Territoriality and beyond: problematizing modernity in international relations', *International Organization*, **47**(1) Winter, pp. 139–74.

158 Walker (1993).

159 Wendt, A. (1988) 'The agent-structure problem in international relations', *International Organization*, **41**, pp. 335–70; Wendt (1992) 'Anarchy'; Wendt (1994) 'Collective identity'; Ringmar (1997) 'Alexander Wendt'; Katzenstein (1996) *The Culture*; Adler and Barnet (1996) 'Governing anarchy'.

160 The structure-agency article of the 'early Wendt' (Ringmar, 1996) is a possible exception from this with its stronger stress on structure as *internal* relations and on structural analysis in terms of 'conditions of existence' (Wendt 1987, pp. 357–64). The Wendt of the 'Anarchy' article, the one who is a self-proclaimed 'constructivist', has – like fellow constructivists – downgraded the structural element, both in the sense of unintended reproduction (cf. discussion above) and in the way of investigating tight, internal relations in larger constellations. Therefore, an impression appears of structures being separate 'rules' open to reconstitutions to the degree that actors get conscious about this and make a new choice.

161 Teubner, G. (1989) 'How the law thinks: toward a constructivist epistemology of law', *Law & Society Review*, **23**(5), pp. 727–57.

162 The analysis is very close to that of post-structuralism in emphasizing the role of dichotomies and how the seemingly opposed always presuppose their common third: the distinction from which they – as opposites – originate. Also, they share the view that all arguments ultimately point back to a performatively installed truth, a self-referential practice, not some empirical fact speaking in a neutral, universal language of self-evidence. Luhmannian autopoiesis and post-structuralism mainly differ in their *attitude*. Where post-structuralism in a partly post-Marxist, partly post-Heideggerian manner wants to 'reveal' dichotomies in order to question and possibly overcome them, Luhmann assumes that these systems have to operate with these dichotomies, that the distinctions even have to be invisible to them. There is no reason to denigrate systems just for being based on dichotomies – they are most likely necessary elements in the continuous differentiation of the modern world and parts of its attempt to handle complexity. cf. Luhmann, N. (1990) *Die Wissenschaft der Gesellschaft* (Frankfurt am Main, Suhrkamp); Luhmann, N. (1990) *Soziologische Aufklürung 5: Konstruktivistische Perspektiven* (Opladen, Westdeutscher Verlag); Luhmann, N. (1997) *Die Gesellschaft der Gesellschaft* vol. 1–2 (Frankfurt am Main, Suhrkamp); Wæver, O. (in preparation) *The Politics of International Structure*.

163 Luhmann, N. (1992) 'Operational closure and structural coupling: the differentiation of the legal system', *Cardozo Law Review*, **13**(5).

164 cf. Rossbach, S. (1994) 'The autopoiesis of the Cold War: an evolutionary approach to international relations?', in EUI *Working Papers in Political and Social Sciences* SPS No. 92/23; Albert, M. (1997) 'Towards generative differentiation: the international political system in world society', paper presented at the workshop 'Identity, Borders, Orders' at New Mexico State University, Las Cruces, New Mexico, 17–19 January.

165 Ruggie (1983).

166 Dessler (1989).

167 Buzan *et al.* (1993).

168 Watson (1990), p. 100.

169 The cultural nearness argument assumes that the question is cultural distance or proximity. In articles like Wight's 'Western values', this is clearly not the case, but the two aspects of the culturalist approach have not been clearly spelled out. This is similar to the argument in the 'democratic peace' debate over whether 'similar systems' generally are more peaceful towards each other, or one specific system is peaceful to its own kin.

170 Manning (1962), p. 110; Manning, C. A. W. (1972) 'The legal framework in a world of change', in Porter, B. (ed.) *The Aberystwyth Papers: International Politics 1919-1969* (Oxford, Oxford University Press), pp. 301-35.

171 Manning (1962), p. 110.

172 Butterfield, H. (1966) 'The balance of power', in Butterfield and Wight (eds), *Diplomatic Investigations*, pp. 132-48.

173 Butterfield (1975).

174 Ibid., p. 7.

175 Butterfield (1966), p. 133.

176 Wight (1977), ch. 6.

177 Mayall (1990).

178 Wight (1977), p. 153.

179 Wæver (1992) 'International society'.

180 Grewe, W. G. (1984) *Epochen der Völkerrechtsgeschichte* (Baden-Baden, Nomos); Der Derian (1987); Bull and Watson (1984) is an impressive study of 'The expansion of international society', but it is somewhat ambivalent as to whether it studies how an almost constant (originally European) core is extended to a still larger part of the globe (cf. the critique in Neumann and Welsh, 1991; Kingsbury and Roberts, 1990, p. 49), or whether these changes in extension actually entail transformations of the code itself. This problem is related to the problem that the different rules and institutions are rarely spelled out, not to say, formalized. It must be assumed that they somehow constitute a layered system, where mutual recognition of sovereignty is the most basic and various principles build on top of it (Buzan, 1992), but then it should be possible to distinguish what is expansion of a European core, and what is shifting rules and codes. With the present vagueness as to what the codes actually are, it is easy sometimes to point to changes (for instance, the principles for admission, the 'standard of civilization', etc.) and at other times show the constant, European core of the system of mutual recognition among sovereign states.

181 Grewe (1984): his cuts are 1494, 1648, 1815, 1919 and 1945.

182 Derrida, J. (1984) 'Guter Wille zur Macht (I): Drei Fragen an Hans-Georg Gadamer' and 'Guter Will zur Macht (II): Die Unterschriften interpretieren (Nietzsche/Heidegger)', in Forget, P. (ed.) *Text und Interpretation* (Munich, Wilhelm Fink Verlag), pp. 56-8 and 62-77; see especially p. 57.

183 Derrida, J. (1977 [1972]) 'Signature event context', *Glyph*, **1**, p. 172.

184 Ibid., p. 182.

185 Gadamer, H.- G. (1984) 'Text und interpretation' and 'Und dennoch: Macht des guten Willens', in Forget (ed.) (1984), pp. 24-55 and 59-61, see pp. 59, 61.

186 Laurelle, F. (1984) 'Anti-Hermes', in Forget (ed.) (1984), p. 81.

187 Lotman, Y. M. (1990) *Universe of the Mind: A Semiotic Theory of Culture* (Bloomington and Indianapolis, Indiana University Press).

188 Wæver (1996) 'Rise and fall'.

189 We can here recall the argument of Butterfield, who in the passage quoted above which stated the cultural basis of international societies (states systems) said: 'It looks as though (in the conditions of the past at least) a states system can only be achieved in a tremendous *conscious effort* of reassembly after a political hegemony has broken down' (1965; emphasis added).

190 Mearsheimer, J. J. (1990) 'Back to the future: instability in Europe after the cold war', *International Security*, **15**(1), 5–56; Keohane, R. O., Nye, J. and Hoffmann, S. (eds) (1993) *After the Cold War: State Strategies and International Institutions in Europe, 1989–1991* (Cambridge, MA, Harvard University Press); Mearsheimer (1995), plus reactions in consecutive issues.

191 Wendt (1992); Wendt (1994).

192 Buzan, B. *et al.* (1990) *The European Security Order Recast: Scenarios for the Post-Cold War Era* (London, Pinter); Wæver (1995); Wæver, O. (1996) 'Europe's three empires: a Watsonian interpretation of post-wall European security', in Fawn, R. and Larkins, J. (eds) *International Society After the Cold War: Anarchy and Order Reconsidered* (London, Macmillan, in association with *Millennium, Journal of International Studies*), pp. 220–60; Wæver, O. (1996) 'European security identities', *Journal of Common Market Studies*, **34**(1), March, pp. 103–32; Wæver, O. (1998) 'Insecurity, security and asecurity in the West European non-war community', in Adler, E. and Barnett, M. (eds), *Governing Anarchy: Security Communities* (Cambridge, Cambridge University Press).

193 cf. Mayall (1991); Roberts (1991); Wheeler (1992).

194 Bull (1977), pp. 254f, 264ff, 285f and 291ff; Der Derian (1987), pp. 70, 79ff; Luke, T. W. (1991) 'The discipline of security studies and the codes of containment: learning from Kuwait', *Alternatives*, **16**(3), pp. 340f; Wæver (1991); Ruggie (1993); Tunander, O. (ed.) (1995) *Europa och Muren: Om 'den andre', gränslandet och historiens återkomst i 90-talets Europa (Europe and the Wall: About 'the Other', the Borderland and the Return of History in the Europe of the 1990s)* (Aalborg, NSU).

195 Farago, B. (1995) 'L'Europe: empire introuvable?', *Le Debat*, **83**, pp. 42–58; Wæver (1996) 'Europe's three empires'; Rufin, J.-C. (1991) *L'Empire et les Nouveaux Barbares* (Paris, Lattés).

196 Buzan, B. (1996) 'The present as a historic turning point', *Journal of Peace Research*, **32**(4), pp. 385–98.

197 Watson (1993), Wæver (1996) 'Europe's three empires'.

198 cf. Rengger (1992); Brown (1995).

199 Keohane (1989), ch. 6; Jervis, R. (1982) 'Security regimes', *International Organization*, **36**(2), pp. 357–78.

200 For instance, in Europe, the concept of 'Europe' becomes so central to what it means to argue about 'German' interests, that the collective identity 'Europe' has gained an indirect stability from the fact that it would take hard work to establish a new narrative of what 'German' means, should 'Europe' (and in this case its main materialization, the EU) be shaken; cf. Wæver, O. *et al.* (in preparation) *The Struggle for Europe*; Wæver, O. (forthcoming) 'Insecurity, security and asecurity'.

201 Buzan (1992); Manning (1962).

202 Watson (1993).

6

The Practice Outruns the Theory

ADAM WATSON

I would like to examine the general maxim that the rules and institutions of an international society are more fixed than the practice, with particular reference to the contemporary scene. I am here concerned with what can loosely be called the theoretical or constitutional legitimacy of an international society, not academic theories about the nature of such societies. Practice is fluid and experimental, inclined to improvise and to look for the expedient. Those practices and arrangements which work - which seem to the leading participants to pay dividends - are then continued and become codified. What is at first simply conduct can become a code of conduct; interpretations of rules, and new uses for institutions, can modify the original purpose; and these revisions gradually become accepted as part of a new conventional legitimacy. This is a general rule; of course, there are exceptions.

One result is that a serious gap can occur between the constitutional legitimacy of an international society - what Hedley Bull calls its rules and institutions - and its practice. People become aware that what happens on the international scene does not correspond very closely with what is supposed to happen. This discrepancy can cause unease, a sense of illegitimacy, a resentment of usurpation, especially by the practice of the most powerful members of the society. In all international societies practice feels obliged to innovate, to deal with new circumstances; but the more the practice appears to conform to the accepted legitimacies, the less unease and resentment there will be.

I discuss the role of legitimacy in the operation of international societies in my book *The Evolution of International Society*. May I quote the following summary from the conclusion.

> Legitimacy in the ancient world was the oil that lubricated the operative machinery of a society. The more its rules and institutions were considered legitimate, the more easily it could change its practices. The experience of the European society confirmed the lubricating role of legitimacy; but it also showed how the anti-hegemonial legitimacy established by the Westphalian

settlement and explicitly confirmed by Utrecht could operate as a check on the swing of the pendulum as it was designed to do. Even so, where the pressures for change were great, practice disregarded legitimacy, or found a way round it; and over a period the legitimacy adjusted to take account of the practice. In the contemporary world the rules and institutions (notably the United Nations) and the nominal values of our international society give a stamp of legitimacy to a very high degree of multiple independence. Even the strongest powers profess to respect the independence of all members; and this reassurance makes the hegemonial reality more acceptable.

Two historical examples

International societies differ from one another; but they have certain resemblances or common characteristics. It may, therefore, be useful to take a brief look at two familiar historical examples. First, the imperial authority of Augustus and his immediate successors. Second, the functioning of the European international society during the hegemony of Louis XIV.

Augustus came to power as a result of victory in civil war, and was constitutionally, if one can use such a term, the last of a number of usurpers of the legitimate authority of the Roman senate and people. In practice, he was a monarch, regulating in different ways the heterogeneous conglomerate of territories that we call the empire - which ranged from client monarchies like Herod and theoretically sovereign allies like Athens to directly administered provinces. He operated largely through his private staff, and most of the expenditure involved came from his personal coffers: especially from Egypt, which he ruled as a private domain. In the east, he allowed himself to be worshipped as divine, like the Hellenistic Kings. But at Rome he was careful to observe the republican forms. He refused titles like rex and Romulus, and called himself just a senator, first among equals (a contradiction in itself); the offices of consul and tribune of the people continued nominally, but in his own or other safe hands; and he had his decisions ratified by the cowed senate. The different expedients were deliberately ambiguous but they were not a farce: they made his rule easier for others to accept, both at Rome and in the east, and, therefore, for him to exercise.

The international society established by the seminal settlement of Westphalia in 1648 was resolutely anti-hegemonial, devised and imposed by the victorious coalition against Hapsburg hegemony. If I may speak in broad generalities, the new society consisted of states which were recognized as independent and those which were in practice able to act as such. The governments of these states were to treat each other as *de facto* equals, based on new concepts of international law, and to refrain from interference in each other's domestic affairs (especially in matters of religion). The makers of the Westphalian settlement recognized the need for international order: the order which they promulgated was anti-hegemonial, as opposed to the hegemonial order which the Hapsburgs had envisaged and to some extent operated. It was one of those brief periods of mirage, like the peacemaking after World War I 'the war to end war', and the great decolonization of the 1960s and 1970s - periods when, as Xenophon said about the defeat of the Athenian empire, men thought that all Hellas might be free. But the mirage soon gave way to the reality of Louis XIV's hegemony. Louis was half a Hapsburg with a Hapsburg wife, and he aimed in practice to impose a new hegemonial order. He controlled the Hapsburg position of Holy Roman Emperor through a German client princeling, and replaced the Vienna-Madrid axis of his cousins with a Versailles-Madrid axis. But he operated as far as possible within the framework of Westphalia: enlisting the other victor allies, using the techniques of subsidy and diplomacy developed by the coalition, and the Westphalian arguments of legitimacy and international law. So his hegemonial practice outran the new anti-hegemonial theory, but made itself more acceptable by operating through and under the cloak of the Westphalian legitimacy.

The contemporary international society

The same is true of our contemporary international society. To start with the legitimacy. The contemporary society is nominally very loosely organized: even more so than the European society after Westphalia, and much more so than Augustus' system. It is theoretically predicated on some 180 plus independent sovereign states, linked by such omnilateral institutions as the United Nations and international law. Both international law and the United Nations assume that sovereign states are equal *de jure*: as Vattel said, a dwarf is as much a man as a giant. The sovereigns accredit ambassadors to each other and to international organizations on a basis of equality (with a few exceptions like the five permanent members of the UN Security Council). This sovereign independence and equal membership of 'international society' was much emphasized during the decolonization of the European seaborne empires (circa 1947-77), and is particularly prized by those formerly dependent states which have acquired or regained their independence as a result of the decolonization process and now make up a majority of independent states. Moreover, it is a society in which the internal affairs of a sovereign member state are, except as provided for in treaties freely signed, in theory its own business, as has been the case since Westphalia. Article 2/7 of the United Nations Charter still debars that body from discussing anything that is wholly or mainly the internal concern of a member state. According to the *New York Times* of 30 January 1992, for instance, 'China, India and some of the third world nations on the Council are resisting any ringing endorsement of such goals as safeguarding human rights and promoting democracy, arguing that by doing so the Council would be involving itself in the domestic affairs of other [sic] countries'. Also, where security and the protection of the weaker against the stronger are concerned the basic rules of our society deal mainly with strategic security and immunity from external coercion, and much less (though increasingly) with collective economic security and the management of international economic activity.

The theory, the legitimacy, has long included the concept of dependent states, such as colonies, which may be legally distinct from the imperial state (such as Hong Kong, la Nouvelle Calédonie), and territories in dispute between two sovereign states, under the occupation of one of them (the Kurile Islands, Peruvian/Ecuadorian Amazonia, the Golan Heights). But it is uncomfortable with theoretically independent states which are clearly dependent in practice. Thus, it balks at the actual situation on the ground of the Lebanon (controlled mostly by Syria and a small part by Israel); Panama; the ex-Soviet republics of Central Asia (military and economic relationship with Russia); ex-French tropical Africa; and other examples. The situation in Palestine (the West Bank and Gaza) is particularly awkward. Perhaps the most glaring example in recent times was the Soviet satellite states of Eastern Europe, which were in theory independent member states of international society but in practice scarcely sovereign at all.

Those examples are not exceptions. They illustrate the truism that the actual practice of the contemporary international society is very different from the theoretical legitimacy.

Let us look, first, at the reality behind the theoretical equality of states; then, at the reality of intervention, with special reference to individual human rights; third, at economic security and aid; and finally at the general concept of sovereignty.

Equality of member states

In our current international society all independent states, or at least all members of the United Nations are treated as juridically equal, in international law and in such minor matters as the precedence accorded to ambassadors. But in practical terms the familiar difference between the strongest and the weakest states is truly immense. We might discuss the following aspects.

The discrepancy between the power of the different members of any international system, and consequently their influence in it, is obvious and inevitable. The influence of a member state in the system is determined not only by its size (both area and population), wealth (a very different criterion, note Singapore and Saudi Arabia), degree of development, etc., but also by its purposefulness, experience in statecraft, and more subjectively its reputation and tradition, and the way in which its capacities and intentions are perceived by others. Therefore, we find that in all known systems the effectiveness of the members, meaning all the above variables taken together, varies very widely. Moreover, the strongest and most effective members exercise a degree of hegemony, some sort of authority explicit or tacit in the system. Hegemonial authority may be exercised by one very powerful state (e.g. Louis XIV), by a diarchy of two collaborating states (e.g. the Athenians and Spartans after the Persian wars), or collectively by a group of great powers (e.g. the Concert of Europe after the Napoleonic wars). Hegemonial authority carries with it privileges but also responsibilities, and derives additional advantages by making the exercise of hegemony acceptable to other members of the society. This is what Butterfield and Wight meant by 'the principles of prudence and moral obligation which have held together the international society of states throughout its history, and still hold it together'.[1]

In our present society, the discrepancy in power is unusually large. The process of decolonization not only re-established Asian and Mediterranean states with millennial traditions of civilization and statecraft, but also made a host of independent but small and undeveloped mini-states from what de Gaulle unkindly called 'the dust of empires'. It is true that an analogous situation existed after Westphalia, when many of the basic principles of the European international society were established. At that time, a number of minor princelings in the Holy Roman Empire had become independent in practice if not yet absolutely in theory. But the analogy, though useful, is not very close: the princes of the Empire and governments of city states like Hamburg were on average as capable, and their realms as 'developed', as the larger members of seventeenth-century European society, so that Voltaire could reasonably describe it as 'une grande république partagée entre plusieurs états'; whereas the same is manifestly not yet true of the inexperienced 'dust of empire' states.

Consequently, the hegemony in our contemporary society is constitutionally tacit rather than explicit, and runs counter to a literal interpretation of the equality of member states; but it is generally acknowledged in practice. The pattern of two antagonistic superstates with rival hemispheres of influence came to an end with the collapse of the Soviet Union, and we now have only one state with a global reach. President Bush in his last State of the Union address put it bluntly: 'A world once divided into two armed camps now recognizes one sole and pre-eminent power, the United States of America.' But though America is temporarily the only superpower, it is not in a position to exercise a single hegemony – to manage international society by itself. First, it needs the co-operation of other 'Great Powers'. This need is especially apparent in all activity short of the actual use of force, where what matters is economic clout, what Diane Kunz calls the importance of having money. The two most important centres of economic power whose collaboration is needed to make an effective world economic concert are Japan and Germany (which is now merging itself into a united Western Europe). Second, if America is not to rely on unilateral pressure, which would be both destabilizing and beyond its strength, and if the exercise of managerial authority is to be broadly acceptable to the other members of international society, the decisions of the Great Power concert need to be implemented through legitimate and constituted channels: particularly the machinery of the United Nations, and multilateral economic organizations like the World Bank and the International Monetary Fund. In other words, it will pay the concert to operate in accordance with the legitimacies.

I, therefore, think that we should recognize the world, not as a hierarchy of states or a suzerain system, but as an international society managed to some extent by a group of Great Powers. This pattern is somewhat similar to the nineteenth-century concert in Europe (in which incidentally the five Great Powers often disagreed, but managed to collaborate or acquiesce often enough to make the concert system work). During the forty years of the Cold War, the US was the leading state of the non-communist world, both strategically and economically, and indeed the only global power. If, today, that eminence is eroding, the association of post-communist Russia as a partner, and the growth of Japan and the West European Community, makes a hegemonial concert perhaps the most likely form of successful management of our international society.

Intervention and human rights

The milder forms of hegemony are usually concerned only with the management of the inter-state aspects of a system. A hegemonial power (or powers) will induce, or in extreme cases compel, other members of an international society to modify their external behaviour to the extent necessary to conform to hegemonial management. For the most powerful state (or directorate of states) to go further than this, and to exercise significant control over the *internal* affairs of other member states, may be called dominion rather than hegemony. The legitimacy of an international society may draw a clear dividing line between the two – that is between inducing members to conform to the society's rules and institutions (which the most powerful members interpret, and may have written) on the one hand, and interference in the internal affairs of members on the other. But the line is notoriously difficult to draw in practice. There is a large grey area of pressure and interference which the interveners justify by the argument that internal developments such as building up a war machine, and especially weapons of mass destruction, affect what is currently called international peace and security, i.e. the orderly management of the system. (The justification is often quite reasonable, but sometimes amounts to casuistry.)

In any case, interference on the grounds of religion, ideology, or in this century the pattern of economic life (discussed below), have been regular practices, especially in times of hot or cold war. There is also a long tradition, one might almost say a norm, of intervention by outside powers in civil wars, overtly and covertly, collectively and by individual foreign states. Collective intervention, and intervention by a single powerful state or group of states acting with the explicit endorsement or tacit consent of the collective institutions of the society (e.g. the Gulf War), are not contrary to the legitimacy. But assigning degrees of legitimacy is usually a secondary issue in the practice. The practical problem with the civil war in Angola, for example, was to manage and contain the various interventions and to negotiate an end to hostilities with the leading interveners, which included both superpowers. The practical problems connected with the spread of nuclear weapons and related subjects are more obviously interventionist, but have acquired a certain legitimacy of their own.

In our contemporary society, the western powers also apply pressure, though less systematically, to ensure minimum standards in the observance of human rights of individuals against their own government. The relationship of a sovereign to his subjects has traditionally been the most quintessentially internal business of a state. The insistence by western governments on human rights in other states now goes very far: for example, the US makes a declaration on the subject a condition of diplomatic recognition of successor states of the Soviet Union. But the western media and large sections of public opinion demand a still stronger attitude. The insistence on human rights is a modern version of the nineteenth-century insistence on a standard of civilization in non-European states wishing to be admitted to the European-controlled international society.[2] China, now as a century ago, plays a leading role in active opposition to demands by the most powerful members of the international system; but the Chinese government's attitude may once again be a rearguard action. Human rights, and the wider issues in international relations which can be subsumed under the rubric 'the Diplomacy of Justice' (on which Professor John Vincent was compiling a book when he tragically died), illustrate how far certain aspects of contemporary international practice outrun the theory.

Economic security and aid

The economic fabric of contemporary international society is perhaps the clearest illustration of the gap separating its practice from the concept of some 180 plus sovereign states all free to run their own domestic economy as they see fit. In an absolute sense, independent governments can exercise this right; and most members of international society do so to some degree. A few states practise autarchy. Some others have resources like oil which enable them to live comfortably, if they or foreign experts produce and export it. But in practice the majority of members are unable at present to generate by themselves the standard of living which their populations have come to expect. To achieve even low standards, they must import both the great range of goods which they can make only at unreasonable expense or not at all, such as electric light bulbs and surgical equipment, and also educational and other managerial services; and this is beyond their unaided means. The problem is often compounded by rapid population increases. Most of the populations, and, indeed, most responsible administrators, of the Less Developed Countries (LDCs) are more concerned with poverty, that is with economic insecurity, than with the threat of foreign invasion and conquest, that is with strategic insecurity.

What, in theory and in practice, are the rich states required to do about the plight of the poorer ones? The notion that the great powers or superpowers in an international society are responsible for the security of the weak is part of *raison de système*, and, of course, not new. Thucydides has the Corinthians tell the Spartans: 'The true author of the subjugation of a state is not so much the immediate agent as the state which permits it though it could prevent it, especially if that state aspires to the glory of being the liberator of Hellas'. Heeren claimed that the obligation to preserve the balance of power was that it protects the weak against the strong. Woodrow Wilson championed the alternative concept of achieving collective strategic security for the weak by means of a league of well-intentioned great powers. But this is surely the first time in history that the economically most developed states have recognized any obligation to supplement the economic and social capacities of weaker states?

International economic responsibility involves the recognition by the economically stronger states that it is in the interest of all the members of an international system that the pressures and constraints caused by their inescapable involvement with one another should be managed as effectively as possible. In other words, it adds a new dimension to the extension of *raison d'état* to *raison de système*. A massive and complex aid programme of bilateral and multilateral government aid provides the LDCs with grants, loans, preferential import regulations, an array of technical experts, and educational and other opportunities. This governmental aid is supplemented by a considerable volume of private investment: which most recipients, from Russia to small Pacific and Caribbean islands, are eager to obtain, in spite of neo-colonialist arguments and many cases of unjustifiable exploitation. A recent Foreign Office enquiry showed that British Embassies and High Commissions in some LDCs were spending up to 80 per cent of their work time on questions connected with aid. Certainly, this aid is in the enlightened self-interest of the donors, as was the Marshall Plan. It is also true that the aid and investment of resources and know-how falls far short of the capacity of the recipient states to usefully absorb it; and that there are various limits to what the donors will do: the resources available, the willingness of democracies to spend abroad resources needed for underprivileged voters at home, and the donors' inexperience of what aid achieves a desired result. Nevertheless, the concept of the responsibility of the economically strongest states (or confederacies) for *collective economic security* exists and is being partially implemented in practice. It is also steadily becoming part of the legitimacy. We might discuss the implications for the society of states.

We should also note that the aid is largely decided and administered hegemonially. International financial organizations operate not on the basis of one member one vote but according to the member's contributions giving the US and other leading donors a hegemonial say. The World Bank and the IMF, as well as the collective hegemony of the Group of Seven, put what is often severe pressure on recalcitrant recipient members to allow a market economy, to show fiscal prudence, to pay some interest on debt, etc. In practice, the conditions set by donor governments and international organizations amount to a degree of control over the domestic economies of recipients. This is not, legalistically speaking, intervention in the internal affairs of member states: it is simply the price of the collective economic security which the weak countries ask for. And, of course, recipient governments, and their sympathizers in rich democracies, demand more aid with less strings. But, in practice, the scope and scale of economic aid is determined by the donors, like so much else in international society.

Sovereignty

On the subject of sovereign independence generally, let me submit for discussion two paragraphs from my book mentioned above.

> The European concept of sovereignty ... as its name implies, was an aim of rulers and princes, who wanted to be masters over all their subjects but to acknowledge no master over themselves. The concept of sovereignty protects the weak prince against the strong. The sovereignty to which Westphalia committed the European society of states was essentially domestic. What a

> sovereign did in the territories recognized as legitimately under its government was not the business of other sovereigns. In principle sovereign princes and states were also free to act as they saw fit in their external relations. Indeed the ability to conduct an independent foreign policy was widely regarded as the test of genuine sovereignty. But the relations of a sovereign state with the other members of the sovereigns' club were constrained by the pressures of the system and by the rules and codes of conduct of the society, and also most of the time by a degree of hegemonial control.[3]
>
> The awareness that states are being constrained into a tighter system, especially in the economic field, has led to increasing doubts about the continuing relevance, and even the reality, of independent sovereignty. The real sovereignty of the *stato*, established by Italian and German princes and maintained by the princes' club and the romantic nationalists, remains precious, especially to the governing élites of states recently emancipated from imperial rule. But the external and internal freedoms of action associated with independent states no longer seem to be bound together into a monolithic whole. In the rhetoric of statehood, the different elements in the bundle - from defence and immigration to currency and human rights - can be assigned to various confederal or society-wide bodies without destroying the identity and ultimate sovereignty of the state. Or to put it more prosaically, the modern successors of the European princes find themselves constrained by the pressures of a tightening system and by the institutions and practices of a more integrated society to act increasingly in ways that deprive them of independence de facto, externally and internally, so that their governments no longer control a *stato*; while leaving intact the symbolic legitimacy of the state and varying degrees of real autonomy.[4]

In a tightening system, the more the symbolic independence of the member states can appear to continue, and the greater the genuine autonomy allowed to the member states by the hegemonial managers of the society, the easier and more acceptable the practice of the society will be.

Concluding questions

The practice of our present international society has outrun its ostensible legitimacy. I must leave the reader with the following questions:

1. It is now a question of:
    a) how much more hegemonial and less 'equal'?
    b) how much more interventionist, especially about human rights?
    c) how much more committed, in practice and in theory, to collective economic security?
    d) how much less sovereign?
2. In which directions is innovative practice moving?
3. How is legitimacy adjusting to practice?

Notes

1 Butterfield, H. and Wight, M. (eds), *Diplomatic Investigations: Essays in the Theory of International Politics* (London, George Allen & Unwin, 1966), p. 13.
2 See Gong, G. W., *The Standard of 'Civilisation' in International Society* (Oxford, Clarendon Press, 1984).
3 Watson, A., *The Evolution of International Society: A Comparative Historical Analysis* (London, Routledge, 1992), p. 316.
4 Ibid., p. 307.

7

Boundaries and International Society*

ROBERT H. JACKSON

Introduction

'Which peoples have the right to draw a line around themselves and constitute a sovereign state?'[1] This deceptively simple question was raised in a discussion of nationhood and nationalism. But it could just as well be asked of international relations because it concerns not only the identities of peoples but also the divisions between them. The question is important because it draws our attention to an immediately practical issue of contemporary world politics. That alone should suffice to capture our interest. The question is also important, however, because it raises significant theoretical issues about a subject which is all too often taken for granted by international relations scholars. This chapter is a preliminary attempt to address these basic issues from an international society perspective.[2]

The question seems to imply that there might be a straightforward answer to the issue of international boundaries based on a principle of group rights. That, however, is not the case. The issue always arises in a historical-geographical setting and the practices by reference to which it is answered change over time. There are no universal and thus unchanging principles which clearly determine who has such a right.[3] There is at best only a general recognition that, in spite of what they may have in common as human beings, the population of the world is divided territorially into local groups, and that members of such groups usually desire not to be ruled by outsiders. In other words they desire independence: a territorial space marked by a frontier or border inside of which people pursue their political lives according to their own ideas and inclinations free from external dictation or intervention.

For most theoretical purposes I believe that international boundaries are

* I wish to acknowledge the helpful comments of Alan James and Georg Sørensen as well as the financial support of the Social Sciences and Humanities Research Council of Canada.

best understood as legal divisions between sovereign jurisdictions. This conception stems from the ontological status of boundaries between human beings: they are not natural divisions even when they follow physical geography such as the Pyrenees mountains between France and Spain; they are entirely the result of human decisions even when they are made to coincide with a physical barrier. Both states and the borders that circumscribe them are social constructs and nothing else. It may be worth quoting Karl Popper on this fundamental point:

> There are no natural boundaries to a state. The boundaries of a state change, and can be defined only by applying the principle of a status quo; and since every status quo must refer to an arbitrarily chosen date, the determination of the boundaries of a state is purely conventional.[4]

International boundaries are historical divisions that define and delimit the various territorial communities - sovereign states - formed by human beings around the world.

The present-day political map of the world is, of course, a map of independent states. A world without such states would be a world without international boundaries although surely not a world without borders of some kind.[5] So international boundaries are a distinctive social relation between human beings organized as sovereign states. And just like the states themselves, the boundaries between them are social constructions: they can be instituted, they can be defended, they can be disregarded, they can be violated, they can be dismantled, they can be moved, and their significance and uses can be changed. The map of Europe of 1400 was different from that of 1700 which was again different from the map of the present time. The ecclesiastical borders of the fifteenth century were not the same as the dynastic borders of the eighteenth century and the national borders of the twentieth century. The first were significant primarily to prelates, the second primarily to princes, and the third primarily to peoples defined as national states. Each kind of territorial border entailed a different type of ruling authority and, beyond that, a different theory of rule.

In short, when we speak of international boundaries we are not speaking of something given in the nature of things or even something which has a historically unchanging institutional character. International boundaries are not outside history; they are historical innovations and adaptations that belong to the era of the modern state and particularly the period since the seventeenth century.[6] They are what states make of them, and that changes over time. We are thus referring to a historical institution invested with different shapes and contents at different times and places. But throughout all historical periods of the modern era and in spite of different functions and significance attached to international borders they have the common and continuous use of delimiting the territorial jurisdictions of ruling authorities. They are inherently juridical arrangements: part of the legal-institutional apparatus of state sovereignty.

International boundaries in theory

The usual starting-point for international relations theory is this historical division of the world's population into independent states. There is, of course, a more extensive subject of human boundaries beyond that of international borders, but I must confine myself to the latter.[7] Our traditional subject is the relations of states across these divisions or in regard to them - war, peace, security, trade, aid, migration, transportation, communication, and the rest. The divisions themselves are not usually a subject of inquiry. However, recent scholarship has interrogated the territorial basis of international relations which indirectly raises questions of borders.[8] I shall try to add something to that scholarship by approaching the subject from the angle of international society theory.

The international society theorists do not have a great deal to say directly about international boundaries. For them, too, it is a residual subject behind more immediate and presumably more important questions, such as: state sovereignty, diplomacy, international order, the balance of power, national interest, arms control, intervention, self-determination, and so forth. When the question arises it tends to be discussed as an aspect of other questions, such as the expansion of the society of states.[9] We mostly have to infer their argument concerning boundaries from their theoretical comments on international society.

Martin Wight addresses the topic of international boundaries indirectly via three major traditions of international relations theory which he and Hedley Bull did much to clarify: realism, rationalism and revolutionism.[10] These are distinctive ways of construing international relations and, in particular, their conceptual shape and normative foundations. Each tradition discloses an interpretation which postulates and emphasizes different features of human life across and beyond the boundaries of sovereign states.[11] Realism emphasizes international anarchy: a plurality of free-standing states which acknowledge no political superior. Rationalism emphasizes international intercourse between independent states: treaties, diplomacy, commerce, communications, and so forth. Revolutionism emphasizes the common humanity and moral solidarity of all men and women in spite of their civic membership in particular political communities or states. Each of these emphases produce different ways of theorizing international boundaries.

Realists see no international society at all and have no theory of membership and no notion of insiders and outsiders. Society is confined to states; civil society is exclusively domestic. States exist on their own: they are separate free-standing realities; they are not members of a society of states and much less are they constituted by that society. The world beyond and between particular states is a state of nature. For realists, strictly speaking, there can be no insiders and no outsiders. Nor can there be any expansion of international society. Boundaries are national but they are not international: each state's external borders are what they are able to erect and maintain. They mark the limits of the territorial control of sovereign states. But they are not a common institution created, shared and operated by the society of states. National boundaries, for realists, define the political community and the domain of political obligation of the citizen to the sovereign. One's own national boundaries are in that respect normative. But the national boundaries of other states, from our own national point of view, are not normative; they are merely instrumental. There is no international obligation to respect them. Whether one respects them or not is a matter of calculated self-interest and is thus an instrumental question and not a moral or legal question.

Rationalists see a society of states and not merely an international state of nature. The international world is not a condition of potential or actual war, as Hobbes famously argued.[12] Rather, as Wight puts it referring to Grotius and Suarez, it is a condition of 'sociability' and 'common intercourse, containing the germ of society': 'a political and moral quasi-society'.[13] Hedley Bull defines international society as a 'group of states' that are 'conscious of certain common interests and common values', 'conceive themselves to be bound by a common set of rules in their relations', and 'share in the working of common institutions'.[14] He firmly distinguishes an international society from an international system: a minimalist condition in which states are merely in contact with each other and, at most, only take each other's self-regarding calculations into account.[15]

Rationalists are the theorists of international society *par excellence*. For rationalists there can be members of international society, and rules which govern such matters as well as both an expansion and contraction of membership. Boundaries are therefore international and not merely national: they mark the limits of the territorial jurisdiction and the domestic society of sovereign states; but they also constitute an institution shared by states and form an important part of an international society between states. One's own national boundaries are moral and legal. But so also are the national boundaries of other states who are members of international society. Boundaries are an institution of the society of states. There is an international obligation to respect boundaries which is defined by international law and is today expressed most clearly by Article 2 of the UN Charter.

Revolutionists, and cosmopolitan theorists in particular, also discern a society of states but it is definitely a second order if not a second-rate society whose moral standing derives from the first-order community of humankind. Each state is indeed a civil society, a *civitas*, but each particular *civitas* is less fundamental than the *civitas maxima*: the cosmopolis, the moral community of humankind itself. Cosmopolitan theorists acknowledge that there can be citizens of particular political communities, or states, who have rights and duties in relation to their government and each other. But bounded independent states and their citizens are secondary in normative terms to the unbounded and unlimited community of humankind.[16] Boundaries are not therefore absolute; they cannot be used to deny or repudiate one's moral responsibility to one's fellow human beings. International boundaries are normative for certain purposes: they mark the limits of the territorial jurisdiction of sovereign states and - for most purposes - the political obligations of their citizens. There may be an international obligation to respect them which is defined by international law. But those political norms and legal obligations are not prior to the moral obligation to assist one's fellow human beings or respect their fundamental human rights. States are not complete communities in themselves. They are merely local normative arrangements for promoting the good of humankind in the area of the world where they are located and when they fail to do that they lose any moral authority they would otherwise have.

These theories constitute three different ways of understanding and evaluating boundaries in international relations and thus provide contrasting normative perspectives on the subject. Wight sums them up by identifying the response of each to the question 'What is international society?'

1. It is not a society, rather an arena.
2. It is a society but different from the state.
3. It is a state (or ought to be).[17]

The first (realism) denies the existence of international boundaries except as instrumental distinctions. The second (rationalism) affirms the existence of international boundaries as normative divisions which carry certain rights and obligations. The third (revolutionism) acknowledges the normative character of international boundaries and the states defined by them, but notes that their normative standing is secondary to that of the unbounded community of humankind. In the next three sections I shall briefly canvass the practice and history of international boundaries. In the final section I shall consider how pertinent these theoretical perspectives are for capturing historical and contemporary experience with the institution. At the end of the chapter I shall comment on the normative point of international boundaries and try to locate the institution on the intellectual map of political theory.

International boundaries in practice

As indicated, international boundaries are presupposed by state sovereignty and hence the right to political independence. According to Martin Wight, there are two grounds by which that international right and thus membership of international society has been claimed historically: prescription and self-determination.[18] The first is associated with the dynastic state, the second with the nation state. By 'prescription' he seems to mean what most lawyers mean: the possession of sovereignty on the grounds of uninterrupted assertion of that claim over a period of time. By 'national self-determination' he seems to mean the possession of sovereignty on the grounds of a group's existence as a distinctive people who occupy a particular territory and have a desire to govern themselves. So the change from prescription to self-determination is basically a shift in international legitimacy and legality from princes to peoples.

Contemporary international practice does not entirely square with either of Wight's grounds - although it does embrace elements of each. It entails prescription - but a form of prescription with a different focus than the traditional practice. That practice focused international legitimacy and legality on ruling authorities. It did not focus it on the populations in the territories they ruled. Territories were transferred back and forth and thus boundaries were drawn and redrawn as a result of war, conquest, treaties, dynastic marriage, purchase and other transactions that largely disregarded the people who made their home in those territories. The people merely came with the territory. Since territories belonged to rulers and not to the people, the drawing of international boundaries was entirely in the hands of the former and entirely out of the hands of the latter. Territory was dynastic property. It was not public property.

The current practice incorporates self-determination but the 'self' in question is not a people or nation in any ethnonational sense. Many such entities do of course assert their right to be sovereign - some successfully. But most are unsuccessful. The populations which claim and exercise the right of self-determination nowadays are not defined by common language, ethnicity, religion or culture. Rather, they are defined by pre-existing juridical boundaries - either international, colonial or internal. A claimant entity already has to be located on the map at a lower level of jurisdiction to be promoted to independent status.[19] Self-determination requires a pre-existing juridical existence of some kind short of sovereignty. Political independence involves elevating a lower jurisdiction to a higher one. The practice is most clearly evident in European decolonization in Asia and Africa where in the overwhelming number of cases only pre-existing colonies became sovereign states. But it is also evident in the break-up of the Soviet Union and former Yugoslavia where only pre-existing and subordinate juridical entities - i.e., 'republics' - became sovereign states.

The contemporary practice thus focuses international legitimacy and legality on existing demarcated territories and regards their boundaries as unalterable without the consent of all states parties touched by them. Sovereigns can dramatically change - as in the cases of Western decolonization or the dismantling of the Soviet Union - but the territorial jurisdictions by reference to which sovereignty is exercised cannot change - without consent all round. Since that is usually very difficult to obtain an important upshot is the juridical freezing of the political map of the world. State jurisdictions no longer migrate as many once did, but instead they are fixed in one location. The map of the world has become a chequerboard - each square of which is the permanent location of a particular named sovereign state.

The late twentieth-century practice, as I discern it, is thus the following: the lines on the map which divide the population of the world into separate territorial jurisdictions are the focus of international legitimacy and legality. Sovereigns can of course change - as happened time and again in the twentieth century with the dissolving of empires. But the boundaries defining populated territories ordinarily cannot change - without mutual agreement of all states parties involved. The alteration and even the attempted alteration of international boundaries without such agreement is an extraordinary event today which is invested with profound concern. The legal principle involved is that of *uti possidetis juris*: respecting the territorial units formed by existing boundaries.[20] That principle of juridical statehood has proved to be remarkably resilient even in the face of widespread and zealous ethnonationalism.

This introduces a new problematic for international politics: in the past, war was the usual arbiter in determining international boundaries, but today the use of armed force to conquer independent territory and redraw the map is illegitimate and illegal - even though it is still attempted from time to time.[21] The new practice is clearly expressed by the UN Charter which forbids aggressive war between states and prescribes a general norm of non-intervention which is the groundnorm of contemporary international society.[22] The main effect of this practice is to freeze the political map of the world in its current geographical pattern. Some problems and paradoxes that result when territorial populations conceive of themselves in contrary terms and refuse to be corseted or partitioned according to this juridical practice are discussed in a later section.

International boundaries in historical summary

This is not the place to investigate the historical expansion of international society. I merely wish to recollect briefly a familiar story as a way of enlarging on the above discussion and as a further response to the question posed at the beginning.[23]

The original members of the European society of sovereign states can be defined, for the purposes of this essay, as the states represented at the Peace of Westphalia in 1648.[24] Those entities were not peoples or nations; in the main they were rulers and dynasties. The peace treaty, among other things, recognized the sovereignty of numerous but previously not fully independent ruling authorities of the Holy Roman Empire. These rulers were henceforth free - according to the principle of state sovereignty - to sign treaties and to engage in other foreign relations on a basis of equality with pre-existing sovereign powers, such as France, England and Sweden. As Adam Watson puts it, 'the Westphalian settlement was the charter of a Europe permanently organized on an anti-hegemonial principle'.[25] Westphalia thus marks the political reconstruction of Europe on the plan of a society of states which were related to each other according to principles and practices of political independence. Alan James characterizes this novel 'international society' as comprising three basic elements: diplomatic communication, international rules (etiquette, morals and law), and 'constitutionally self-contained' or sovereign states - which are the basis of the scheme.[26]

This novel society of states was a European political innovation in response to a previously existing medieval world which was organized according to a contrasting principle of transnational imperialism and religious unity. Westphalia represents a formal repudiation of that world which by the mid-seventeenth century was dying anyway, if it was not already dead. 'Thus the modern state came into existence; a narrower and at the same time a stronger unit of loyalty than medieval Christendom.'[27] For several centuries its membership consisted entirely of European states and also, at a later period, European-immigrant states in the Americas. Prescription was the basis of the original membership of international society with an unstated assumption that members shared a common race, religion and culture associated with Europeans. That assumption became explicit when European international society expanded outwards into other continents and oceans on the heels of European trade, conquest and colonization and encountered peoples of different race, religion and culture.

The original practice of prescription continued long afterwards. For example, Turkey and Japan entered international society largely on this basis once it became clear by about the mid-nineteenth century that European race, Christian religion and western culture could no longer be used to bar non-western powers from membership. But new members still had to accept the diplomatic practices, the positive international law, the institutions and the customs of the western-centered international society they entered. Thus the Turks and the Japanese had to abandon any traditional practices that were contrary to those of the West. The main one was their self-conception as a suzerain state in relation to all outsiders and their conduct of external relations on the basis of their own postulated superiority. These secular and universalist requirements henceforth took the place of the older Eurocentric assumptions and prejudices already noted.[28]

At about the same time that international society was encroaching on the rest of the world the practice of prescription was gradually challenged from within Europe by the contrary right of self-determination as the only valid ground for determining membership of international society. Most scholars date this challenge from the time of the French revolution in 1789. But it is prefigured by the Glorious Revolution a century earlier and the subsequent Act of Settlement by which, as Martin Wight puts it, 'the English had imposed upon Europe a principle of national sovereignty against Louis XVI's doctrine of dynastic legitimacy'.[29] The Americans later forced the same practice on the British.

Although the transition was long and winding, with many reverses, over time peoples displaced princes as the legitimate entity for claiming a right to independence.[30] Thus, the mid-nineteenth-century unification and independence of Germany and Italy - each on the basis of a common language - spelled the loss of independence and submergence of numerous, smaller pre-existing territorial jurisdictions mostly based on dynastic legitimacy. At a later date differences of language defined the contraction and eventual disintegration of large pre-existing multinational empires - German, Austro-Hungarian, Turkish - and the emergence of more numerous but smaller independent states in Central and Eastern Europe based, very awkwardly, on the nationhood principle.

After the First World War, self-determination seemed to displace prescription as the only valid ground for asserting a claim to membership of international society. In its provisions for minority protections and a mandate system the new League of Nations suggested as much even though the principle of self-determination was not formally written into its Covenant.[31] By that time numerous new national states were emerging, or had emerged, in Eastern Europe and were assuming membership in international society. In all of this extensive relocating of international boundaries, however, sovereign jurisdictions never coincided exactly with linguistic communities and most new states encompassed substantial ethnic minorities. And post-war Germany was explicitly denied the right to draw its new borders according to the principle of self-determination.

The next great expansion of international society occurred in the decades following the end of the Second World War in areas outside Europe, mainly Asia and Africa. In that period membership of international society increased about threefold. All of these emergent states claimed a right of sovereignty and membership of the United Nations on the grounds of self-determination. In this respect their emergence was consistent with the birth of states in Central and Eastern Europe after the First World War. There were important differences, however. The newly independent states of Asia and Africa were almost without exception former overseas dependencies of Western colonial powers: Britain, France, Holland, Belgium, Italy, Spain, and Portugal. They were defined - with few exceptions - by boundaries drawn by the colonial powers and not by the borders of indigenous tribes, nationalities or nations. This elevation of pre-existing subordinate territorial jurisdictions is the prevalent practice in the definition and admission of new members of international society in the twentieth century. It recalls the experience in Latin America a century earlier where international boundaries which defined newly independent states were approximately the same as the external and internal frontiers of the previously existing Spanish and Portuguese empires. An element of prescription focused now on colonially defined territories thus became international practice: *uti possidetis juris*.

The most recent expansion of international society following the end of the Cold War was also brought about by the disintegration of what were empires in all but name: the Soviet Union and former Yugoslavia. And even though the claims for independence were expressed in the rhetoric of self-determination, the actual practice by which the new members were defined as territorially sovereign was exactly the same as the practice in Latin America, Asia and Africa: the existing internal borders of the former USSR and Yugoslavia were henceforth recognized as international boundaries separating independent states. The sovereign members of the Commonwealth of Independent States occupy territorial jurisdictions that are identical to those of the former constituents of the Soviet Union. Likewise, the new international borders of the Balkan peninsula recognized to date are identical to the internal borders of the former Yugoslav Federation. In all these cases preexisting borders in some places dating back to the Austro-Hungarian and Russian empires were the lines of reference for defining the territorial sovereignty of the successor states.

To sum up. The right of independence noted at the beginning is usually asserted when empires or quasi-empires disintegrate and international boundaries have to be redrawn. In the twentieth century that has happened on a significant scale at one time or another in every continent except North and South America - where it took place in the previous two centuries. It is thus a major feature of international relations. As indicated, the question posed at the beginning of this chapter is usually answered by recognizing pre-existing colonial or internal borders as international boundaries. It is not usually answered by drawing new boundaries around claimant nations or nationalities - despite the fact that there are many such entities which assert their right to self-determination on these occasions and at other times. Only existing bounded territories are legitimate, and any change in their borders requires the agreement of all affected states parties. The contemporary practice is not consistent with self-determination in the sociological meaning. Yet neither is it consistent with the traditional practice of prescription because, as indicated, in the twentieth century it is inherited boundaries and their territorially contained populations and not merely rulers or even governments which are prescribed as legitimate. The new practice clearly is a hybrid.

International boundaries today

Important events in the former Soviet Union and the former Yugoslavia since the end of the Cold War indicate that these same borders, while they may be the only legitimate reference points for international society, are not legitimate for all the peoples enclosed or partitioned by them. Indeed, in some cases they may be profoundly illegitimate. Thus, while territorial prescription has predominated internationally, the right of self-determination in the sociological sense has been asserted by certain nations or nationalities aimed at changing international boundaries to conform to ethnic patterns of residence. That has happened in a number of newly independent states and former republics of the USSR including most notably Russia, Ukraine, Moldova, Georgia, Armenia and Azerbaijan. However, I must restrict this brief analysis to two noteworthy cases in ex-Yugoslavia.

Following the independence of Croatia and Bosnia-Herzegovina in 1992 armed conflicts broke out (in Croatia) over territory substantially populated by Serbs and (in Bosnia-Herzegovina) over territories substantially populated by Serbs and by Croats. The new Croatian government in Zagreb not only accepted the inherited internal borders of Yugoslavia - which had been drawn by Tito - but unfortunately insisted on portraying the independent Croatian state defined by those borders in exclusively ethnic-Croatian terms. Croatia clearly was a new state in territorial terms, but the government operated as though its borders were the markers of a historic ethnonation. That left the Serbian minority out in the cold. The Serbs resorted to the use of armed force to take control of territories within the new state of Croatia in which they, the Serbs, were concentrated: mainly eastern Slavonia and Krajina. I think it is fair to say that neither the government in Zagreb nor the Serb minority were prepared to accept the multinational principle of territorial legitimacy outlined above which involves a respect for both existing borders and ethnic minorities. That belligerent attitude was behind the war.

In Bosnia-Herzegovina, however, the government of the new state was officially and avowedly multiethnic. But that evidently made no difference to the Serbian minority which was not prepared to acknowledge the legitimacy of the new multinational state. Serb militias took up arms with the apparent aim of unifying all Serb-populated territory, and perhaps any additional territories they could occupy by force, and forming an ethno-political association with Belgrade comparable to that which already existed between Serbia and Montenegro. The Bosnian Serbs instituted their own ethno-national government in the territories they forcibly seized from the new state of Bosnia-Herzegovina supposedly as a preliminary to eventually uniting with Serbia.

These episodes disclose all too clearly the unwillingness of certain ethnonational groups to live side by side peacefully within the territorial framework of a single multi-ethnic state when they lack the will to do so and they have an opportunity and an excuse (at least in their minds) to resort to armed rebellion. The Bosnian Serb leader - Radovan Karadzic - publicly complained time and again that the only viable and enduring basis for peace was separation of the principal ethnonational groups by international boundaries to form ethnically homogeneous national states. Maybe he is right. But because such groups in the Balkans (and most other parts of the world) are inextricably intermingled on the ground they cannot be separated in practice without uprooting large numbers of people from their homes and villages: the infamous process that has come to be known as 'ethnic cleansing'.

In the past and indeed until as recently as 1945 such a revision of boundaries by force would have been acknowledged, however reluctantly, by international society whose attitude in that regard was fundamentally realist. At the end of the Second World War there was not only a redrawing of international borders by the victors but also a massive relocation of ethnic populations under international auspices that was little different from ethnic cleansing. That is no longer accepted practice, however. Today the norm of territorial prescription together with its companion, nonintervention, constitute foundations of international society proclaimed by the UN Charter, the Helsinki Final Act, the Charter of the Organization of African Unity, and other international covenants. Those norms were reiterated by the 1990 Paris Charter and subsequent pronouncements of the CSCE and the Council of Europe which articulated international standards of conduct for the post-Cold War era in Europe. They were also reiterated by the 1992 London Conference which - in connection with the conflicts in former

Yugoslavia - called upon all parties to respect existing international boundaries and the rights of national minorities.

To date international society has proved deeply reluctant to give up on the post-1945 and post-colonial practice of legitimating inherited boundaries. I am not aware of any evidence for arguing that self-determination based on ethnonational group identity is a legitimate claim if it involves changes of existing international boundaries against the will of any affected sovereign state. That has never been a practice of international society. The world of national states is a juridical order and not a sociological order.

Normative theory and international boundaries

International boundaries are an institution created and operated jointly by states which have them in common and generally conduct themselves without violating them. Whether a state respects an international boundary is not merely a question of narrow self-interest: an instrumental question. Rather, it is a moral and legal question because states are bound to respect them: a question of international obligation.

The foregoing analysis suggests that rationalism is more apt than realism or cosmopolitanism for understanding the character and *modus operandi* of international boundaries. Indeed, the discussion in previous sections has been expressed almost entirely in that discourse alone. Realism has difficulty comprehending the borders between states as a shared institution that imposes a common obligation. Cosmopolitanism has difficulty comprehending those borders as embodying fundamental rather than merely secondary normative value. If realist theory were pertinent to the subject there would not be the international normative concern that there obviously has been about violations of borders in former Yugoslavia. If cosmopolitan theory were pertinent the value of preventing human suffering and defending human rights would take normative precedence over the value of respecting existing borders. Yet there obviously is a profound international concern to preserve those borders unless all affected states parties consent to boundary changes. States are inclined to defend international boundaries even in cases, such as the former Yugoslavia, where that may involve turning their back on serious human rights violations.

Realists might say that the motive states have for respecting international boundaries is, ultimately, that of international order. It would I think be difficult to disagree. But international order is not the narrow self-interest of one state or even the coincidence and sum of the narrow self-interests of many states. International order is a generally recognized value or good which commands a shared or common interest, as Bull might put it.[32] It does not happen by accident or even by the unintended consequences of the pursuit of narrow self-interest of states. It is constructed and defended and, from time to time, it is undermined and even occasionally knocked down by the conflicts of states.

International boundaries are thus a fundamental building block of contemporary international order: a standard of conduct behind which all sovereign states can rally. They express a rare international consensus that gets beyond culture, language, race, religion, ideology, wealth and all other non-juridical divisions between members of the society of states. Of course, that does not mean that every state is likely to be satisfied with its current borders: many states may be dissatisfied. It means something more fundamental: that however awkward or unsatisfactory those borders may be in any particular case, they are a generally accepted point of reference for everyone. Most countries today are multinational or multiethnic in social composition. That means that a majority of the members of international society would be adversely affected if the current practice were abandoned or even called into serious question. If that happened in Croatia or Bosnia-Herzegovina, for example, it could encourage demands for independence and possibly armed challenges to the sovereignty of existing states by frustrated nationalities or nations on grounds of ethnonational self-determination. There is thus a compelling common international interest springing from numerous national interests in supporting the current groundnorm. Understood in that light, international boundaries are a basic stabilizing institution of world society.

The problem with the classical theorists of international society, such as Martin Wight and Hedley Bull, is that they usually stop here and do not go on to probe the fundamental point and basic values of international society and its institutions. When they do occasionally probe it, as Bull does, they sometimes arrive at a conclusion which is at odds with the main normative presuppositions of international society. The fundamental point is not international order, or even world order, for that matter. I disagree with Hedley Bull where he writes: 'World order is more fundamental and primordial than international order because the ultimate units of the great society of all mankind are not states (or nations, tribes, empires, classes or parties) but individual human beings.'[33] The fundamental point of international society is the good life of human beings on the planet as they endeavour to construct it in historical time. Human beings are not significant as primordial entities; they are significant as historical agents who construct social and political communities within which far more than a primordial existence hopefully is available. The fundamental point of international boundaries is that they provide a framework within which humans anywhere on the planet can attempt to build their local good life according to their own values and capacities. Some will succeed, some will fail, but everybody will have the chance if boundaries and the corollary rule of nonintervention are respected in accordance with international law.

If the analysis in earlier sections of this chapter is correct it suggests that sovereign states operate with something far closer to a communitarian theory than a cosmopolitan theory as an underlying justification of international boundaries: by 'communitarian' I mean the assumption that states have, or could have, independent normative value well beyond the primordial value of the human beings who compose them; states are actual or potential political communities.[34] Boundaries are primarily about that particular value and only secondarily about international order. Order is a value, but it is not an end value. The main point of international society on a global scale such as exists today is to accommodate the plurality of human social organization: diverse cultures, religions, political systems, legal institutions, family institutions, and other distinctive ways of collective life on the planet. Boundaries are a principal element of the institutional framework, the society of states, that gives effect to this communitarian and pluralistic morality of the society of states. Here, as elsewhere, I take inspiration from the writings of Isaiah Berlin: 'In the house of human history there are many mansions. ... This doctrine is called pluralism.'[35] International boundaries are a universalist element which prevents communitarianism and pluralism from descending into relativism.

Notes

1 'The warmth of nationhood', *Times Literary Supplement*, 19 February 1993, p. 14.

2 Anybody who takes an interest in theorizing international boundaries is soon made aware of the elusive character of the subject. But that should not be a reason for avoiding the subject.

3 Here I am referring to political and moral principles and not to legal principles. I cannot get into the huge and complex international law of boundaries. There is an emergent political and ethical theory on the subject. See, for example, O'Neill, O., 'Justice and boundaries', and Pogge, T. W., 'Cosmopolitanism and sovereignty', in Brown, C. (ed.), *Political Restructuring in Europe: Ethical Perspectives* (London and New York, Routledge, 1994), pp. 89–122. See also Hont, I., 'The permanent crisis of a divided mankind', in Dunn, J. (ed.), *Contemporary Crisis of the Nation State?* (Oxford, Basil Blackwell, 1995), pp. 166–232.

4 *The Open Society and Its Enemies, Vol. I: The Spell of Plato* (Princeton, NJ, Princeton University Press, 1966), p. 288, n. 7.

5 There are of course many other kinds of territorial borders: provincial, municipal, electoral, judicial, etc.

6 Clark, G., *The Seventeenth Century*, 2nd edn (London, Oxford University Press, 1960), Ch. X.

7 Boundaries figure prominently in anthropology, sociology, psychology, feminist studies, and even biology: the types of boundaries commonly identified include cultural, racial, colour, class, ethnic, gender and biological.

8 See, for example, Kratochwil, Friedrich, 'Of systems, boundaries and territoriality', *World Politics*, **38** (October 1986), pp. 27-52; Herbst, Jeffrey, 'Challenges to Africa's boundaries in the new world order', *Journal of International Affairs*, **46** (Summer 1992), pp. 17-30; Ruggie, John Gerard, 'Territoriality and beyond: problematizing modernity in international relations', *International Organization*, **47** (Winter 1993), pp. 139-74; Barkin, J. Samuel and Cronin, Bruce, 'The state and the nation: changing norms and the rules of sovereignty in international relations', *International Organization*, **48** (Winter 1994), pp. 107-30; 'Sovereignty, interdependence and international institutions', in Miller, Linda B., Keohane, Robert O. and Smith, Michael Joseph (eds), *Ideals & Ideals: Essays in Honor of Stanley Hoffmann* (Boulder, CO, Westview Press, 1993), pp. 91-107; and Philpott, Daniel, 'Sovereignty: an introduction and brief history', *Journal of International Affairs*, **48** (Winter 1995), pp. 353-68.

9 See, for example, Bull, H. and Watson, A. (eds), *The Expansion of International Society* (Oxford, Clarendon Press, 1984).

10 Wight, G. and Porter, B. (eds), *International Theory: The Three Traditions* (London, Leicester University Press, 1991).

11 Wight, M , 'An anatomy of international thought', *Review of International Studies*, **13** (1987).

12 Hobbes, T., *Leviathan*, ed. M. Oakeshott (Oxford, Basil Blackwell, 1946), Ch. 13.

13 Wight, *International Theory*, pp. 38-9.

14 Bull, H., *The Anarchical Society* (London, Macmillan, 1977), p. 13.

15 Ibid., p. 14.

16 One of the best discussions of this relationship is Linklater, A., *Men and Citizens in the Theory of International Relations* (London, Macmillan, 1982).

17 Wight, *International Theory*, p 48.

18 Wight, M., 'De systematibus civitatum', and 'International legitimacy', in Bull, H. (ed), *Systems of States* (Leicester, Leicester University Press, 1977).

19 The expression 'lower' is used to state the normative standing of a border in relation to state sovereignty; it is not intended to imply any normative evaluation

20 For the origins and development of this practice in the emergence of independent states in the new world see Parkinson, F., 'Latin America', in Jackson, R. H. and James, A. (eds), *States in a Changing World* (Oxford, Clarendon Press, 1993), pp. 240-61.

21 The latest being the Iraqi invasion, occupation and attempted annexation of Kuwait in 1990.

22 See Article 2.

23 See Bull and Watson, *The Expansion of the International Society*.

24 This date is of course hotly debated. See the discussion in Wight, M.,'The origins of our states-system: geographical limits', in Bull (ed.), *Systems of States*, pp. 110-14.

25 Watson, A., *The Evolution of International Society* (London, Routledge, 1992), p. 182.

26 See James, A., 'International Society', *British Journal of International Studies*, 4 (July 1978), pp. 91–106.
27 Wight, M., *Power Politics*, 2nd edn (Harmondsworth, Penguin Books for Royal Institute of International Affairs, 1986), p. 25.
28 Gong, G. W., *The Standard of 'Civilisation' in International Society* (Oxford, Clarendon Press, 1984).
29 Wight, 'International legitimacy', p. 160.
30 One of the best summaries is still Lyon, P., 'New states and international order', in James, A. (ed.), *The Bases of International Order* (London, Oxford University Press, 1973), pp. 24–59.
31 See the helpful legal analysis in Shaw, M., *Title to Territory in Africa* (Oxford, Clarendon Press, 1986), Ch. 2.
32 Bull, *The Anarchical Society*, pp. 13–14.
33 Ibid., p. 22.
34 This point is convincingly made by Rengger, N., 'A city which sustains all things? Communitarianism and international society', *Millennium*, **21** (Winter 1992), pp. 353–70. For an insightful analysis of normative international relations theory in contrasting cosmopolitan and communitarian terms, see Brown, C. *International Relations Theory: New Normative Approaches* (New York, Harvester Wheatsheaf, 1992).
35 Berlin, Isaiah, *The Crooked Timber of Humanity* (New York, Vintage Books, 1992), p. 79.

8

Intervention in International Society: Theory and Practice in Contemporary Perspective*

JAMES MAYALL

Political cartoonists are quicker than most to expose the humbug which so often surrounds liberal talk of a New World Order. On the day the Americans were due to land in Haiti, JAK of the *Evening Standard* portrayed two GIs in front of a voodoo shop whose most prominent display was a row of pin-cushion dolls replete with pins. The caption read 'How much are those Jimmy Carter dolls?'[1] The cartoon was, no doubt, mainly intended to illustrate the US military's frustration at not being allowed to get on with the job, but it inadvertently threw light on another aspect of the current debate about the use of force in post-Cold War international society. How should governments respond to displays of tyrannical or barbarous behaviour on their doorstep, or even further afield? More specifically, should they intervene in the affairs of other countries, not to repel or deter an aggression, nor even to pre-empt the possibility of one, but to change the character of alien and repressive regimes?

This question is hardly new, but during the Cold War it was seldom discussed. Since then, however, it has re-emerged with a vengeance, not just as a concern for those with a professional interest in political ethics or the theory of international society, but in a series of deadly crises that have been brought before the United Nations Security Council. It would be difficult to claim a high level of success for any of the recent UN interventions in civil conflicts and it is worth asking whether there is any general explanation for this failure.

The failure of the 'English School' of international society theorists to make much of the concept of humanitarian intervention is understandable. It stems largely from their preoccupation with carving out a middle position between the extreme realist proposition that social relations are impossible

* Earlier versions of this paper were discussed at the ECPR Limerick Conference in 1993, the Carlisle Club and the LSE Ford Foundation seminar on International Society since the End of the Cold War.

in the absence of government and the utopian vision of a community of humankind or world society. Against these rival positions they have continued to argue for an international society of sovereign states which, in the last analysis, is bound together by its members' commitment to non-interference in each other's domestic affairs. It follows from this view that intervening in civil conflicts contravenes the fundamental rule of international society. As we shall see, there are formidable practical difficulties to overcoming this aspect of the morality of states. Nonetheless the preoccupation of the English School with a narrow conception of international society does have the inevitable consequence, as Chris Brown has argued, of marginalizing the normative theory of international relations within the wider philosophical debate between cosmopolitanism and communitarianism, where he believes it belongs.[2] The protagonists in this debate *are* concerned with the ethics of intervention, although it is not clear (at least to this author) that they have advanced our understanding of the issues involved much further than the international society theorists.

In practice, the issue is more often debated at the political level between conservatives and liberals, who have seldom thought deeply about the external world, and generally carry into it the values and prejudices to which they remain attached at home. For many conservatives the failure of recent UN interventions was inevitable, the result of basing policy on the mistaken assumption that there can be obligations to outsiders, other than those freely entered into within an Alliance to meet a specific threat. For Maurice Cowling, for example, 'the only permanent claims are those which arise from the national interest defined in terms of sovereignty, historic continuity and national identity, and beyond these no other focus of loyalty is either necessary or desirable'.[3] On this view, presumably, reference to international society would make little sense since there is no such society. States are justified in using force when they are attacked or to protect vital interests, such as free access to raw materials on which they have come to rely over time. The only relevant criteria in weighing the merits of intervention are the interests of the intervening state and prudence without which no sovereign power can be maintained.

Conservative thinkers are not generally concerned with questions about origins, but with the preservation of an actual state of affairs, so that if an empire exists they will regard national and imperial interests as synonymous. But conservatism cannot generate an ideology of empire, in the sense of a justification for subordinating one sovereignty to another on a permanent basis, since the establishment, rather than maintenance of empire, is manifestly a radical project involving upheaval for the conquering and the conquered populations alike. No doubt, few present-day conservatives would accept my caricature of their position where obligations stop at the border. Most would probably concede that the world has become so intertwined in a commercial, technological and even military sense that it is difficult to be sure where obligations end and interests take over as the basis for political action. And some might agree that the attempt to drive a wedge between interest and moral behaviour was always mistaken.

Treaties - the most uncontentious source of international law - certainly reflect the interests of the contracting parties but they could not be negotiated without a bare minimum of shared value to reassure the signatories that promises will be kept. It is true that the maxim *pacta sunt servanda* is generally accompanied by the qualifying *rebus sic stantibus* but the fact that the tension between principle and contingency is expressed in an international language, albeit a dead one, itself suggests that while the concept of society may not always have been world-wide, it was certainly not confined to a single country.

If, then, international society exists, our present confusion over the rights and wrongs of intervention cannot simply be blamed on the incoherence of liberal ideas. Conservatism can be shown to be equally incoherent. A rigorous insistence on non-intervention can be reached by either conservative or liberal reasoning, but so can the justification of the right, even the duty, to intervene under certain circumstances.

The real problem raised by the recent spate of international interventions - in former Yugoslavia, Africa and Central America - is quite different. It concerns the attempt to ground international society on principles of internal legitimacy as well as external sovereignty. The UN Charter, with its attempt to entrench a set of inalienable human rights alongside state sovereignty, fore-shadowed the recent internationalization of civil conflicts in the name of constitutionalism. So did the Cold War, if you follow Samuel Huntington in viewing the ideological contest between capitalism and communism as an internal quarrel within the European Enlightenment.[4] But the nuclear stand-off that accompanied it ensured that the implications and limits of the putative international constitution were never tested in practice. Now we have the chance to reflect on what is involved in trying to police a minimum standard of civilization. This kind of intervention is certainly a departure from the historical pattern. The conventional view is that international society is a society of states only. It is a consequence of this view, moreover, that Article 2.7 of the Charter, which prohibits intervention in the domestic affairs of other states, can only be overridden to deter or repel a direct threat to international peace and security.

There is much to be said for this parsimonious interpretation in both theory and practice. Theoretically, non-intervention is a logical entailment of a system formally and legally based on sovereignty and mutual recognition. At the end of the European wars of religion, the princes were only able to frame a contract of peaceful co-existence by guaranteeing each other's ideological supremacy within the area of their exclusive territorial jurisdiction - hence the principle of *cuius regio eius religio*, the direct forerunner of Article 2.7. It is true that in the centuries that followed the Peace of Westphalia, the European powers interpreted this formula in a discriminatory way. Treaties could be contracted with barbarian states, roughly speaking those which belonged to non-Christian civilizations, such as the Indian princely states or the Ottoman Empire, but they could be set aside more easily than agreements between Christian states. Treaties concluded with savage peoples, i.e. those who lacked either a literate culture or centralized political institutions or both, were even more dispensable.[5] During the founding years of the United States, slavery was debated as a moral problem, but the position of the Indian population was barely considered since Indians were not members of civil society. Treaties that had earlier been made with indigenous leaders during the colonial penetration of North America were swept aside in the name of Christian civilization and manifest destiny. The underlying rationale was the same for the European expansion in Asia and Africa.

After 1945, not only were these convenient, if self-serving distinctions, abandoned but there was an attempt to persuade sovereign powers to put themselves under a measure of self-enforced restraint: the use of force was confined to defence, and collective intervention was only to be sanctioned under Chapter 7 of the Charter to deter or repel aggression. By implication, conquest, the most traditional way of settling disputes, was proscribed.

It is at this point that a divide opens up between the theory and practice of international society. For those who framed the UN Charter it was one thing to accept the principle of *uti possidetis* as the basis of the post-Second World War political map, quite another to accept that conquest might change that map in the future. To have challenged the former principle would have opened up a Pandora's box of claims and counter claims from which no government would have been safe, but to have conceded the possibility of future conquests after the defeat of fascist aggression would in 1945 have been tantamount to admitting that a right could be derived from a wrong. By contrast the three authors who are generally considered to have founded the English School, Herbert Butterfield, Martin Wight and Hedley Bull, had a more ambiguous attitude to the role of force in world politics and a tendency to accept, however reluctantly, war as an institution of international society. In this sense the liberal ideology of the major western powers was ahead of the pessimistic conservatism of the leading international society theorists.

One reason why the Gulf War had such an impact on public perceptions of international society was that it appeared - with a hindsight it seems erroneously – to narrow the gap between both theoretical and practical and liberal and conservative conceptions of justified intervention. Saddam Hussein's invasion of Kuwait in August 1990 threatened the geopolitical and economic interests of the western powers, and greatly alarmed the majority of Iraq's regional neighbours, which no doubt explains why the Americans found it relatively easy to put together so wide-ranging an alliance to oppose him. But Iraq's occupation of Kuwait was also an unambiguous breach of the rules of international society. With no threat of a veto, it also allowed the Security Council to respond more or less as had originally been intended.

The resolutions under which Operation Desert Storm was mounted were confined to repelling Iraq's aggression, and were careful not to call in question either the country's territorial integrity or even the legitimacy of Saddam Hussein's regime.[6] Nothing that happened between August 1990 and February 1991 suggested that there was widespread support for sanctioning intervention in civil conflicts. What happened in the aftermath of the war was a different matter and I will return to this shortly.

There are also strong practical grounds for refraining from such intervention. From this point of view, the non-intervention rule not only underpins the sovereignty of states but cautions their governments from embarking on foolhardy projects, on the basis of inadequate information, and from which it will be difficult and costly to extract themselves. The use of force, even when the military goals are clear and the political objectives obtainable, always involves risks, but these will escalate dramatically where what is at stake is not the defeat of an enemy but the transformation of a society. Nonetheless, it has long been held that in the face of events so barbarous that they 'shock the moral conscience of mankind' it may be necessary to intervene on the side of the victims. The establishment of safe havens for the Kurds and the Shi'ites, which, unlike the ejection of Saddam Hussein from Kuwaiti soil, did not have the unanimous support of the Security Council, is generally held to have fallen under this head.

The creation of safe havens in Iraq was not the original intention of the coalition leaders, but a policy which they devised hurriedly and largely in response to public opinion. In this it had much in common with the immediate background to other recent interventions in former Yugoslavia, Somalia, Rwanda and Haiti. This comparison was unfortunate since the issues involved – and the justifications that can be offered in support of them – were very different. I have argued elsewhere that the Iraqi safe havens were justified because, having encouraged the Iraqi people to depose Saddam Hussein, western leaders could not escape responsibility for the fate of the Kurds when predictably he suppressed their rebellion.[7] In the 1860s, John Stuart Mill advanced an analogous argument when he defended the British conquest of the Indian princely state of Oude. He wrote:

> A civilised government cannot help having barbarous neighbours: when it has it cannot always content itself with a defensive position, one of mere resistance to aggression. After a larger or shorter interval of forbearance, it either finds itself obliged to conquer them or to assert so much authority over them … that it has become morally responsible for all evil it allows them to do.[8]

Moral responsibility can be attached to agents; it cannot sensibly be attached to abstract and contested structures such as imperialism, capitalism or communism. On this view, despite Chinese, Indian and African fears that the permanent members of the Security Council were about to sanction a new form of imperialism – they either abstained or voted against Resolution 688 which condemned the Iraqi attack on the Kurds – the coalition *was* responsible for the post-war conflict in Iraq in much the same way as the British, in Mill's view, were responsible for the civil corruption of Oude.

But it is not obvious that any outside power could be held similarly responsible for the crises in former Yugoslavia, Somalia, Rwanda and Haiti. The Cold War certainly contributed to the disintegration of the state in Somalia since the superpowers and others had flooded the Horn of Africa with weapons. This hardware fell into the hands of rival warlords who eventually overcame the tyrannical rule of Siad Barre, before turning with equal ferocity on one another. But in this context the Cold War is a convenient shorthand term for a diffuse set of relationships, involving not merely superpower efforts to extend their spheres of influence, but the determined efforts of local actors to manipulate their patrons for their own quite different ends. In an interdependent world there is no doubt a sense in which we are all guilty of complicity, but there is no reason to believe that the Serbs, Croats and Bosnian Muslims, the Somalis, Hutus and Tutsis and Haitians are not primarily responsible for their own miseries.

Why then, should the international community intervene, and to what end in cases where no great power interest is involved, and no direct responsibility can be identified? The first question is easier to answer than the second. It is also easier to say why decisions to intervene were taken in practice than to provide theoretical justifications for them. In each case, the operation was mounted very largely in response to the pressures of special interest groups, NGOs, the media and more generally public opinion. The immediate objective was to ensure the delivery of relief aid to the victims of civil war and famine, to act as a firebreak between rival factions wherever they could be persuaded to separate and, in the case of Haiti, to restore to office the elected president. If there were specific interests involved – to prevent the crises triggering a flood of refugees, to stop at source the contagion of political instability and religious fundamentalism, to prevent any backtracking on democratic commitments, a kind of free world version of the Brezhnev Doctrine – these remained firmly in the background, rationalizations rather than genuine justifications. There seems little doubt that the primary motivation in each case was humanitarian.

Public opinion is notoriously fickle. The public's conscience can be aroused, but democratic politicians remain fearful that it will turn against them if there is a serious risk of casualties. Nor is there a clear theoretical argument with which to counter their equivocation. The relief of avoidable suffering is perhaps a necessary part of any ethical theory of intervention, but it is hardly sufficient since it does not stipulate how much suffering a population must undergo before outside powers may justifiably override the non-intervention rule; nor is it clear what are the limits of the intervention. How long is it to last and how is the abused population to be reassured that any amelioration of its plight will be permanent?

One has only to read eyewitness accounts of the Rwandan massacres in 1994, in which the killings were not carried out just by the militias but by ordinary people including women and children, to realize that it is a real, not an abstract, problem.[9] For more than two years Rwanda was a substantially depopulated country, with more than a million of its people corralled in squalid refugee camps in the then Zaire and Tanzania. Since, by their own admission, so many ordinary people were involved in the attempted genocide, they were unlikely to be reassured about their future treatment by a Rwandan Patriotic Front (RPF) government promise to put only their leaders on trial for crimes against humanity. In these circumstances, the international community was frequently accused of aiding and abetting the next round in the cycle of violence, namely the Hutu revenge on the RPF.

International society, as at present constructed, is incapable of dealing with societal breakdown, where all public authority is destroyed. The initial response, illustrated by the Security Council resolutions covering the interventions in Bosnia and Somalia,[10] was to define these crises as threats to international peace and security justifying UN forces to 'take all necessary measures', i.e. including force, to restore order. But placing a UN operation under Chapter Seven cannot itself translate an intractable civil conflict into an international problem to which there is a military or a political solution.

UN commanders in the field understandably felt let down by governments which have repeatedly failed to provide the resources which would enable them to implement the Security Council resolutions under which they operate. The increasing tendency of the Council to will the ends but not the means is indeed a problem, but it is more a symptom than a true cause of the failure. The reason why international society cannot cope with societal breakdown is that, as the English School theorists rightly diagnosed, it is first and foremost a society of states not peoples. In other words when public authority collapses it is not clear with whom foreign governments should deal and on what legal or institutional basis.

Once it had become clear, in October 1993, that the Somali operation had failed, the Security Council sounded the retreat from Chapter Seven. The new orthodoxy was the return to principles of peacekeeping, as devised and tested during the Cold War. The two foundation principles of peacekeeping are that intervention requires the consent of the parties and that UN forces should be strictly impartial. In other words before the UN can perform a useful role in a civil conflict there has to be a ceasefire, and therefore a peace to keep. It was because these preconditions no longer held that the United Nations initially withdrew from Rwanda when the precarious ceasefire between the government and the RPF broke down irretrievably in April 1994.

This decision may have been disastrous but it was perfectly consistent with the traditional and limited conception of the society of states. However, the withdrawal to Chapter Six, under which the international community confines itself to mediation and good offices in civil conflicts, could not be maintained in the face of the enormity of the human catastrophe and the incessant demands that 'something must be done'. The problem to which the expanded role of UN intervention since the end of the Cold War has drawn attention - that is, the problem of savage anarchy in collapsed states - unhappily seems unlikely to go away. Nor can it easily be defined out of existence. If this conclusion is accepted there are in principle, it seems to me, only two ways in which the problem can be resolved, neither of which is likely to command wide support. Let me conclude by considering each briefly in turn.

The first resolution would be for the Security Council to abandon its policy of impartiality. Intervention is not peacekeeping. If a people can only be saved from its enemies, or from itself, by the application of outside force, then the decision to intervene should follow the identification of those primarily responsible for terrorizing, abusing or massacring the population and should treat them unequivocably as the enemy. This is, of course, what many critics of the United Nations have demanded in former Yugoslavia and in Rwanda. Assuming its feasibility, such a policy would require the commitment of resources on a scale that governments have so far been unwilling to countenance. But one may reasonably question whether it is feasible. In Somalia the UN was almost certainly right in naming Mohammed Aideed as responsible for the action that led to the killing of 20 Pakistani peacekeepers, but nothing contributed more to the collapse of the operation's credibility than the attempt to single him out from among the other Somali warlords, none of whom were seriously committed to political reconstruction on a national basis.[11] And how could peace be restored in Rwanda by supporting the Tutsis, who, before the latest bloodletting, constituted at a maximum 15 per cent of the population, and whose reconquest of the country reversed an earlier Hutu uprising which had forced the Tutsi leadership into exile in Uganda a generation previously. It is almost a definition of civil war that responsibility is shared and the battle lines shifting and unclear. If the international community declares itself for one or other side, it will almost certainly become part of the problem rather than the solution.

The second resolution is imperial. If the case for intervention rests on state collapse - and if one doubts this, one need only ask why no one has seriously proposed taking on the government in Khartoum over its repression in the Southern Sudan or the government in Jakarta over East Timor - then it is no use pretending that Humpty Dumpty can be put together again. In Somalia, the stated purpose of both the American task force and the UN force which took over from it was to hold the ring while Somalis themselves worked out a programme of reconstruction. But those who held the power over most of the country had no interest in this agenda. Once the UN withdrew at the end of 1994 Somalis reverted to their traditional pattern of political rivalry and manoeuvre. If there was no return to the anarchic war of all against all this was not because the Somalis had agreed to make peace or reconstruct their state, even less out of respect for the norms of international society, about which most Somalis remain profoundly ignorant; it was simply that the balance of forces in the country prevented any one faction from imposing its will.

A coherent strategy would require the intervening force to assume full responsibility for the reconstruction of the state and the rehabilitation of the citizenry. When Sir Brian Urquhart, the former assistant to UN Secretary General in charge of peacekeeping, proposed the revival of the Trusteeship Council to preside over operations of this kind,[12] the idea was generally dismissed on two grounds. It was feared that any such proposal would be strongly opposed in Asia and Africa and almost certainly vetoed by China. (This is no longer necessarily so, at least if one listens to senior African diplomats and academics who are increasingly apt to argue that the time has come to reimpose government, where it does not exist, either through trusteeship or by absorbtion in neighbouring states.) Secondly, none of the countries with the capacity to provide military and administrative personnel were prepared to take on costly, probably unpopular and open-ended commitments of this kind. In this sense the bottom has fallen out of the empire market, probably for good.

There remains, however, the theoretical question of whether a people can be made free by intervention, against its own history and inclinations. Modern liberals generally opposed empire on the grounds that even if the intentions were good, the necessary subordination of one people to another amounts to a denial of universal human rights. Mill, as we have seen, took a rather more robust view, holding that where moral responsibility could be attributed, the conquest of a barbarian state should be regarded as a duty. But in other cases he was only prepared to countenance intervention in support of a people that had already demonstrated its ability to live under free institutions but which might 'be unable to contend successfully for them against the military strength of another nation much more powerful'.[13] The collapsed states that confront international society with its most immediate challenge fall into neither category, although they are closer to the first than the second.

If the international community is to undertake the reconstruction of these states there will have to be a revival of something approximating to imperial responsibility. But even if the Security Council, perhaps acting through neighbouring states, could be induced to take over these countries, it is unclear how long it will take to transform their societies, or even what is involved. The last time the United States intervened in Haiti in search of a quick democratic fix, they stayed nineteen years and left the country not much better than they found it. It is still too early to be confident that the final outcome will be any different this time. In the mid-nineteenth century Sir Charles Napier was instrumental in eradicating suttee from Sind, but despite his willingness to hang the culprits he despaired of doing anything about the abuse of women and female infanticide. Although the methods are more discreet, it would be a brave person who could argue that either evil had been eradicated from the Indian subcontinent. These observations are not intended to ridicule all intervention in civil wars - it would be hard to deny that thousands of lives have been saved in former Yugoslavia - but they do point to the need for caution in attempts to democratize international society by this means.

Notes

1 The *Evening Standard*, 21 September 1994.
2 Brown, Chris, *International Relations Theory, New Normative Approaches* (London, Harvester Wheatsheaf, 1992).
3 Cowling, Maurice (ed.), *Conservative Essays* (London, Cassell, 1978), p. 16.
4 Huntington, Samuel, 'The clash of civilisations?', *Foreign Affairs*, **72**(3) (Summer 1993), pp. 22-49, and 'If not civilisations, what? Paradigms of the post-Cold War world', *Foreign Affairs*, **76**(5) (November-December 1993), pp. 186-94.
5 I have discussed the slow evolution of the principle of non-discrimination in international society in 'International Society and International Theory', in Donelan, Michael (ed.), *The Reason of States: A Study in International Political Theory* (London, George Allen & Unwin, 1978), pp. 122-41.
6 Between 2 August and 29 November the Security Council adopted twelve

resolutions under Chapter VII of the Charter on different aspects of the crisis. See Urquhart, Brian, 'The UN and international security after the Cold War', in Roberts, Adam and Kingsbury, Benedict (eds), *United Nations, Divided World* 2nd edn (Oxford, Clarendon Press, 1993), pp. 82–7.

7 'Non-intervention, self-determination and the "New World Order"', *International Affairs*, **67**(3) (July 1991), pp. 421–9.

8 Mill, J. S., 'A few words on non-intervention', *Dissertations and Discussions* (London, 1867), pp. 168–9.

9 See, for example, Block, Robert, 'The tragedy of Rwanda', *New York Review of Books*, 20 October 1994, pp. 3–8.

10 Security Council Resolution 770, 13 August 1992 and Resolution 794, 3 December 1992.

11 See Lewis, Ioan and Mayall, James, 'Somalia', in Mayall, James (ed.), *The New Interventionism: UN Experience in Cambodia, Former Yugoslavia and Somalia* (Cambridge, Cambridge University Press, 1996).

12 'Who can police the world?', *New York Review of Books*, 12 May 1994.

13 Mill, J. S,. 'A few words', p. 176.

9

Hedley Bull's *The Anarchical Society* Revisited: States or Polities in Global Politics?

YALE H. FERGUSON

The subject of 'international society' inevitably calls to mind the work of Hedley Bull, especially his masterwork, *The Anarchical Society.*[1] Others like Evan Luard[2] and John W. Burton[3] have written eloquently, thoughtfully and extensively about international society, but - perhaps partly because Luard adopted the perspective of historical sociology and Burton has concerned himself primarily with conflict resolution - Bull's contribution tends to be better known and more highly regarded. Bull was a major figure in contemporary international relations theory, mainly because *The Anarchical Society* was such an unusually important and influential book. That it is still widely read today on both sides of the Atlantic and around the world, nearly two decades after it appeared, is not something that one can report about many of its contemporaries or, indeed, predict for most of the volumes on international relations theory that continue to swell our library shelves.

Bull is very much with us yet and doubtless will be for many years to come. *The Anarchical Society* is deservedly famous, but it is far from obvious that the world of scholarship needs any further assessments of a book that has already been so widely reviewed. There has also been one significant retrospective collection of essays about the nature and impact of Bull's ideas.[4] And, of course, I am a theorist from the wrong side of the Atlantic.

Nevertheless, the English School of IR theory is wont to celebrate and periodically re-examine 'great books', and my rereading of Bull's modern classic convinced me not only that I had previously treated it a little unfairly but also that some of its most interesting implications have never been adequately explored. I have once again been reminded of the dangers of commenting upon a book based solely upon one's recollection of what it said. In a recent article, Richard W. Mansbach and I grouped Bull with other 'traditionalists' in the debates of the 1960s whom we suggested were 'as intolerant of competing visions as the then-upstart prophets of the scientific revolution because they were supremely confident of their own "tradition," which essentially was realism'. We continued: 'Even those venturesome traditionalists like Hedley Bull, who insisted that there was something worthwhile in the notion of 'international society' and thereby tapped into a competing nonrealist tradition, remained comfortable with the realist assumption that sovereign states are the building blocks of global society.[5]

Upon reflection, it was misleading to have implied guilt by association with realists, from whom Bull earnestly sought to distance himself.[6] The second statement was entirely correct and will be the focus of some of the discussion to follow, but it did not capture the fact that there is more to Bull's work than his vision of a society of states. John Vincent, another distinguished IR theorist who sadly, like Bull, died in his prime, put it well:

> [Bull's] intellectual legacy is simply that of one who has done fundamental work in his subject. On almost every page of *The Anarchical Society* it is possible to find a foundation on which further work could build ... [H]e was an excavator and foundation-builder: his superstructure was left for others. And his openness of mind makes him accessible to diverse approaches.[7]

James L. Richardson, in his own tribute to Bull, wrote: 'The best service to [his] memory is not to endorse his conclusions but to approach his work in the critical, but ultimately constructive, spirit which he brought to the subject.'[8] This is what I shall seek to do in the present essay.

The three Hedley Bulls

I shall argue that there are at least three different, major dimensions to Bull's work. The first dimension is that of a cautious, yet determined innovator who interposed his 'Grotian' or 'neo-Grotian' conception[9] of 'international society' squarely between the then-dominant Hobbesian or realist tradition and the tradition of Kantian universalism/cosmopolitanism/'revolutionism' or what realists like to term 'idealism.'[10] Bull assumed neither constant conflict in world politics nor a necessarily broad harmony of interests only waiting to be discovered, rather a limited but highly significant level of co-operation in the midst of 'anarchy' - in his memorable characterization, an 'anarchical society'. He asserted:

> A society of states (or international society) exists when a group of states, conscious of certain common interests and common values, form a society in the sense that they conceive themselves to be bound by a common set of rules in their relations with one another, and share in the working of common institutions.'[11]

In his view, the idea of international society - traceable in inspiration, if not in all its contemporary manifestations, to Grotius - was nothing less than 'one of the several paradigms in terms of which we have thought about international relations in modern times, and that, for better or worse, provides the constitutional principle in terms of which international relations are in fact conducted.'[12]

A second dimension of Bull's work was that it was also, in some respects, profoundly conservative. His was a militantly 'traditional' or 'classical' approach, which expressed itself in two main respects. One respect was methodological. In his best-known article on this subject, he lauded:

> the approach to theorizing that derives from philosophy, history, and law, and that is characterized above all by explicit reliance upon the exercise of judgment and by the assumptions that if we confine ourselves to strict standards of verification and proof there is very little of significance that can be said about international relations, that general propositions about this subject must therefore derive from a scientifically imperfect process of perception or intuition, and that these general propositions cannot be accorded anything more than the tentative and inconclusive status appropriate to their doubtful origin.[13]

The target at which he aimed this convoluted salvo was, of course, the self-styled 'scientists' or 'behavioralists' who in the late 1950s and 1960s appointed themselves leaders of a quest to transform the study of international relations into a scientific discipline similar to the natural sciences. This was the era when so many otherwise extremely sensible scholars found themselves afflicted with an acute case of physics envy. 'Models' were so much in fashion that, as Bull notes, the term came to be applied to mere analogies, and 'number crunchers' laboured their way through mountains of data to produce, at best, very modest results and more often the crudest of correlations.

Looking backward at the theoretical debates of the sixties from the vantage point of the present is instructive. That was a critical juncture in the development of IR theory, and Bull played a major role in keeping most British and Commonwealth scholars on the path of 'understanding', while what the postmodernists are fond of calling the big American car carried many a gifted theorist lumbering down a road that dead-ended in never-never land.[14] Martin Indyk observed:

> Bull managed to encapsulate all the reservations of the British school and its Australian offshoot to behavioural approaches. It was therefore easy for Australian academics to breathe a sigh of relief and get back, with clear consciences, to what they had been doing. Bull saved everybody else the trouble of taking the behaviouralists seriously.[15]

Roy E. Jones and others[16] have complained that the 'English School of International Relations', thus reassured of their own superiority, failed to engage in genuine dialogue and learn what they might have from the upstart American scientists. Perhaps so, but the scientists, too, were uninterested in dialogue. John Vincent used to say that British IR scholars are continually engaged in a trans-Atlantic tennis match, in which the Americans are always serving. Bull on that occasion helped the English School refuse to play under the proposed new rules, and I personally believe more was gained through preservation of a valuable classical tradition[17] than was lost to calcification and missed opportunities.

Today, as Richardson suggests, the IR field has moved on. He is correct that 'the behaviouralist school is far from vanquished, but lives on vigorously, retaining a prominent place in the leading American journals'.[18] Yet it is significant that many others who do not share their faith are also publishing in leading journals and that several leading journals[19] are *not* American. Whereas realism has proved amazingly resilient and adaptive – evolving into Waltztian neorealism,[20] power transitions,[21] and Keohanean institutionalism – an unqualified faith in science appears to be waning with the gradual passing of an earlier generation who failed to convince enough disciples to carry forward the crusade. However, even as we may soon miss the Cold War, we may soon be yearning for actual data-gatherers.[22] They seem to be losing pride of place to rational choice/game theorists, for whom the world exists solely as intellectual abstractions, a kind of modern-day idealism that would have astounded Woodrow Wilson.

One of the most recent challenges in IR theory has come from the postmodernists, whose attack on the scientific method and 'positivism' generally makes Bull's scepticism appear mild by comparison. Like the postmodernists and some more 'mainstream' theorists like myself and Mansbach,[23] Bull consistently denied that work in the field could or should be 'value-free', and this was one of his objections to the gospel preached by the true-believer scientists. However, Bull did not believe that work in the IR field could or should be entirely science-free in the sense of non-empirical or unsystematic. As Stanley Hoffmann notes, Bull's own scholarship 'is a blend of intelligent social science and humanism'.[24] Bull declared:

> What is important in an academic inquiry into politics is not to exclude value-laden premises, but to subject these premises to investigation and criticism . . . I believe in the value of attempting to be detached or disinterested, and it is clear to me that some approaches to the study of world politics are more detached or disinterested than others. I also believe that inquiry has its own morality.[25]

This position is a far cry from the almost complete relativism of the most extreme postmodernists. After all, Bull did describe his notion of international society as a 'paradigm'. There is at least some basis for an intersubjective 'understanding' of international politics or enough consensus to make for a meaningful debate as to the most convincing 'explanations' of phenomena mutually observed. This is less-demanding 'science', rather like what Hans J. Morgenthau meant when he claimed that realists had produced a 'science of politics', however deficient others of us might regard realist explanations.

Mention of Morgenthau and realism is entirely appropriate, for the other respect in which Bull's work is profoundly conservative is his views that international society is 'formed' by states, that states remain the only members of international society, and that whatever mitigation of anarchy exists derives exclusively from the common interests that states perceive in upholding certain rules and institutions. He distinguishes between an international society, where states share some elements of the same culture and civilization and therefore recognize some significant common interests and values; and an 'international system', where states regularly interact and affect one another's behaviour but do not recognize common interests and values and thus do not form a society. His example is the international society of the classical Greek city-states versus the international system that included the Greek city-states plus Persia and Carthage. He does acknowledge that there are borderline systems, 'where a sense of common interests is tentative and inchoate'.[26] Hoffmann comments that a missing element in Bull's work is a classification of different types of international society, based on the extent to which a common culture exists. However, in Bull's conception, either in an international society or an international system, states are the important members and the key consideration is the degree to which states recognize common interests.

I shall have much to say in due course about the deficiencies of this conception, but at this juncture it might be well to establish the relationship of Bull's international society to several other approaches. A Grotian link is evident in the importance Bull attached to common culture and norms, yet there is none of Grotius's belief that natural law helped to shape them. In fact, Bull's stress on states' recognition of common interests seems almost closer to that of legal positivists, not far from the narrow view of UK courts that recognizes no international legal obligations - for example, 'customary' rules - that have not been explicitly accepted by domestic political authorities. Although Bull was intrigued by their arguments, he firmly rejected Richard A. Falk's contention that the international community was moving from 'consent to consensus' as a means of establishing obligation in international law and the position of 'legal realists' like Myres S. McDougal that international law can be understood as the 'flow of decisions' about its content. Bull insisted that we had quite enough rules to which states had already assented, thank you, and there was no need to concern ourselves with any wider set of norms.[27]

Perhaps because Bull was put off by what he termed 'Falk's radical global salvationism', he dismissed these American international lawyers much like he did the scientists. He was surely correct about Falk's rather utopian policy prescriptions, but we will never know where Bull's analysis of the normative context of international society might have taken him had he been a little more receptive to some of their other ideas. Consider, for example, Falk's emphasis on the behaviour of states rather than the rules they accept formally: 'A horizontal norm is a descriptive proposition about what nations will probably do in the light of the interplay of event, interest, conscience, and rule; it is a predictive generalization that acts as a comprehensive ground rule for behaviour.'[28] Even more potentially suggestive was McDougal's description of 'a dynamic process in which decision-makers, located in many institutional positions and contexts, are continually creating, interpreting and reinterpreting rules'.[29] Following McDougal, when we wish to know 'what the law is', we must ask the question 'who are the relevant decision-makers?' The answer, he explained, involves considerations of both 'formal authority' and 'effective control' and inevitably leads us to examine the roles of a wide variety of actors.

There are also some similarities between Bull's international society and regime theory, which came into fashion not long after *The Anarchical Society*, despite the fact that Bull was never particularly interested in the problems of international political economy that inspired the regime theorists. John Ruggie introduced the concept of 'regime' in 1975, defining it as 'a set of mutual expectations, rules and regulations, plans, organizational energies and financial commitments, which have been accepted by a group of states'.[30] Donald J. Puchala and Raymond F. Hopkins went so far as to argue that 'a regime exists in every substantive issue-area in international relations where there is discernibly patterned behaviour'. They concluded that '[w]herever there is regularity in behaviour some kinds of principles, norms or rules must exist to account for it'.[31] Bull would not have approved of Puchala's and Hopkins' definition of regime, because of its reliance on behaviour rather than state voluntarism and formal rules. But he would not have quarrelled - except perhaps to ask 'So what else is new?' - with the insistence of Robert O. Keohane's 'institutionalism' that regimes certainly do not rest upon pie-in-the-sky idealism. Keohane wrote:

> [I]nternational institutions help to realize common interests in world politics. An argument for this view has been made here not by smuggling in cosmopolitan preferences under the rubric of 'world welfare' or 'global interests,' but by relying on Realist assumptions that states are egoistic, rational actors operating on the basis of their own conceptions of self-interest. Institutions are necessary ... in order to achieve *state* purposes.[32]

Bull and regime theorists thus were implicitly united regarding the irrelevance of such basic questions as to what extent actual or perceived interdependencies allow states the option of choosing whether they will or will not pursue co-operative strategies, do regimes impact upon states' interpretation of common interests, are some regimes themselves autonomous actors, and what are the true sources of 'state' policy (who or what is 'the state')? Subsequently, although Keohane and other institutionalists have not renounced their realist foundations, they have begun to acknowledge that state learning may take place as a result of experience with regimes and that domestic politics, too, has been an unfortunate 'blind spot' in their theories.[33] There is growing interest in what Robert D. Putnam has termed two-level games, in which domestic interests influence the conceptions of 'national interest' held by a state's decision-makers, while states in turn negotiate the evolution of international institutions.[34] In fact, what is opening up in the study of international relations generally is a much broader and more interesting question about actor/structure interrelationships on many different levels in world politics.[35] However, these sorts of theoretical issues appear not to have occurred to Bull any more than they did early on to regime theorists.

Bull may have been profoundly conservative in some respects, as we have discussed, but there is also a third dimension to his work that moved beyond innovative to venturesome or even radical insights. It is these insights that, to me, make *The Anarchical Society* not just a landmark on the long road to international theory, but a book to build on.

One major insight was Bull's recognition that the difference between 'international' and 'domestic' spheres was overrated in much of the traditional literature. He emphasized the order in the modern international system that resembles order within states, while, unfortunately (as we shall see), neglecting to consider the implications of the disorder within many states that resembles 'anarchy' in international relations. Bull pointed out some of the limitations of 'the domestic analogy, the argument from the experience of individual men in domestic society to the experience of states, according to which states, like individuals, are capable of orderly social life only if, as in Hobbes's phrase, they stand in awe of a common power'.[36] The international system, he insisted, is 'anarchic' only in that its member states do not recognize a common government, and anarchy in this limited sense does not mean that a Hobbesian state of nature always prevails. Indeed, he suggested, Locke's vision of a relatively orderly 'society' without government may often offer a better overall description of day-to-day relations among states.[37] In the last analysis, for Bull, the nature of the international system depends upon the time-frame, regional sub-systems, issues, and decision-maker personalities involved. He wrote: 'In different historical phases of the states system, in different geographical theatres of its operation, and in the policies of different states and statesmen, one of these three [Hobbesian,

Kantian, Grotian] elements may predominate over the others.'[38] This characterization is obviously far from classical realism's simplistic description of international relations as a struggle for power!

Bull's characterization is much closer to more recent work by 'neo-liberals'/'neo-idealists' and 'constructivists'. He doubtless would approve neo-liberals'/neo-idealists' assertion that international organizations and international law are both increasingly significant, and (considering one of his possible scenarios for the future) he *might* now be willing to accept their suggestion that state control is seriously being undermined by the likes of transnationalism, breakaway ethnicities, or other divisions within civil society.[39] As for the constructivists, he would recognize Alexander Wendt's statement that 'Anarchy is what states make of it'[40] as being very nearly what *The Anarchical Society* was all about, and find persuasive Friedrich V. Kratochwil's position that rules and norms play a major role as virtual system structures, through their influence on the reasoning of decision-makers, in 'defining the game of international relations'.[41] Given Bull's negative reaction to the more permissive legal realists, he would especially applaud Kratochwil's insistence that 'explicit rules' are 'necessary in cases in which the interacting parties do not share a common history or culture' or whenever there may be ambiguity of interpretation or practice.

Another aspect of Bull's work - more potentially than actually radical, because he never adequately followed it up - stemmed from his recognition that there is more to world politics than 'international society', that students of the subject must also consider the full implications of the existence of a wider 'international system' and broader patterns of 'world order'. He asserted:

> [S]tates are simply groupings of men, and men may be grouped in such a way that they do not form states at all. Moreover where they are grouped into states, they are grouped in other ways also. Underlying the questions we raise about order among states there are deeper questions, of more enduring importance, about order in the great society of all mankind.[42]

What is the range of such groups, we might ask, and how are they interrelated horizontally and vertically in world politics? How do their particular domains affect 'order in the great society of all mankind'? Queries like these raise issues of 'global governance' that are currently in the IR theory spotlight. Bull always disdained what a colleague of mine likes to refer to as 'globaloney', but surely he would have been pleased to see the recent founding of a journal on *Global Governance: A Review of Multilateralism and International Organizations* (and might well have served on the editorial board). Yet James N. Rosenau's article in the first issue of that journal,[43] as well as Rosenau's and Ernst-Otto Czempiel's collection on

Governance Without Governments: Order and Change in World Politics,[44] advance notions of 'governance' that are much less state-centric than anything Bull ever seriously addressed.

Unfortunately, Bull himself gave his primary attention, not to the 'deeper questions' he identified, but to his international society of states, because he believed that he was thereby getting at most of what was significant anyway. Unlike many theorists, he expanded the concept of 'state' to embrace such entities as the Greek city-states, so that studying 'international society' could include such regional historical examples as ancient Greece, the Hellenistic kingdoms, China during the Period of Warring States, and ancient India.[45] However, in the modern period, 'international society' became more all-inclusive, when Europe spread its states-system and the norms that sustained it all over the globe. In Bull's words, 'the political structure to which these developments gave rise was one simply of a global system and society of states'. 'Order on a global scale has ceased to be simply the sum of the various political systems that produce order on a local scale; it is also the product of what may be called a world political system.'[46]

Bull was slightly interested in what he labelled 'primitive stateless societies', but his Eurocentric bias seemed to lead him to believe that most of these had been eliminated by the conquering Europeans, and that they in any event lacked 'government' and were therefore not part of the study of 'international relations'. As he expressed it:

> In parts of Africa, Australia, and Oceania, before the European intrusion, there were independent political communities held together by ties of lineage or kinship, in which there was no such institution as government. Entities such as these fall outside the purview of 'international relations', if by this we mean (as we generally do) not the relations of nations but the relations of states in the strict sense. The relations of these independent political communities might be encompassed in a wider theory of the relations of *powers*, in which the relations of states would figure as a special case, but lie outside the domain of 'international relations' in the strict sense.[47]

Bull's last sentence about a 'wider theory,' I submit, pointed up a line of inquiry he should have explored more fully but, regrettably, did not.

Moreover, Bull's further discussion of such 'primitive stateless societies'[48] betrays a lack of in-depth knowledge and consequent tendency to stereotype them as much as he does modern states. For instance, he suggests that the political leaders of such societies 'do not have any … exclusive rights in relation to the persons that make them up' comparable to state sovereignty.[49] Yet the demands that some 'primitive' societies assert can be formidable, and the governments of some modern states are far less secure and authoritative. He contends that non-state societies 'usually have a less clearly defined relationship to territory', which is generally true only if one means borders laid out on a map. Territoriality has been an important feature of most polities since the dawn of time. In addition, Bull maintains that the societies in question are somehow different because they rest on a culture that is not only homogeneous but also includes 'the element of magical or religious belief'. To be sure, modern culture has become somewhat more secular and less superstitious, but belief in a political ideology - even the state itself, for traditional Marxists, Nazis, or realists - can approach devotion.[50] Moreover, religion itself is still a leading source of personal identity, closely associated with national identity in places like Poland and Iran, and a major factor in world politics. Finally, Bull points to the disparity in size between international society and primitive stateless societies. He might have emphasized similar contrasts among today's states, let alone disparities between some states and the political subdivisions of other states. For example, compare the territory and economy of Texas with most developing-world states - or the financial resources of many of the latter, with major globalized firms and banks.

Be that as it may, Bull was radical enough to think seriously and write provocatively in Part 3 of *The Anarchical Society* about possible 'Alternative paths to world order.' He examined whether the 'Contemporary states system' was experiencing 'decline' or 'obsolescence' and what the 'alternatives' might be. In this exercise his European blinkers - by providing the historical example of the Middle Ages - had some utility.

Bull grouped his alternatives into five general categories. A 'system but not a society', might develop if East-West and North-South ideological cleavages grew so severe that few common norms and interests could be perceived. 'States but not a system' might result if world technological civilization were somehow to collapse - presumably because of war, resource scarcity, environmental disaster, or other calamity - and states were to be isolated from one another. Although 'world government' seemed particularly unlikely, it could conceivably develop through agreement or conquest. And, of course, some unprecedented and therefore completely unpredictable 'non-historical alternative' might emerge.[51]

However, Bull gave most of his attention to what he termed 'a new mediaevalism' that he viewed as the most plausible alternative in the foreseeable future. Comparison of the late-twentieth-century world with the Middle Ages is commonplace today (e.g. in a recent BBC television series), but not when Bull was writing. In his assessment, several trends in world politics provide '*prima facie* evidence' of 'a secular reincarnation of the system of overlapping or segmented authority that characterized mediaeval Christianity'. These trends include the regional integration of states, the internal disintegration of states owing to nationalist secessionist pressures, terrorism and other forms of non-state or private international violence, the growing presence of transnational organizations like multinational corporations and international non-governmental associations, and the technological 'shrinking' of the globe.[52] At a minimum, Bull wrote, 'there is now a wider world political system of which the state system is only part,' that is, a 'world-wide network of interaction that embraces not only states but also other political actors, both "above" the state and "below" it'. Within states, political groups 'do not simply affect world politics through the influence they may have on their own state's foreign policy' but also enter into direct relations with foreign states, international organizations, and political groups in other states.[53] Daring stuff!

At this point, I submit, Bull had tapped into a vein of analytical gold that was not unrelated to the possibility of a 'wider theory' he had mentioned casually in connection with 'primitive stateless societies'. He was thus at the brink of exciting theoretical advance when his fundamental conservatism pulled him back into orthodoxy. '[I]t would be going beyond the evidence', he concludes, to hold 'that "groups other then the state" have made such inroads on the sovereignty of states that the state system is now giving way to this alternative.'[54]

In support of this conclusion, he advances several arguments that range from persuasive to astonishingly lame. He makes a good point, drawing on Raymond Aron, that high levels of interdependence or 'transnational society' are not a new phenomenon in world history and certainly existed in Europe prior to 1914 without threatening state sovereignty.[55] Fairly convincing is his contention that states have succeeded in regulating many activities of multinational corporations, although, of course, this ignores a growing range of inadequately regulated multinational and other private-sector activities that have grave implications for the welfare of states.[56] Positively silly are his final assessments of the implications of contemporary integration in Europe and of nationalist challenges to established states. A fully integrated European Community would just be 'a European super-state' or 'simply a nation-state writ large', while anything short of full integration would only produce some sort of regional 'hybrid entity' that would not necessarily threaten the concept of state sovereignty elsewhere in the world. Nor should we worry about nationalist upheavals, as long as the intention of breakaway movements is to form new sovereign states.[57] What an amazing preoccupation with form over substance! Instead of fretting that nothing in his international-society-of-states framework has anything to tell us about the most dynamic features of world politics in our time, Bull is most concerned about preserving the idea of sovereignty.

An international society of states?

In sum, as I view it, Bull's notion of an international society of states is far too restrictive to serve as a model for world politics and is even ultimately unsatisfactory on its own limited terms. States *qua* states are not actors in international relations; and sovereignty is little more than a legal concept of state autonomy that never was and never will be realized in practice to any significant degree. To be sure, realism is a parsimonious model, but it is largely wrong. Realists in the classic tradition and modern-day neo-realists, no less than the strict scientists, have found their own dead-end road to never-never land.

Mansbach and I have argued elsewhere,[58] the realist/neo-realist, normative/legal conception of an international society of sovereign states presents only about as accurate a vision of the 'real world' as a Hollywood western stage-set built in the desert does of the old American West. The façade is reasonably authentic, yet behind it is a vast landscape of hot air. It is not *entirely* a fiction, but it is *primarily* a fiction, that is, no more than *pseudo-realism*.

Let me, then, begin by establishing the degree to which the stage-set is a true picture. *To what extent* does the sovereign state actually 'exist' and/or contribute as a concept to our understanding?

Some would maintain that the state is a symbol which many persons around the world would give their lives to defend and advance. Such analysts have been seeing too many films on the Third Reich or reading musty Marxist tomes – and misinterpreting them at that. Hitler's appeal was that of German ethnic nationalism (and relief from interwar value deprivation), and Marxism's appeal was a promise of socialist equality. The state is a means to other ends, not an end in itself. Loyalty to the state has always been contingent upon its delivering on its promises and often, as well, upon its capacity to associate itself with other identities. Today, almost no one 'heils' the state *qua* state any more, except some political scientists and a few beleaguered European socialists.

All individuals have multiple identities and associations, and loyalty to the state usually comes far down the list of priorities – if it is even on the list. Individuals tend to care about their own welfare, their families and friends and property, their business firm or labour union, and such things as clan, village, tribe, town, city, ethnic group, religion, political party, or political ideology. Concerns like these everywhere constrain government policies and can be downright subversive or dangerous. Few governments rule mainly through coercion, and the most successful ones do not have to. Citizens[59] obey because they believe they are getting worthwhile things in exchange, including material and/or psychological benefits inherent in group identity. Locke's notion of governmental contract is thus not far from the mark.

Fear of Soviet military repression is part of the explanation for why the USSR held together as long as it did, yet this is far from the whole story. Most Ukrainians, for example, were reasonably content with their material lot, felt some pride at being an integral part of the Soviet superpower, and were allowed to express their ethnicity in folk dances and other ways deemed harmless to the Soviet state. They therefore were willing to suppress their nationalism and Greek Orthodox Catholicism. However, Ukrainians rebelled when the gap between Soviet ideology and practice became too great, Gorbachev's 'New Thinking' provided an opening, and the USSR's empire began to collapse. Where, oh realists, is the Soviet state and all its power capabilities today? In a fundamental sense, it lost its *raison d'état.*

That observation about the Soviet state presents a logical bridge to another argument advanced primarily by historical sociologists like Michael Mann,[60] that the state represents a concentration of power at the centre. How impressive are the government buildings, the extensive bureaucracies, the military on parade, the intelligence and police networks, and above all the tax revenues at the state's disposal! All this is to some extent genuine. Nevertheless, when one's looks closer, a true 'centre' is just as elusive as the state itself.

For starters, states *qua* states are not actors in politics at any level. Governments act in the name of the state, but they not only do not speak for all citizens but also are themselves far from unified actors. Who decides who will pay what taxes and how the accumulated revenues will be spent - or, for that matter, any governmental policy at all? Ask any scholar focusing on policy analysis, with whom IR theorists should have regular conversations, just how complicated and contingent the process from agenda-setting through implementation stages can be.

Part of the factionalization in the policy-making process stems from the activities of legislatures, which are growing in prominence and assertiveness around the world. Moreover, the very expansion of bureaucracy at the centre that statist theorists regard as so important makes unified governmental action - sometimes, it appears almost any effective action at all - much more difficult to achieve. Citizens the world over despise bureaucrats, sometimes for good reason. They tend to advance their own perceptions or parochial interests wrapped in the flag of the 'national interest', so that the substance of 'state' policy often consists of little more than the 'win' of one bureaucracy over another or a least-common-denominator compromise among several bureaucracies. And we still haven't factored in political parties or the influence of non-governmental political interest groups, lobbying in legislative corridors and clustering like barnacles around particular bureaucracies. Cabinet governments like that of the United Kingdom perhaps come closest to the pole of unity, but they, too, can be deeply divided, with ministers and prime ministers close to resignation, and government leaders and much of parliament at loggerheads on important issues like the ratification of the Maastricht Treaty.

This brings us to the degree of control exercised by the state. Like that of state, the concept of sovereignty is vastly overrated. We always seem to be discussing arcane matters like whether sovereign is absolute or can be divided, when much more important questions are to what extent do particular polities exercise effective rule over what issue domains, and why? No government enjoys the degree of autonomy and control that the sovereignty concept implies. Bull remarks:

> [S]tates *assert* the right to supremacy over authorities within their territory and population and independence of authorities outside it; but, on the other hand, they also exercise, *in varying degrees*, such supremacy and independence in practice. An independent political community which merely claims a right to sovereignty ... but cannot assert this right in practice, is not a state properly called. (emphasis added)[61]

His hedging somewhat on this score suggests that he was not entirely unaware that the sovereign might have no clothes or only tattered garments. In fact, I agree entirely with his second sentence. How many 'states' in the world can fully live up to the standard?

Few governments can even exercise control over themselves. They are routinely challenged by malaise, insubordination, and corruption in their own administrative bosoms. The military establishment is often more of an internal threat than a safeguard against foreign attack. The vehicles paraded in Red Square seemed rather less patriotic when they encircled civilian leadership in a coup attempt. Every *aficionado* of the idea that the military contributes to power at the centre should also consult with generations of Latin American civilian politicians - not to mention Africans or the current leaders in China. The selfsame military that put down the student demonstration in Tienanmen Square may one day overthrow party rulers or even, should China fragment along traditional provincial lines, transform itself into private armies backing regional warlords.

Yet central governments are models of coherence alongside of entire states. In many countries significant authority and control must be shared with regional and local governments, and all sorts of federal and confederal experiments seem to be the wave of the future in the former Soviet empire. Then there is the vast private sector to consider. Private-sector resources dwarf those in government coffers, except in socialist states, which are privatizing as fast as possible because of their governments' proven inability to manage the resources they had. In by far the majority of states in the world, the government has little idea what resources the private sector owns and is producing, let alone how to go about taxing those resources effectively. In Italy, for example, most of what honest entrepreneurs produce goes undocumented - which is the main reason EU statisticians have never been able to decide how the size of Italy's economy ranks among its peers - and nearly everything else is controlled by organized crime. Criminal networks like the Mafia and Colombian druglords prosper within what are sometimes, almost literally, states within a state - or, more accurately, transnational organizations - because they are able to offer their adherents a great deal more than the governments they defy and corrupt. If these challenges were not enough, governments must also often contend with separatist movements, ethnic and tribal conflicts, guerrilla bands, terrorist bombings, religious fundamentalists, and militant citizens demonstrating 'people power' in the streets. Governments may claim, with Weber, that theirs is the only legitimate exercise of violence, but that view clearly is not shared by significant sectors of the population.

Because of such pressures, the boundaries of not a few sovereign states today are being rearranged, so to speak, from the inside. As for the external side of sovereignty, widely accepted legal independence and boundaries are still significant, although, again, the question is to what extent? Most state members of international society favour maintaining the status quo in boundaries, because they are keenly aware of how illogical many boundaries (perhaps their own) are; once the rearranging starts, where does it stop?[62] The response to Saddam's attempt to annex Kuwait appears to suggest that it remains unacceptable to violate a boundary with military force from outside. Of course, the oil dimension makes it difficult to generalize from the Gulf War. Query: would a similar reaction greet, for example, a Hungarian intervention to protect persons of Hungarian ethnicity in greater Serbia? Be that as it may, most states have at least a limited capacity to defend their boundaries militarily. Boundaries also continue to act as something of a barrier to unwanted immigration and trade, and they define an area of legal jurisdiction that a government can attempt to enforce. Finally, being a recognized sovereign state is normally required to be a member of an international governmental organization.

However, let us not confuse formal independence and boundaries on a map with a state's having genuine autonomy in the international system - any more than, as we have seen, they denote the existence of unified state actors. Trade protectionists in the United States have had little more success countering fundamental trends in the global economy than the authors of stricter immigration laws did in curbing the flow of illegal immigrants from Mexico. Not for nothing is migration, legal and illegal, currently one of the hottest topics in international studies. European governments, Mexico and even the United States similarly find their national currencies at the mercy of a booming international financial market. Also in Europe, decisions are now made within the EU over many matters that traditionally were in the exclusive province of member governments. Neo-realists will stress that the states involved 'voluntarily' surrendered sovereign rights in stages and still retain important areas of domestic jurisdiction, but surely equally or more significant is the fact that control over some key issues and patterns of decision-making have gradually been transformed. Nor should we take at face value the voluntary nature of the surrenders that have occurred, for it is by no means clear that individual countries can afford to opt out, for long, when others are willing to proceed without them.

If anything, the challenges to state autonomy and control are rapidly increasing in the present exceptionally 'turbulent' or 'postinternational' era (Rosenau's terms) in world politics.[63] However, it is important to see events since 1989 as merely the surfacing of long-range trends. In 1974, Burton had a clearer grasp than Bull of what was happening on a number of different levels in world society:

> There has been an erosion of authority of central governments because they cannot contain revisionist minority movements which win support in the wider world society. Central authorities have failed to deal effectively with the complex problems of inflation, unemployment, housing and education. Major industrial societies are moving toward forms of government that are sub-system dominant, many of the sub-systems being international. The life of the ordinary person - whether or not he has adequate education for his children, what is the real value of his savings, whether his particular job is secure and whether he has the prospect of a job - is largely determined by decisions taken outside his national environment, and frequently at a non-governmental level. The role and nature of government is altering, away from defensive postures toward assisting adjustment to change.[64]

Startlingly contemporary as Burton's description seems, the world has become only 'more so' in recent years. There has been a steady growth in the number and significance of international organizations and regimes. Yet the members of most IGOs, by definition, are states, while the world itself is increasingly being (re)organized in other ways. NGOs and INGOs are assuming an ever more prominent role and may be more effective in delivering such goods as education for democracy and famine relief. The elevation of economic issues to 'high politics' has highlighted both the relative autonomy of many transnational firms and banks and the globalization of the world economy generally. Financial flows from trade, bank lending, currency speculation, and foreign investment have reached record proportions. It has always been difficult in some countries to draw a clear distinction between public and private sectors, but now, with investment and component parts from around the world, it is hard even to identify the national origin of products. Alliances among firms seem as salient as, and certainly more productive than, alliances among governments. The technological shrinking of the globe noted by Bull has accelerated, with a veritable revolution in communications and information. Those citizens around the world who have the skills and equipment to 'plug in' to this revolution are increasingly difficult for governments to govern, and those citizens who do not are beyond the capacity of most governments to help.

Developments that cross boundaries and overarch states are having a decided impact *within* them, as such astute commentators as Rosenau, Luard and Mark W. Zacher remind us. Zacher speaks of 'the decaying pillars of the Westphalian temple',[65] Rosenau perceives a shift in loyalties, and Luard declares:

> Politics has been globalized in part because inexorable technological change has had the effect that national endeavours are no longer adequate to achieve the goals which are everywhere demanded. ... But political action is globalized also because, with the decline in distance, the goals themselves are transformed. A new political vision is created. Citizens are no longer content with the narrow and distorting aspirations created by parochial national political systems. ... They know, and know increasingly, that they live on a small, and still shrinking, planet. They will not any longer obediently confine their responsibilities, and their concern, to conform with the lines that have been drawn at random across the atlas. On a planet so small they no longer have any choice but to be citizens of the world as a whole.[66]

Luard waxed a little too lyrical, but it is undeniable that macro-level developments are having a dramatic micro-level impact. The ideologies of political democracy and market capitalism have swept the world, albeit with widely varying results. There has been a momentous resurgence of ethnic identity and mini-nationalisms. Ironically, largeness has encouraged smallness; economic and political integration, fragmentation. (Rosenau, inelegantly but accurately, combines the overall divergent processes into 'fragmegration'.) National self-determination as a goal seems more than ever within reach, not only because others are demanding it too, but also because of the growth of the European Union, as well as a free trade area in North America; the revitalization of the United Nations and existence of numerous other international organizations and regimes; the proliferation of NGOs and INGOs; and the vast resources of transnational corporations, banks, and other institutions in the global marketplace. Breakaway ethnicities and other sub-groups no longer see the need to maintain old ties that bind, when they appear to have a host of potential new relationships to replace them.

Polities in global politics

However confident he was of his own conception of international society, Bull was not close-minded. He wrote:

> The classical theory has held sway not because it can account by itself for all the complexity of universal politics, but because it has provided a truer guide to it than alternative visions such as that of an imperial system or cosmopolitan society. A time may come when the anomalies and irregularities are so glaring that an alternative theory, better able to take account of these realities, will come to dominate the field. If some of the trends towards a 'new mediaevalism' that have been reviewed here were to go much further, such a situation might come about.[67]

I submit that the time for an alternative theory that Bull almost seemed to foresee has arrived - and is actually long overdue.

At the end of the day, Bull's conception of international society is far too narrow because the only significant members are states who share certain goals and a common European diplomatic culture. He failed even to appreciate the full significance of 'the expansion of international society' that the collection he edited with Watson spotlighted. Europe only partially succeeded in homogenizing world culture; in other respects, the introduction of European ideas and forms around the globe made matters extraordinarily more complex.[68] The colonies eventually inherited the form of the European state without the substance. Successor governments were weak reflections of their European parents, and the main identities continued to be tribal, ethnic, and/or religious.

The central problem lies with a definition of 'international society' that allows for only one important polity type, the state, and only those values derived from European diplomatic culture that state polities hold in common. By contrast, any but the simplest actual societies have numerous significant groups, and the contest between values held in common and those in dispute - not to mention the policies to implement shared values - are the very stuff of politics. I see no reason why our understanding of international society cannot be expanded to include a more 'pluralistic' conception of political actors, the values they control or advance, and the ideological and other foundations of political authority. If not, then we must return to the more analytically neutral notion of an 'international system' or 'world political system' with various 'open' (i.e., non-discrete, interlocking) sub-systems.

However we accomplish it, we have to recognize that the 'interstate' and 'intrastate' political arenas enshrined in the classical tradition are actually a single arena that encompasses countless individuals as well as layered, overlapping, and interacting political authorities. These polities, in turn, are variously engaged in many, often interrelated, issues. In this perspective, there is no 'international politics' or 'domestic politics' – there is only 'politics', and that is the subject we should be studying.

The POLITIES project[69] that Mansbach and I have been engaged in for some years uses as organizing concepts 'polities' or 'authorities', the human identities and loyalties that uphold or undermine them, and the ideologies that help to legitimate particular relationships. In our definition, each 'polity' has a measure of identity, a degree of institutionalization and hierarchy (leaders and followers), and the capacity to mobilize persons and other resources for political purposes (that is, for value satisfaction or relief from value deprivation). As we see it, at any given time, the world is composed of innumerable polities of different types: families, tribes, cities, firms, IGOs, INGOs, and so on. Each polity type is just an ideal type, encompassing a wide range of actual forms. The Westphalian state is merely one type of polity, distinguishable solely by its peculiar legal status. Is there a global or world polity? Yes, to the extent (and only to the extent) that entities like the UN and regimes like the WTO have identity, institutionalization and hierarchy, and capacity to mobilize persons and other resources. Anything else is globaloney.

The domain of a polity consists of the persons who identify with it, the resources it can command, and the 'reach' it therefore has with respect to territory, space in a broader sense (e.g., markets), and issues. Polities typically share some or all of the same political space, that is, physical space and/or influence over some or all of the same issues. Political space should be viewed both horizontally and vertically. Seen in these perspectives, the 'structure' of any system is considerably more complex than neo-realist reductionist models like bipolar or multipolar, based on a supposed distribution of capabilities, might suggest. Polities may expand horizontally and thereby encounter and sometimes incorporate other polities, which more often become 'nested' rather than disappear entirely. Virtually all polities must contend with others within its domain.

Rosenau appears to have been thinking along somewhat similar lines when he suggests:

> [W]ith the globe becoming smaller and more interdependent, with causal flows cascading among and within collectivities in crazy-quilt patterns ... we can break free by conceiving of humanity, not as a collection of countries or relations among states, but as congeries of authority relationships, some of which are coterminous with countries and states and others of which are located within or extend beyond state boundaries.[70]

Most IR theorists have been reluctant to attribute authority to anything but states, because, to such theorists, authority implies legitimacy and the only legitimate authorities in the restrictive legal/normative framework recognized by realists are states. However, Rosenau is again correct: It is essential to '[r]ecognize that what makes actors effective in world politics derives not from the sovereignty they possess or the legal privileges thereby accorded them, but rather lies in relational phenomena, in the authority they can command and the compliance they can thereby elicit.'[71] Mansbach and I regard all polities as authorities that 'govern' within their respective domains. Governance thus does not necessarily require 'governments' in the Westphalian state sense. 'Authority' is effective control or significant influence within a domain, and it should be stressed that authority need not be exclusive and, in fact, is often shared. Nor need authority be legitimate, although authority that is widely regarded as legitimate is inherently more secure. Law is only one source of legitimacy.

We argue that among the most important questions confronting all students of politics are the following: What are the polities involved, what is the scope of their respective domains, and how do we explain the authority patterns observed? Politics typically involves relationships of co-existence, co-operation, and conflict among different types of polities. Also, most actual polities are always changing, sometimes coming from or moving toward another polity type, although political evolution is not necessarily unilinear. Accordingly, another key question is how and why do polities change? How and why do they expand and incorporate other polities, fragment, and expire - and why do polities sometimes reappear in whole or in part? Part of the explanation for the latter is obviously the fact that old identities and loyalties often linger on long after the demise or eclipse of the polities originally associated with them.

This essay is clearly not the place to discuss the POLITIES project in further detail. I hope I have at least said enough to demonstrate that there are other ways of looking at the world, outside of the classical tradition, that may explain more of the things we urgently need to understand. It is regrettable, indeed, that Hedley Bull can no longer participate in the discussion. Who knows how his thinking might have continued to evolve, not least in response to all the momentous developments in the world since 1989?

In any event, let us close with yet another reference to *The Anarchical Society*. Bull told the familiar story of a man who was lost somewhere in Scotland and asked a farmer how to get to Edinburgh. The farmer is supposed to have replied: 'Oh sir, if I were you, I shouldn't start from here.' Wrote Bull: 'The fact is that the form of universal political organization which actually prevails in the world is that of the states system, and it is within this system that the search for consensus has to begin.'[72] My position in this essay is that the farmer offered sage advice. Whether one is looking to contribute either to world order or progress in IR theory, I should not start from an international society of sovereign states. One cannot get to Edinburgh or anywhere else, except never-never land, from there. Rather, let us explore the great variety of polities engaged in global politics. That is the road to true understanding, and we should start our journey along it without further delay.

Notes

1 Bull, H., *The Anarchical Society: A Study of Order in World Politics* (London, Macmillan, 1977).

2 See especially the following by Luard, E., *Types of International Society* (London, Macmillan, 1977); *Economic Relationships Among States* (London, Macmillan, 1984); *War in International Society* (London, I. B. Tauris, 1986); and *International Society* (London, Macmillan, 1990). The last book is a summary of the other three.

3 cf. Burton, J. W., *Systems, States, Diplomacy and Rules* (Cambridge, Cambridge University Press, 1968) and *World Society* (Cambridge, Cambridge University Press, 1972).

4 Miller, J. D. B. and Vincent, R. J. (eds), *Order and Violence: Hedley Bull and International Relations* (Oxford, Clarendon Press, 1990).

5 Ferguson, Y. H. and Mansbach, R. W., 'Between celebration and despair: constructive suggestions for future international theory', *International Studies Quarterly*, **35**(4) (1991), p. 369.

6 I am grateful to Hidemi Suganami for having set me straight on this score.

7 Vincent, R. J., 'Order in international politics', in Miller and Vincent (eds), *Order and Violence*, p. 63.

8 Richardson, J. L., 'The academic study of international relations', in Miller and Vincent (eds), *Order and Violence*, p. 185.

9 cf. Bull, H., 'The importance of Grotius in the study of international relations', in Bull, H., Kingsbury, B. and Roberts, A. (eds), *Hugo Grotius and International Relations* (Oxford, Clarendon Press, 1990), pp. 65–93. This entire volume is an excellent compendium and assessment of Grotian thought. See also especially Bull, H., 'The Grotian conception of international society', in Butterfield, H. and Wight, M. (eds), *Diplomatic Investigations: Essays in the Theory of International Politics* (London, George Allen & Unwin, 1967), pp 51–73; and Cutler, A. C., 'The "Grotian tradition" in international relations theory: a critique', *Review of International Studies*, **17**(1) (1991), pp. 41–65.

10 Bull, *The Anarchical Society*, pp. 24–7.

11 Ibid., p. 13.

12 Bull, 'The importance of Grotius', p. 93.

13 Bull, H., 'International theory: the case for a classical approach', *World Politics*, **18**(3) (1966), p. 361.

14 See Puchala, D. J., 'Woe to the orphans of the scientific revolution', in Rothstein, R. L. (ed.), *The Evolution of Theory in International Relations* (Columbia, SC, University of South Carolina Press, 1992), pp. 39–60.

15 Indyk, M., 'The Australian study of international relations', in Aitken, D. (ed.), *Surveys of Australian Political Science* (Sydney, George Allen & Unwin, 1985), p. 276. Quotation and citation from Richardson, 'Academic study of international relations', p. 154.

16 Richardson cites Jones, R. E., 'The English School of international relations: a case for closure', *Review of International Studies*, **7** (1981), pp. 1–13; and Ogley, R. C., 'International relations: poetry, prescription or science?', *Millennium*, **10** (1981), pp. 170–85.

17 For a discussion of this tradition, see Suganami, H., 'The structure of institutionalism: an anatomy of British mainstream international relations', *International Relations*, **7**(2) (1983).

18 Richardson, 'Academic study of international relations', p. 155.

19 For example, *Review of International Studies*, *Millennium*, and the *European Journal of International Relations*.

20 cf. Waltz, K. N., 'Realist thought and neorealist theory', in Rothstein, *The Evolution of Theory in International Relations*, pp. 21–37.

21 cf. Doran, C. F., *Systems in Crisis: New Imperatives of High Politics at Century's End* (Cambridge, Cambridge University Press, 1991).

22 For a thoughtful assessment of the unexplored potentialities of a scientific approach, see Vasquez, J. A., 'The post-positivist debate: reconstructing scientific inquiry and IR theory after Enlightenment's fall', in Booth, K. and Smith, S. (eds), *International Political Theory Today* (Cambridge, Polity Press, 1995), pp. 217–40. Vasquez argues that empirical research has suffered mainly because it has proceeded from realist premises.

23 See especially Ferguson, Y. H. and Mansbach, R. W., *The Elusive Quest: Theory and International Politics* (Columbia, SC, University of South Carolina Press, 1988).

24 Hoffman, S., 'International society', in Miller and Vincent, *Order and Violence*, p. 18.

25 Bull, *The Anarchical Society*, xv. Compare Bull's stance with that of James N. Rosenau, a leading IR theorist on the other side of the 1960s' debates, who remains committed to the advancement of science and yet is increasingly cognizent of the limitations inherent in the application of the scientific method: 'Inevitably, therefore, science is not so much a value-free enterprise as a value-explicit one. It requires observers to be clear about their presence in the research, to acknowledge biases and idiosyncratic perspectives that may skew their interpretations. Most of all, it demands that observers alert their readers to the dangers of being taken in by the analysis, and remind them that what they are reading is not so much a detached view of the world as one analyst's perspective, with all the possibilities of distortion that may be involved. In this way, science insures that its findings can be checked and, if need be, revised or rejected.' This quotation from Rosenau, J. N., *Turbulence in World Politics: A Theory of Change and Continuity* (Princeton, NJ, Princeton University Press, 1990), p. 33.

26 Bull, *The Anarchical Society*, pp. 13–15.

27 See especially ibid., Ch. 6; and Bull, H., 'International law and international order', *International Organization*, **26**(3) (1972), pp. 583–8.

28 Falk, R. A., *Law, Morality, and War in the Contemporary World* (New York, Praeger, 1963), p. 78.

29 McDougal, M. S., 'International law, power and policy' in Academie de Droit International, *Reçueil des Cours*, **82** (1953), pp. 182-3.

30 Ruggie, J. G., 'International responses to technology: concepts and trends', *International Organization*, **29**(3) (1975), p. 570.

31 Puchala, D. J. and Hopkins, R. F., 'International regimes: lessons from inductive analysis', *International Organization*, **36**(2) (1982), p. 247.

32 Keohane, R. O., *After Hegemony* (Princeton, NJ, Princeton University Press, 1984), pp. 245-6.

33 Keohane, R. O., 'International institutions: two approaches', *International Studies Quarterly*, **32**(4) (1988), pp. 379-96. He makes a distinction between 'rationalistic' and 'reflective' approaches to regimes. The debate goes on. cf. Snidal, D., 'International cooperation among relative gains maximizers', *International Studies Quarterly*, **35**(4) (1991), pp. 387-402; Moravesik, A. 'Negotiating the Single European Act: national interests and conventional statecraft in the European Community', *International Organization*, **45**(1) (1991), pp. 19-56; and Strang, D., 'Anomaly and commonplace in European political expansion: realist and institutional accounts', *International Organization*, **45**(2) (1991), pp. 143-62.

34 Putnam, R. D., 'Diplomacy and domestic politics: the logic of two-level games', *International Organization*, **42**(3) (1988), pp. 427-60. See also Evans, P. B., Jacobson, H. K. and Putnam, R. D. (eds), *Double-Edged Diplomacy: International Bargaining and Domestic Politics* (Berkeley, CA, University of California Press, 1993).

35 'Structuration theory' is most clearly identified with the work of British sociologist Anthony Giddens. For a useful overview of his ideas, see Cohen, I., *Structuration Theory: Anthony Giddens and the Constitution of Social Life* (London, Macmillan, 1989). Also cf. Onuf, N. G., *World of Our Making: Rules and Rule in Social Theory and International Relations* (Columbia, SC, University of South Carolina Press, 1989); Wendt, A. E., 'The agent-structure problem in international relations theory', *International Organization*, **41**(3) (1987), pp. 335-70; Wendt, A. E., 'Levels of analysis versus agents and structures', *Review of International Studies* **18** (1992), pp. 181-5; and Carlsnaes, W., 'The agency-structure problem in foreign policy analysis', *International Studies Quarterly*, **36**(3) (1992), pp. 245-70.

36 Bull, *The Anarchical Society*, p. 46.

37 Ibid., p. 48.

38 Ibid., p. 41.

39 cf. Baldwin, D. A. (ed.), *Neorealism and Neoliberalism: The Contemporary Debate* (New York, Columbia University Press, 1993); Kegley Jr., C. W. (ed.), *Controversies in International Relations Theory: Realism and the Neoliberal Challenge* (New York, St Martin's, 1995); and Kegley Jr., C. W., 'The neoidealist moment in international studies? Realist myths and the new international realities', *International Studies Quarterly*, **37**(2) (1993), pp. 131-46. See also Powell, R., 'Anarchy in international relations theory: the neorealist-neoliberal debate', *International Organization*, **48**(2) (1994), pp. 313-44.

40 Wendt, A., 'Anarchy is what states make of it: the social construction of power politics', *International Organization*, **46**(2) (1992), pp. 391-425.

41 Kratochwil, F. V., *Rules, Norms and Decisions: On the Conditions of Practical and Legal Reasoning in International Relations and Domestic Affairs* (Cambridge, Cambridge University Press, 1989).

42 Bull, *The Anarchical Society*, p. 20.
43 Rosenau, J. N., 'Governance in the twenty-first century', *Global Governance*, **1**(1) (1995), pp. 13–43.
44 Rosenau J. N. and Czempiel, E. O. (eds), *Governance without Government: Order and Change in World Politics* (Cambridge, Cambridge University Press, 1992).
45 Bull, *The Anarchical Society*, pp. 15–16.
46 Ibid., pp. 20–1. See also the splendid collection of essays assembled by Bull, H. and Watson, A. (eds), *The Expansion of International Society* (Oxford, Clarendon Press, 1984). The editors commented in their 'Introduction': 'The present international structure of the world – founded upon the division of mankind and of the earth into separate states, the acceptance of one another's sovereignty, of principles of law regulating their co-existence and cooperation, and of diplomatic conventions facilitating their intercourse – is, at least in its most basic features, the legacy of Europe's now vanished ascendancy. Because it was in fact Europe and not America, Asia, or Africa that first dominated and, in so doing, unified the world, it is not our perspective but the historical record itself that can be called Eurocentric' (p. 2). Nonetheless, Adam Watson investigated a far longer historical record, much of which is not European, in his pioneering work *The Evolution of International Society: A Comparative Historical Analysis* (London, Routledge, 1992).
47 Bull, *The Anarchical Society*, p. 9.
48 Ibid., pp. 63–5.
49 In private correspondence with the author, Mary Bull explained that his interest here was primarily in a comparison of what anthropologists call 'tribes without rulers' – governed only by councils of elders with different areas of competence – with the workings of the international anarchical society.
50 However, Mary Bull is correct that no modern secular ideology holds that certain forbidden acts are offensive to the ancestors and will bring down such direct sanctions upon the perpetrator as the failure of crops or the death of children.
51 Bull, *The Anarchical Society*, pp. 248–64.
52 Ibid., pp. 264–76.
53 Ibid., pp. 276–7.
54 Ibid., p. 275.
55 Ibid., pp. 278–9
56 Ibid., pp. 271–3.
57 Ibid., pp. 264–8.
58 Ferguson and Mansbach, 'Between celebration and despair', p. 370. See also Ferguson, Y. H. and Mansbach, R. W., *The State, Conceptual Chaos, and the Future of International Relations Theory* (Boulder, CO, Lynne Reinner, 1989); and *The Elusive Quest*, Part II. The balance of this essay draws heavily upon the theoretical critique and research agenda discussed in 'Between celebration and despair' and other works in the POLITIES project cited later.
59 Even traditional dictatorships like those of Trujillo, Somoza, or Batista in Latin America had to provide adequate rewards for a ruling élite. Yet the middle and lower classes became increasingly politically active over time, with serious destabilizing results. Today, though there are still political élites, mass politics in one form or another is characteristic of most of the world.

60 cf. Mann, M., *The Sources of Social Power: A History of Power from the Beginning to A.D. 1760* (Cambridge, Cambridge University Press, 1986).

61 Bull, *The Anarchical Society*, pp. 8–9.

62 See Jackson, R. H., *Quasi-States: Sovereignty, International Relations and the Third World* (Cambridge, Cambridge University Press, 1990). Jackson explains that in Africa and elsewhere in the Third World a sort of 'negative sovereignty' prevails. Corrupt élites oppose changing boundaries that reflect former colonial administrative divisions, because the tribal nature of society makes almost any boundary highly artificial and élites have a personal stake in the status quo.

63 See Rosenau, J. N., *Turbulence in World Politics: The United Nations in a Turbulent World* (Boulder, CO, Lynne Rienner, 1992); and Rosenau, J. N. and Durfee, M., *Thinking Theory Thoroughly: Coherent Approaches to an Incoherent World* (Boulder, CO, Westview Press, 1995). See also especially Rosenau's 'Governance in the twenty-first century'; 'Powerful tendencies, startling discrepancies, and elusive dynamics: the challenge of studying world politics in a turbulent era', Harrison Lecture, University of Maryland, 1 December 1994 (ms); and 'Multilateral governance and the nation-state system: a post-Cold War assessment', paper for a Study Group of the Inter-American Dialogue, Washington, DC, April 1995 (ms).

64 Burton, J. *et al.*, *The Study of World Society: A London Perspective*, as reprinted in Vasquez, J. A. (ed.), *Classics of International Relations*, 2nd edn (Englewood Cliffs, NJ, Prentice-Hall, 1990), pp. 100–1.

65 Zacher, M. W. 'The decaying pillars of the Westphalian temple: implications for international order and governance', in Rosenau and Czempiel (eds), *Governance Without Governments*, pp. 58–101.

66 Luard, E., *The Globalization of Politics: The Changed Focus of Political Action in the Modern World* (London, Macmillan, 1990), p. 191. Luard's conception of world society appears to have become gradually less state-centric, although, of course, he always had a keen interest in international organization. Compare, for example, his stress on states and the lack of 'community' in *International Society* (especially pp. 1–10), a book published the same year as *The Globalization of Politics* but summarizing his earlier work.

67 Bull, *The Anarchical Society*, p. 275.

68 The two final essays (by Bozeman, A. and Dore, R.) in Bull and Watson (eds), *The Expansion of International Society*, argue the cases for multiculturalism and unity, respectively. Both positions are essentially correct, depending upon what features of world politics and especially which polities one wishes to emphasize. It should also be noted that Bull was planning another book, based on his Oxford lectures on 'the revolt against Western dominance', that would have explored the development of non-western ideas about the organization of international society.

69 An initial discussion of the POLITIES perspective appeared in Ferguson and Mansbach, 'Between celebration and despair'. See also Ferguson, Y. H. and Mansbach, R. W., *Polities: Authority, Identities, and Change* (Columbia, SC, University of South Carolina Press, 1996); 'The past as prelude to the future: changing loyalties in global politics', in Lapid, Y. and Kratochwil, F. (eds), *The Return of Culture and Identity in IR Theory* (Boulder, CO, Lynne Rienner, 1996); and 'Beyond inside/outside: political space in a world of polities', *Global*

Governance, **2**(2) (1996), pp. 261–87. In addition, see Ferguson, Y. H., *Ancient Regimes* (Cambridge, Cambridge University Press, forthcoming).

70 Rosenau, *Turbulence in World Politics*, p. 39.

71 Ibid., p. 40.

72 Bull, *The Anarchical Society*, pp. 295–6.

10

International Society, Cleavages and Issues

FULVIO ATTINÁ

In the last two decades, the function of rules and institutions as causes of conformity and regularity in the international system has been emphasized by scientists. To call attention to such regularity was the merit of Hedley Bull with his 'international society approach' to international politics and order. Bull's seminal book *The Anarchical Society*[1] had the effect of turning a small theoretical stream into the English School of international relations. Years after the publication of Bull's study, the neo-institutional approach was proposed by students of international relations in the United States. Without making reference to the English School, they stressed the importance of consented restraints on foreign policy; specifically, they focused on the role of regimes as factors limiting the international conduct of states. Both the international society approach and the neo-institutional approach are important steps forward in the theory and analysis of contemporary international politics. They point to factors inducing continuity and regularity not taken into consideration in classical theories of international relations. This makes these schools relevant and innovative explanations of international politics, but it does not impede us from calling attention to their weakness, especially in the definition and interpretation of change in international politics.

This essay is concerned with social and political factors of change that have been neglected in contemporary research on international relations, especially by the English School. In spite of the acknowledged importance of the social aspects of international relations, this School disregards social variables as relevant determinants of state actions and system characteristics. The aim of this essay is to present the obverse side of the English School approach. Bull was interested in the definition of the international society and, consequently, stressed the importance of factors inducing community and peaceful co-existence rather than separation and division. He disregarded the fact that, even in a single society, conflict is not only the product of the will of single actors but the result of social structures and cleavages. Factors of order and community must be considered together with factors of disorder and separation. The main contention, and a much neglected and even disputed aspect of international theory, is that in order to explain continuous change in the international system, it is necessary to take this combination of factors into consideration. The international society approach regards the rivalry of great powers as the only important cause of international change. The analysis of international change proposed in this essay, instead, underlines the importance of collective and concurrent actions taken by states placed on the opposite sides of social cleavages in the world. The present approach contrasts also with the American-born school of international regimes. Such an approach regards international change as the transformation caused by single governments or small groups of governments well equipped with resources specifically relevant to the regime undergoing a process of change; it disregards the importance of the expectations and actions of cleavage-ridden groups of states which favour the change of rules, procedures and institutions through which the political and economic issues of the international system are managed.

The concepts of organization and change of the international system are preliminarily defined in this essay. The concept of international cleavage is subsequently presented and three cleavages of contemporary international politics are analysed. Lastly, the influence of social cleavages on the change of the rules and institutions which organize the international system and determine the setting of the agenda of today's global politics is examined.

On organization and change in the international system

The organization of the international system is made up of rules and institutions which induce regularity and conformity in the actions and policies of states concerned with their reciprocal relations and with the allocation and use of goods, resources and values of the world system. Beside rules and institutions, the role played by some states in the formulation, conservation and transformation of rules and institutions is an important element of system organization. Organizational roles are held by states able to make new rules and create new institutions when an international system is reorganized. The role of constituting the organization of an international system has been usually exercised at the end of great or world wars by the victorious state(s). Today the situation is different; various kinds of states and groups of states influence the evolution of the international organization and play various and differently important organizational roles.

Classical theories of international relations focused on the rivalry of major powers as cause of change; they considered military means as the exclusive instrument for the control of the system. Contemporary states are complex social entities; their primary subjects - men and women - have different kinds of needs. To respond to individual and collective needs, governments cannot limit their international duties to preserve territorial security and political independence. They have to do much more. For that reason, the international system is regulated by rules and institutions made for organizing not only sovereignty and territory but different domains of goods, values and relations like finance, trade, communication, energy transportation, culture, human rights, and so on. For that reason, the change of the organization of the international system is the change of the major rules and institutions concerned with the most important goods and values of the system. Great powers are primary actors of such a change, but the evolution of the system organization is also a matter of competition involving large groups of states. More exactly, the change of the organization of the international system is the result of great power rivalry and of two kinds of related competitions: those arising from social cleavages and those arising from specific issues.

Rules and institutions

State systems are regulated by rules and institutions. Generally speaking, international rules are those principles, norms and conventions commonly observed by governments as guides to behaviour and actions in the system of international relations. Fundamental organizational rules - those determining the form of an organization in a definite time period - may be classified as social principles, international law norms and rules of the game or operational rules. *Social principles* prescribe the proper conduct for the preservation of the system and the plurality of its membership. Non-interference in domestic affairs and restriction in the use of violent means for the defence of national interests are examples of these principles. They are voluntarily and commonly observed by governments, but frequently the definition of compliance and violation depends on the subjective evaluation of concerned governments. The violation of social principles is sanctioned by moral reprobation, sometimes by political isolation and, according to favourable circumstances, by economic boycott and military acts. The inventory of the social principles of the international system can be made by the examination of solemn diplomatic declarations, the statutes of inter-governmental organizations (like the Preamble to the Charter of the United Nations) and specific parts of national written constitutions. New social principles have been recently introduced - for example, the principle of preserving the biosphere and the principle of collective disposal of global commons - while traditional principles have been given new attention and importance - for example, the principle of humanitarian intervention in the territory of another state and the principle of *ingérence* in domestic affairs for the sake of protecting human and people rights. New principles, generally enunciated in fundamental documents of multilateral conferences, collide with traditional principles. For example, humanitarian intervention and *ingérence* are in evident opposition with the traditional principle of non-intervention and non-interference; the principle of the conservation of environmental resources collides with the principle of territorial sovereignty.

When social principles are formally accepted by governments, they take the form of *norms of international law*. This, however, is not a mere collection of agreed rules but a system of norms on international matters (sovereignty, nationality, diplomatic relations, state liability, coercive use of force, etc.) and today also of norms about matters traditionally taken as domestic matters such as the law of human rights and the regulation on the protection of the environment. In spite of the absence of an authority punishing the violations of international norms, governments normally respect international law in order to interact in a frame of certainty. They violate it only when the cost of undergoing other states retaliation is considered lesser than the cost of complying with norms.[2] The nuclear non-proliferation treaty (NPT) is a good example of treaty norms concerning the organization of the contemporary international system. It was explicitly intended to contain the disposal of nuclear arms in the hands of a couple of states in order to limit the number of top countries in the organization of the system.

The *rules of the game* or operational rules pertain to states' relational contexts not regulated by written agreements. They are formulated through tacit negotiation and observed for the sake of reducing the waste of resorting to violence and the disadvantage of interacting in a frame of uncertainty. For this sake, the rules of the game put restrictions and exceptions to social principles. An operational rule results from repeated demonstrative acts and unilateral declarations which usually leave ambiguities about the real significance and content of the rule. Rule violation is usually denied with the argument of being in an unprecedented situation which makes the context completely different from the originally regulated one. Operative rules are usually specific to restricted groups of states – usually of a geographic region – but the governments of states which obtain the top role of the system, create rules for the entire system organization. This has been the case of the 'rules of the bipolar game' invoked by many analysts of contemporary international politics. These analysts emphasized the existence of such rules, but a list of these has never been agreed upon. It may be asserted that such rules were concerned with the conservation of nuclear strategic parity, the respect of zones of influence (apparently the two parts of Europe), the avoidance or exclusion of direct military confrontation (apparently in the wars of the peripheral regions) and the commitment to direct and good faith negotiation in case of serious crisis. The dissolution of the Soviet Union has resulted in the dissolution of such rules. However, observance was neither conforming exactly nor constant for all of bipolar rules.

In the 1990s, the making of new rules of the game seems to be taking a new form. Instead of rules made by the major powers of the system, important operational rules are made through collective and multilateral decision-making. The best example of this rule-making is the formulation of the operational rule of multilateral intervention for humanitarian purposes, in defence of ethnic minorities threatened in their existence. So, the social principle of humanitarian intervention is linked to formation of the operational rule of its enforcement only by multilateral (for example, NATO) or systemic (the United Nations) institutions.

The institutions of the international system are permanent sets of procedures, norms and, in most cases, administrative and operational bodies or inter-governmental organizations established by governments for the sake of giving adequate solutions to important common problems.[3] The contemporary international system has two principal kinds of institutions: inter-governmental organization and economic regimes.

Not all *intergovernmental organizations* are important for the organization of the international system. The case may be restricted to those created for solving political and security problems. In the present international system such kinds of organization are represented by the United Nations and by less important regional bodies like the OSCE. The functioning of an inter-governmental organization is conditioned by the formal and informal roles held by some states and by the antagonism of groups of states. Conflicting groups may block the activity of an inter-governmental organization and hinder its functioning as an institutional factor of international politics. The same result is achieved by governments enjoying hierarchical positions: they usually aim at driving the organization to accomplish goals coherent with their strategy.[4]

Regimes are institutions on which governments converge for the management of separate areas of economic interdependence like finance, trade, transportation and exploitation of material resources.[5] Regimes are a necessary means to deal with problems of interdependence which cannot be controlled through ordinary co-operation or by the coercion of participating states. Regimes give advantages (especially reduction of management costs and increase of information) but governments must also bear international and domestic obligations. Regimes may be consisting only of norms and procedures but the complexity of contemporary co-operation often requires the establishment of permanent bodies to accomplish different tasks like monitoring, assistance and rule-making. When regime costs are asymmetrically distributed - a frequent situation because states normally differ in resources pertaining to specific regimes - these exhibit an hierarchical structure and give to privileged countries the opportunity to use their regime role for getting a privileged position in the organization of the system.

The globalization process, experienced by the contemporary world, has increased the number of regimes formed with the decisive contribution of non-state actors such as transnational corporations, networks (for example, epistemic communities) and other kinds of transnational actors.[6] The increasing importance of non-state actors in the functioning of regimes gives these institutions a role in the organization of the international system which is partially autonomous from the action of state governments. However, the 'autonomous' influence of the institutions on the organization of the international system is a general phenomenon and not one specific of the present situation. The autonomy of institutions is essentially the product of their internal structures and procedures which are, in some degree, 'discontinuous' with the system organization: in the last two or three decades, for example, the United Nations turned out to be increasingly discontinuous with the hierarchical form of the international system organization.

Forms of organization of the international system

Inequality is generally taken as the single fundamental aspect of international relations. This is not true. Equal sovereignty and unequal disposal of resources are the inherent nature of states and the essential ingredients of the rules and institutions which lead governments to comply with the overall organization of the international system. The principle of territorial integrity is a clear example of equalitarian rule; the norms of the NPT restricting the possession of nuclear arms to a couple of states are an example of hierarchical rule. The 'veto power' of the permanent members of the Security Council makes the United Nations an institution with a high level of formal inequality and an international organization less equalitarian than the League of Nations; however, other important structural and procedural attributes reduce the hierarchical nature of the United Nations. Economic regimes are, almost all, unequal institutions, based - as they are - on the unequal distribution of material resources.

Examining the nature of the rules and institutions of an international system, analysts may define the form taken by its organization in a specific period of time. This operation may be conceived as locating an organization on a continuum of different possible forms of organization. At one end of the continuum, state autonomy is generally respected; at the other end, the dominance of the most powerful state(s) is fully and unreservedly observed. Towards the former, rules and institutions are predominantly equalitarian and a 'world parliament' or a network of equalitarian institutions lead the system in a functionalist way; toward the latter, the organization is hierarchical and centralized and the most powerful state(s) impose rules and institutions. When one state controls the system as well as the internal affairs of other states without meeting considerable resistance by those states, the world has a 'domestic' organization - at that point the system is no longer a state system but an empire.[7]

The analytical continuum gives the possibility of comparing the organization of different systems and the forms of one system at different times. Undoubtedly, the international system organization always fell close to the inequality end of the continuum whether as hegemonic organization (one state performing the highest organizational role though not as an imperial power), bipolar (two states performing the leading role) or pluralistic (a small number of states sharing the directive role). Precarious and imperfect equalitarian organizations have been occasionally established; the organization of the system in the early period between the two world wars is an example of it.

Watson[8] has compared a great number of historical international systems and has demonstrated the usefulness of such a spectrum for interpreting international system development. According to Watson, state systems move either towards the empire extreme or - under the effect of a gravitational force - towards the centre of the spectrum. Great powers impose hierarchical rules and place the system in the imperial part of the spectrum but the reaction of other states exerts a counter pressure and the system goes back to a more equalitarian organization form.

Watson emphasizes two conservation effects: the material benefits enjoyed by the majority of states and the legitimacy of the rules based on the cultural traditions and recent experience of the states of the international system. These factors induce governments to accept hierarchical rules and institutions. It is here argued that the introduction of legitimacy as an inherent attribute of the organization points to the bi-dimensional nature of the organization of the international system. For that reason, it must be represented not on a one-dimension continuum but on a two-dimensional space (Figure 10.1). System organization changes according to the quantity of hierarchy of its major rules and institutions and the level of legitimacy the governments attribute to the major rules and institutions of the organization. The first dimension is ascertained by analysing the scope and depth of the restrictions put on state autonomy by the most important rules and the most important procedures and outputs of the institutions of the system. The second dimension is ascertained by analysing the occurrence and importance of the violations to rules and institutional regulations, especially by the states placed in the high ranks of the system hierarchy.

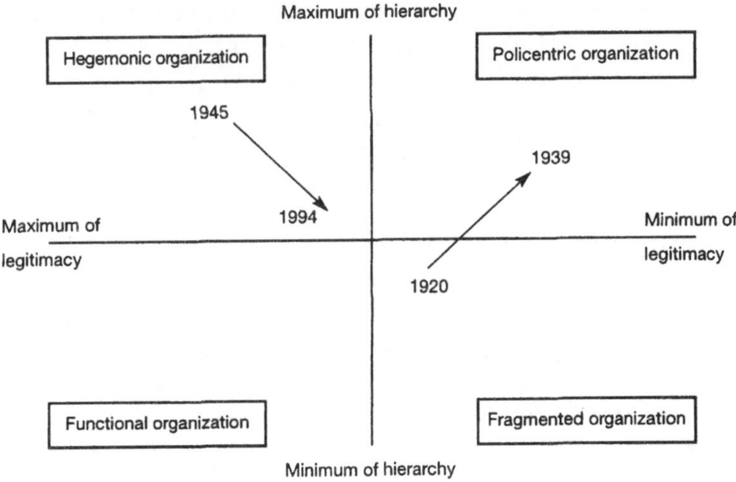

Figure 10.1 Space of the organizational forms of the international system

The axes of the two-dimensional space create four areas of systemic organization which are here named hegemonic, policentric, fragmented and functional organization areas.

In the hegemonic area, moving upward and leftward from the centre, rules and institutions become increasingly hierarchical in nature and accepted by states. The leading organizational role is held by a very small number of states. In the upper part of the area, one state (the hegemon) is positioned better than all other major powers in the most important institutions of the system. Making use of its position, the hegemon is able to promote its own interests and provide the system with public goods like military assistance and economic capitals necessary to the stability and development of the system; consequently, many governments react with co-operation to the actions of the hegemon and sustain the existing hierarchical organization.

In the policentric area, the legitimacy of rules and institutions decreases and the importance and frequency of violations increase. The organization is policentric because the making and enforcement of rules and institutional decisions depend on antagonistic powers; the number of these powers is smaller in the upper side of the area, larger in the lower. They impose to 'client' states the respect of universal and regional rules and regulations. The further we go to the right lower part of the area, the more the system organization becomes discontinuous and regionalized.

In the area of fragmented organization the largest number of rules concerns region-wide matters and is observed by regional groups of states. The regulations of world economic regimes present many exceptions. Regional inter-governmental organizations are more effective than global organizations in the management of political conflicts and local crises.

Finally, in the area of functional organization, rules and regulations respect the sovereign equality of states. Regional and system institutions, endowed with specific competencies for dealing with functions previously exercised by states, exercise all major organizational roles in co-operation with a small number of functional global institutions.

In the above Figure the evolution of the contemporary international system is graphically represented and compared with that of the period between the two world wars. By investigating the present state and nature of rules and institutions, we can argue about the evolution of the organization of the international system either towards the area of policentric or fragmented organization or even towards the area of functional organization if such trends like the trend of regionalization of the world economy and the increased activity of the United Nations and regional institutions like the OSCE continue to take place.

From a theoretical point of view, it is important to stress the fact that general wars are points of discontinuity in the evolution of system organization though they are not the exclusive condition of organizational change. General wars are (could we say 'were'?) the ultimate verdict on the attribution of leading organizational roles: they give government(s) of the victorious state(s) the capacity to dictate new rules of the game and to model new institutions, especially inter-governmental organizations for the control of political and territorial conflicts, and functional regimes for the government of world economic and financial issues. However, general wars do not occur frequently and - though they result in wide and great transformations imposed by (and in the interests of) the victors - fundamental social principles and basic legal norms are of long duration and scarcely depend upon the will of a few governments which win a global war. Moreover, though victors are able to prescribe new legal norms and rules of the game concerning political and territorial integrity and national security and also create the principal economic regimes and inter-governmental organizations of the new system, they are unable to keep their role unaltered for a long period of time. After a sufficient lapse of time, their leading position tends to decay and the existing organization turns out to be conditioned by political competitions which cause the evolution of the form of the organization.

In the following sections the importance of great power rivalry is taken for granted and will not be considered; attention is put on competitions engendered by social cleavages and on competitions concerned with the regulation of the new issues of global politics since the two are strictly connected.

International cleavages

Generally speaking, social cleavage is the division of the members of society on the basis of some criteria. Cleavages divide society members into opposite groups and cause political conflict when reciprocal hostile attitudes and actions arise in the opposite groups. Cleavage analysis has been applied to the study of the formation of European political parties and the evolution of the party system in Western Europe. Stein Rokkan[9] and other political and social scientists[10] have analysed the historical origin and features of social cleavages and explained how class, religion, ethnicity, geography and socio-economic factors like modernization and industrialization influence the political system of Western European countries.

International political scientists are invited to regard social cleavage analysis as an important tool for their investigations and interpretations. Social cleavages have the same effect on the international political system that domestic social cleavages have on domestic politics and competition. The latter lead to the formation of political parties and influenced party competition; the former create various kinds of *aggregation* of states which co-ordinate government actions on specific issue-areas and favour the adoption by governments of policies, either joint, collective or individual, aimed at changing the cleavage structure and influencing the evolution of the organization of the international system.

The cleavages of a society may be numerous and intertwined; they often overlap and usually influence each other. To discover important cleavages is the first analytical problem. Researchers must be sure of making the right selection of a cleavage at the exclusion of another. Second, they have to make the right separation of one cleavage from others and examine the origin, features and development of the different cleavages in order to discern the specific effect of each cleavage on political competition. Third, research on a long period of time runs into the problem of cleavage decay and substitution.

All these problems considered, at least three cleavages are relevant in the analysis of the organization of the contemporary international system: two of them extend over a long period of time, the other one spans a few decades and then falls apart. The first cleavage of long duration concerns the international division of labour in the world economy, the interdependence of national markets and today the relations between national economies as well as between state and non-state actors of the global market. I suggest it be called *North–South cleavage*; however, this name does not refer only to the confrontation between the so-called developed and developing countries but to the confrontation between different groups of states on altering or keeping unaltered the world economic regimes which favour in a decreasing way the groups of states which are located from the top to the bottom of the world economy. The second cleavage of long duration was created by the extension of the European state system and the diffusion of the European civilization and culture to the rest of the world and, then, by the resistance of extra-European peoples and states to that diffusion and to the Euro-American cultural and political pre-eminence in the world. I call it *Centre–Periphery cleavage*. The third cleavage is the well-known *East–West cleavage*. It was about two alternative conceptions of property rights as fundamental principles of domestic economic and political regimes - the private/capitalist and the collective/socialist conception. This cleavage was very important in the first decade after the end of the Second World War, when the formation of the hierarchical organization of the contemporary international system took place. Since the mid-1950s, the importance of the East–West cleavage progressively declined and in the second part of the 1980s it completely vanished.

The importance of cleavage analysis and the relevance of the three cleavages in contemporary international relations is confirmed by the fact that in the last three decades the existence of traditional military and diplomatic alliances of states has been substituted with the creation of cleavage-made aggregations of states. In the past, the co-ordination of foreign policies was achieved by alliance treaties and the formal definition of roles and commitments of the contracting parties. Since the mid-1950s the formation of formal alliances has progressively run out of contemporary international politics. Undoubtedly, contemporary governments have almost abandoned this kind of political co-operation. Many alliances disappeared in recent years and only the alliances linked with cleavage politics have had a strong chance of lasting. After the Second World War, flexible ties and *ad hoc* co-ordination have been preferred to rigid and well-defined relations of assistance based on military means. The Atlantic alliance - the only major alliance still working - has always been a military alliance and also much more than that. It has been an aggregation placed at the intersection of the three cleavages and an instrument for co-ordinating foreign policies in the three cleavage domains (to contend with socialist countries, to formulate common economic strategies, to concert on political and military crises in the Third World, etc.).

By all means, in the post-World War Two international system, a great deal of foreign policy co-ordination has been connected with affinities directly related to the three cleavages: affinities in the domestic political and economic system (East–West cleavage), in the economic structure and policies (North–South cleavage) and in the cultural and political constitution of the states (Centre–Periphery cleavage). The term *aggregation* is adopted to indicate a stable group of states with the same position on an international cleavage and with similar foreign policy perspectives. The members of an aggregation adopt various forms of collaboration, solidarity and co-ordination which do not demand - nor exclude - the subscription of formal treaties. Common structures and explicit agreements may not exist, be restricted to a small number of 'core states' or be the very form of an aggregation. The list of the major aggregations of contemporary international politics shows a variety of cases. It includes, at least, the Atlantic and the Soviet aggregation, the aggregation of non-aligned countries, the aggregation of the seven most industrialized countries and the Group of 77. These aggregations show many differences in decision-making, political style and performance, but they all contribute to international politics in the same way: by aggregating expectations, resources and actions of the associated governments with the aim of changing the rules and institutions of the organization of the international system in order to reinforce the position of their members against the position of the opposite aggregate members.

Origins of the international cleavages

The origin of the three cleavages is differently placed in the history of the international system: East–West is the most recent one; North–South and Centre–Periphery were rooted in a more distant past and, after the Second World War, took new forms and features.

The establishment of the socialist regime in Russia in 1917 was opposed by the major European states who were determined to impede the diffusion of socialism. Stalin's programme of reinforcing socialism in one country and the Nazi threat to Europe postponed the struggle between socialism and capitalism until the end of the Second World War, when Stalin opted for bringing socialism to Europe and Asia and sustained the transformation of the social and economic regimes of the East European states, China and North Korea. This fact created the condition for making the *East–West* cleavage a major factor of post-war international politics. The formation and conservation of the aggregations on the two sides of the cleavage line was a strong factor in establishing the hierarchical organization of the new international system and contrasting the counter-efforts of the opponents.

The *North–South* cleavage and the competition for the control of the world economy may be traced back to the formation of the world capitalist market in the seventeenth century (as world-system analysis maintains) but the essential features of contemporary economic relations materialized in the second half of the nineteenth century when the second industrial revolution prompted a great competition among major European industrial countries. At the same time, two extra-European newcomers - the United States and Japan - attacked the core of the world economy and started their rise to the upper position. However, the North-South cleavage took its present features with the structuring of the major economic regimes in the afterwards of the Second World War and, lately, with the growth of the gap between industrial and developing countries and the precarious re-structuring of those regimes in the last two decades.

The *Centre-Periphery* cleavage is present in the international system as in all the territorial political systems in which the extension of the political control, the diffusion of the cultural models and the imposition of the economic interests of the 'central' area hurt the politics, culture and economy of the rest of the system. In the central area, the making of a single political system on a territorial unit has its inception; in this area the major economic and political actors and decision-makers of the system are permanently located. The origin of the Centre-Periphery cleavage in international politics may be found in the reaction of Japan to the invasion of Asia by the European great powers at the end of the last century. This cleavage took on new features after the Second World War when new Asian countries asked for participation in the leading roles of the system, for the true end of colonialism and the elimination of all the conditions making them 'penetrated' states or states whose major decisions are made with the involvement of actors who support the interests of the centre.

Evolution of the international cleavages

At the end of the Second World War, the United States undertook the reorganization of the international system in the main political and economic domains. They were deeply convinced of the necessity for an institution designed to put under international control the political and territorial conflicts which could destabilize the post-war settlement. The idea took the form of the United Nations which substituted the almost totally unsuccessful League of Nations. Under American pressure, the equalitarian structure of the League - which had proved ineffective - was changed into the structure of the new institution characterized by few but important hierarchical elements. On the economic side, from 1944 to 1947 Washington acted to lead the world out of uncertainty, disorder and restraints. This aim was pursued with the creation of economic regimes consistent with the position of the American economy in the world market. These regimes have been, above all, the monetary and financial regimes, based on the IMF and the World Bank, and the commercial regime, based on GATT.

The United States was successful in putting its hegemonic position in the international system on the solid foundations of those political and economic institutions, but it had to face the strong opposition of the Soviet Union. The Soviet-American rivalry concerning the leading role of the organization of the system took great strength from the East-West cleavage and its aggregations - NATO, the Warsaw Pact and the less structured and viable aggregations of Asia, the Pacific and the Middle East (Seato, Anzus and Cento). The East-West competition contributed to strengthen the infant hierarchy of the system organization and to support it for a couple of decades. At the same time, the remaining two competitions were contributing to push it back. The opposition became irreversible in the 1960s when the two great powers could perceive the limited nature on their control on the organization of the system.

EAST-WEST

East-West competition and Soviet-American rivalry have been two different things; however, they proceeded together and made for what is named the Cold War.[11] In the early phase of the contemporary international politics, the East-West competition was an instrument in the hands of the two global rivals to reinforce their hierarchical roles; but progressively it lost its power of explicating such a function. The United States and Soviet Union wanted to extend their socio-economic system to the whole world, but neither of them were inclined to risk direct confrontation leading to war for that aspiration. According to the already cited rules of the game, they preferred to give military aid to friendly governments and to carry on 'proxy wars'. On the other hand, when one of the two was convinced of the necessity for direct intervention (as in Vietnam or Afghanistan), both of them cautiously avoided direct confrontation. Soviet and American leaders soon admitted that winning converts everywhere to capitalism and socialism was an attempt doomed to fail; implicitly they converted the East-West cleavage into a transient factor of the international system without abandoning the use of its rhetorical appeal. In fact, this cleavage was overcome by the other two. Because of the cycles of growth and decay of the world economy (North-South cleavage), a steady movement of domestic structures towards capitalist and socialist patterns could not be induced by foreign assistance and intervention in all the countries of the world. In those parts of the world where new states were consolidating their precarious social and economic structures, the United States and Soviet Union simply attempted to convince local political leaders to support their stance in the global rivalry without any real expectation of advancing their position in the East-West competition. On the other hand, the ascendancy of the East-West by the Centre-

Periphery cleavage took also the form of explicit foreign policies of important extra-European countries which firmly refused to be involved in the East-West competition (like India) or to play a subordinate role in it (like China).

NORTH-SOUTH

The constitution of the post-war economic regimes brought unexpected growth and development all around the world. The competition among states on economic matters was reduced for some years. The North-South cleavage became politically important again only in the late 1950s when Gaullist France protested against the political economy of the American administration, the inadequacy of the gold-dollar exchange rate and the spread of American multinational corporations through all Western Europe. The controversy seemed to be solved with the reform of the IMF and the Kennedy Round, but new problems came on the forefront when under-development became a major political issue and a new political aggregation, the Group of 77, was formed with the United Nations sponsorship at the first conference on trade and development (UNCTAD) in 1964.[12] The economic take-off of new countries was expected to result either from appropriate decisions taken by individual governments, namely import-substitution policies which proved to be successful only under special conditions, or from international aid which turned out to be a problem-perpetuating, rather than a problem-solving, strategy.

In the 1960s, signs of economic crisis appeared all around the world but the worst came in the following decade. Economic recession - a consequence of the first (1973) and second (1979) oil crises as well as of the political economy of the American government - caused stronger competition among the most industrialized countries. If the American economy kept its primacy and the Washington administration its control over financial and trade regimes, the position of Western Europe and Japan in the world market gradually improved and, at the end of the 1970s, the formal rank of the United States in the world economic institutions was substantially reduced. The control of the monetary regime, for example, shifted from the directive and formal rules of the IMF to a flexible model based on repetitive negotiations and almost continuous rearrangements agreed upon by the Treasury Secretaries of the Group of Seven, then of Five and finally of Three (United States, Japan and Germany).

During the time of the erosion of the major economic regimes (namely, IMF and GATT) and the failure to constitute a new institutional framework for the government of the world economy, the resentment of the developing countries increased and no effective solution was found for protecting their scarcely equipped economies from suffering further injuries. Briefly, in the competition of the North–South cleavage the United States retained the hegemonic role but in a framework of growing economic contest and restrained hierarchical regulations. In the last decade, regional groupings (North America, Western Europe, and East Asia-Pacific) progressively showed on the stage, further undermining the efficacy of the existing regimes.

CENTRE-PERIPHERY

The Centre–Periphery cleavage has been shaped by the foundation of the world system through the imposition of European and, later, Euro-American models and interests to the rest of the world.[13] The conflict between the centre and the peripheries of states are usually multi-dimensional - they are featured by cultural, economic and political matters. The same is true at the international level. In the years of de-colonization, the international Centre–Periphery cleavage was mainly linked to political autonomy. Examples of that dimension are the foreign policies of the early Asian neutralist countries (like India, Burma, Cambodia) in the early 1950s and the constitution of the Non-alignment Movement with its demand for effective sovereignty and democracy in the organization of the international system. The economic dimension gained importance in a later period. In the 1970s, when the Centre–Periphery competition merged with the North–South competition, the documents issued in the conferences of the Non-Aligned Movement were predominantly concerned with economic issues. Finally, though the defence of extra-European cultures has been a persistent theme in the competition activated by the Centre–Periphery cleavage, the cultural dimension has got new impetus in the last decade, mainly with the mobilization of Islamic movements.

The Non-Aligned Movement is the principal aggregation experience of the Centre–Periphery cleavage. Though fraught with many contradictions and inconsistencies, it has been for a long period of time the only collective support to the autonomous aspirations of the peripheral countries and the only world-wide aggregation of the Periphery. However, international cleavages do not only cause aggregate behaviour, they also give specific qualities to the foreign policies and actions of single countries. Examples of individual policies of peripheral governments inspired by this competition are that of India, Iran after Khomeini's revolution, China after the rupture with Moscow, the former Yugoslavia, Egypt and Libya. The foreign policies of peripheral countries have been mostly 'volatile'[14] because their governments oscillated between the two superpowers and accepted ties with the superpower most inclined to help them to solve domestic and international problems.[15] Still, those governments never cut all links with the aggregations (the Non-Aligned Movement and the Group of 77) and other governments resistant to the superpowers and the influence of the centre.

The foreign policies of peripheral countries inspired by this cleavage are predominantly non-violent when the country is sufficiently large, powerful, or unpenetrated (like China or India), but tend to take violent forms - like terrorism and even international war - when those features are absent and the governments of the centre heavily frustrate the aspirations of the peripheral country; this has been the case with Iraq, Libya, Syria and Iran.

Iran is a good example of the importance taken by the Centre–Periphery cleavage in the evolution of contemporary international politics. In the first phase of contemporary international relations - the phase of high hierarchy and intense East–West competition, extinguished in the late 1950s - Iran was involved in all-important events of the East–West cleavage in Central Asia and the Middle East. It adhered to all the aggregative initiatives taken by western governments in those regions, namely to the Baghdad Pact in 1955, the Eisenhower Doctrine in 1957 and the Central Treaty Organization (CENTO) in 1959. In the mid-phase of contemporary international politics - from the late 1950s to the mid-1970s - Iran changed its foreign policy orientation; it ceased to orientate toward the East–West competition, set its relationship with the United States on a bilateral and inter-governmental base, and concentrated on the North–South competition. The economic cleavage offered Teheran the advantage to play a major role in system organization politics by making use of the oil card. In the third phase, started in the early 1980s and characterized by the reinvigoration of the Centre–Periphery competition and the Reagan administration efforts to restore American hegemony in the Third World, Shi'ite Iran changed its foreign policy again and definitely took its place on the periphery side of the cleavage stressing the cultural and political dimension of its confrontation with the countries of the centre and American hegemony.

Social cleavages, global issues and agenda-setting

The end of the East–West competition creates scepticism about the importance of cleavage analysis for the study of the organization of the international system. A major argument of writings on present international politics is that the sharing of problems by all the states of the world is stronger than any form of social division between them. The degradation of the environment, the danger of severe nuclear incidents, the offenses to people and human rights, the diffusion of epidemics (like AIDS) and the growth of international crimes (like drug trade and money laundering) are major examples of global problems binding the states together no matter how different they are in social, economic and cultural terms. In opposition to this opinion, it can be argued that the factors which create interdependence and togetherness do not exclude the continuous effect of social cleavages. The economic (North–South) and the cultural (Centre–Periphery) cleavages persist and continue to act on the organization of the international system. They are very important because they shape the position of states on the solution of global problems. These problems have different possible solutions. So, they are real issues of global politics because governments have different preferences on the alternative solutions according to their position on the cleavage lines of world society. Briefly, social cleavages influence conflict and negotiation on the solution of global issues.

Territorial integrity and political independence are typical problems of the international system since its origin. Monetary and trade issues have been added to the agenda in our century while the reduction of the development gap became a political issue only thirty years ago. Finally, in the last twenty years, the United Nations and its agencies - often by means of international conferences (for example, the first United Nations conference on the environment in 1972) - have been called, in co-operation with all the governments of the world, to take care of a number of new global issues. Today, the list of major global issues includes at least the following: safeguarding the biosphere and reduction of industrial pollution; defence of human rights and expansion of democracy; protection of ethnic minorities and appropriate execution of the principle of self-determination; reduction of migration for economic reasons and of mass dislocation for political reasons; use and exploitation of the global commons (space, atmosphere and oceans); repression of transnational crimes and prevention of illegal trade (drugs, arms, 'new slaves', money laundering); struggle against world-wide health problems (epidemics like AIDS and great diseases like cancers).

The appearance of global issues has been produced by the globalization process which invested the domestic politics of practically all the countries of the world in the last decades.[16] Technological innovation applied to communication and transportation, and the development of the capitalist economy created the global society at the same time that the competencies of governments extended to practically any aspect of human and social life. The interdependence and inter-connection of national economies and politics, produced by the globalization process, draw governments to international co-operation and co-ordination in order to carry out their old and new functions in delicate fields like public security, economic development and social security. In other words, the application of technological innovation to economic relations and structures and the diffusion of social, political and cultural aspirations which cannot be completely contained by national borders nor submitted to government control for a long time, engender international problems which cannot be solved effectively at the national level nor by unilateral governmental actions, but require a multilateral strategy and the production of regulations by the international institutions with the collaboration of non-state actors in a growing number of cases.

Conclusion

Though no analytical and theoretical approach to the present form of organization of the international system can avoid considering the actors and processes of the transnational or 'multicentric world',[17] governments continue to play the predominant role. Therefore, the regulation of global issues largely, but not exclusively, depends on factors pertaining to the international political system. The regulation and regimentation of a global issue - that is, its management through rules and regimes accepted all around the world - is conceivable only when the issue is included in the agenda of the international or inter-governmental system. On the setting of this agenda, major states have great importance, but no less important are the cleavages which gave origin to different groups of states with different orientations toward that agenda.

The evolution of the present organization of the international system calls upon political scientists to give more attention to the process of agenda-setting in global politics and to the processing of the issues on the agenda.[18] The introduction of any issue onto the agenda - that is, the explicit agreement expressed by the large majority of governments and especially by the governments with major organizational roles - and the result of the negotiation on the regulative solution of the issue - that is, the production of rules and regimes on the issue - largely depend on social cleavages. In fact, on one hand, cleavages separate states into groups which are differently exposed and sensitive to the issues of the system; on the other, social cleavages result in aggregations which strongly influence political alignment and governmental coalitions in multilateral negotiation for giving formal solution to global issues.

It is also true that any formal agreement on the treatment of any global issue - either through the formulation of new rules, the constitution of new regimes or the extension of the competencies of an existing regime - may produce a change in the organization of the system moving its form on the two-dimensional space of the organizational forms which has been considered in the first part of this essay.

Finally, the importance of considering the different sources of inter-state conflict in the contemporary world must be stressed. This essay has pointed to some of these sources, namely to the social and issue sources of competition and conflict. Rule and institution convergence is as important as power distribution in organizing international politics; however, neither power rivalry nor great power diplomacy account for all the factors relevant to the explanation of international political change. Social and issue cleavages are among these factors. An effort has been made to demonstrate the advantage of considering them within the general perspective of the approach of the organization of the international system.

Notes

1 Bull, H., *The Anarchical Society: A Study of Order in International Society* (New York, Columbia University Press, 1977).

2 On the political relevance of international law see, among others, the classical book by Henkin, L., *How Nations Behave: Law and Foreign Policy* (New York, Columbia University Press, 1979), originally published in 1968, and the more recent Nardin, T., 'International ethics and international law', *Review of International Studies*, **18**(1) (1992), pp. 19–30.

3 International relationists, as other social scientists, attribute different meanings to the concept of institution. See Keohane, R. O., 'International institutions: two approaches', *International Studies Quarterly*, **32**(4) (1988), pp. 379–96, for a remarkable theoretical survey of the concept.

4 On different aspects of inter-governmental organizations as institutions of the international political system, see Archer, C., *International Organization* (London, George Allen & Unwin, 1983); Haas, E. B., *When Knowledge is Power: Three Models of Change in International Organizations* (Berkeley, CA, University of California Press, 1990); and Gallarotti, G. M., 'The limits of international organization: systematic failure in the management of international relations', *International Organization*, **45**(2) (1991), pp. 183–220.

5 The extended use of the concept of regime to different areas (such as money, arms, shipping, telecommunication, human rights, etc.) makes it too loose and confusing. I favour the use of the term only to indicate institutions regulating wide areas of *economic* interdependence like finance, trade or energy.

6 See McGrew, A. G. and Lewis, P. G. (eds), *Global Politics: Globalization and the Nation-State* (Cambridge, Polity Press, 1992); Stopford, J. and Strange, S., *Rival States, Rival Firms: Competition for World Market Shares* (Cambridge, Cambridge University Press, 1991).

7 On the difference, see especially Wesson, R. G., *The Imperial Order* (Berkeley, CA, University of California Press, 1967); Wesson, R. G., *State Systems: International Pluralism, Politics and Culture* (London, Collier Macmillan, 1978).

8 Watson, A., *The Evolution of International Society*, (London, Routledge, 1992).

9 Rokkan, S., *Citizens, Elections, Parties* (Oslo, Universitets Forlaget, 1977).

10 For example, Rae, D. W. and Taylor, M., *The Analysis of Political Cleavages* (New Haven, CT, Yale University Press, 1970); Lane, J. and Ersson, S. O., *Politics and Society in Western Europe* (London, Sage, 1991).

11 On the East–West competition see, among many others, Aron, R., *Paix et guerre entre les nations* (Paris, Calmann-Levy, 1962); De Porte, A. W., *Europe Between the*

Superpowers: The Enduring Balance (New Haven, CT, Yale University Press, 1979); Romer, J., *Détente et Rideau de Fer* (Paris, Publications de la Sorbonne, 1984); Halliday, F., *The Making of the Second Cold War* (London, Verso, 1986); and Kaldor, M., *The Imaginary War: Understanding the East-West Conflict* (Oxford, Basil Blackwell, 1990).

12 On North-South competition, besides the international political economy literature, see Krasner, S. D., 'Transforming international regimes. What the Third World wants and why', *International Studies Quarterly*, **25**(1) (1981), pp. 119-48; Jones, C. A., *The North-South Dialogue: A Brief History* (London, Frances Pinter, 1983); Cox, R. W., *Production, Power, and World Order: Social Forces in the Making of History* (New York, Columbia University Press, 1987); Augelli, E. and Murphy, C., *America's Quest for Supremacy and the Third World: A Gramscian Analysis* (London, Pinter, 1988); and Chase-Dunn, C., *Global Formation. Structures of the World-economy* (Cambridge, MA, Basil Blackwell, 1989).

13 On center-periphery competition see: Bandyopadhyaya, J., *North over South: A Non-Western Perspective of International Relations* (New Delhi, South Asian Publishers, 1982); Bull, H. and Watson, A. (eds), *The Expansion of International Society* (Oxford, Clarendon Press, 1984); Singham, A. W. and Hune, S., *Non-alignment in an Age of Alignments* (London, Zed Books, 1986); Amin, S., *L'Eurocentrisme: Critique d'une Ideologie* (Paris, Anthropos, 1988); Halliday, F., *From Kabul to Managua: Soviet-American Relations in the 1980s* (New York, Pantheon Books, 1989); Mazrui, A. A., *Cultural Forces in World Politics* (London, James Currey, 1990); and Strang, D., 'Global patterns of decolonization, 1500-1987', *International Studies Quarterly*, **35**(4) (1991), pp. 429-54.

14 Ayoob, M., 'The Third World in the system of states: actor schizophrenia or growing pains?', *International Studies Quarterly*, **33**(1) (1989), pp. 67-80.

15 It should be remembered also that the political movements and forces of the peripheral regions of the states demand more political and cultural autonomy as well as more economic assistance.

16 On the globalization process, see especially McGrew and Lewis (eds), *Global Politics*; and Camilleri, J. A. and Falk, J., *The End of Sovereignty? The Politics of a Shrinking and Fragmenting World* (Aldershot, Edward Elgar, 1992).

17 Rosenau, J. N., *Turbulence in World Politics: A Theory of Change and Continuity* (New York, Harvester Wheatsheaf, 1990).

18 An interesting study of this point is Livingston, S. G., 'The politics of international agenda-setting: Reagan and North-South relations', *International Studies Quarterly*, **36**(3) (1992), pp. 313-30.

11

The English School and the Political Construction of International Society

R. J. BARRY JONES

Introduction

Thought about international relations requires wide-ranging concepts that allow such complex phenomena to be simplified, ordered and endowed with significance. The sets of ideas suggested by such wide-ranging concepts rarely, if ever, constitute proper *theories*, by the demanding, but also limiting, criteria traditionally associated with the empirical 'sciences'. Such sets of ideas, rather, form the bases of *metatheories*, which, while being incapable of generating strictly verifiable (or falsifiable) laws or propositions serve a less formal, but no less vital, intellectual function.[1]

The employment of such metatheories may be acceptable, indeed essential, in the study of human activity. However, such devices confront the 'social sciences' with a singular difficulty. The character of metatheory is such as to rule out strict testing against empirical 'reality'. Moreover, the reality against which metatheories must eventually be tested, in some manner, exhibits marked levels of complexity, change and ambiguity. The empirical world can thus provide some support for all but the most extreme of metatheories and complicate the task of establishing criteria of choice between such alternative, and often competing, interpretations.

The difficulties facing students of international relations are not merely epistemological, however. First-order epistemological issues concern questions about how knowledge about the world external to the observer is to be established. Students of human affairs are certainly confronted by such, but they also face additional questions about the nature of human activity itself. The issue here is whether human activity, in any of its various forms, can be treated as identical to the 'behaviour' of most of the other elements of the natural universe. This issue is most acute when attention is directed to the behaviour of aggregates of human beings - groups, 'societies', or 'states'.

Many of the 'great debates' within modern international studies have turned around the core epistemological and ontological issues. Behaviouralists have sought to reject the use of metatheories, with rather limited success. 'Realists' have generally found difficulty with the notion that theirs is but one amongst a number of equally valid metatheoretical approaches to international relations. Moreover, proponents of most of the more prominent theoretical 'schools' have, until recently, adopted a rather simplistic view of the essential character of human activity.

The so-called 'English School',[2] and its core concept of 'International Society', encounters the whole range of issues confronting students of international relations. Despite Hedley Bull's vigorous diatribe against the 'scientific' pretension within the study of international relations,[3] the position of the 'English School' on these epistemological and ontological issues does not appear to be either clear or consistent. Such a lack of clarity and consistency is not surprising, however, for it reflects difficulties inherent in the notion of an 'International Society' and the sources of such a 'society' in reality.

International society

A popular and significant concept within the study of international relations, the notion of 'International Society' offers the apparent promise of a tolerable condition within world affairs. The 'English School' locates such a notion at the heart of its theorizing about 'modern' international relations. 'International Society' remains, however, a contested and problematical concept, with critics ranging in the depth and nature of their rejection. For some, 'International Society' is seen to be merely unnecessary; for others it stands condemned as a pernicious distortion of prevailing international realties.

Many of the difficulties and uncertainties arise from the central notion of an 'International Society' and its proposed role, both analytical and existential. In conventional usage a 'society' is something composed of real, cognisant human beings. It is in the patterned interactions of such real people that 'normal' societies find their 'reality'. Interactions amongst abstract entities like states are difficult to accommodate to such a notion of 'society'.

A partial answer to the problems posed by according a 'social' character to the interactions of states is provided by the distinction drawn between *Gemeinschaften* - or 'real' social communities - and *Gesellschaften* - looser 'communities' bound by common beliefs and values, rather than by continuing personal interaction.[4] The problem is not finally resolved by this distinction, however, for the agents that collectively generate *Gesellschaften* remain real human beings. A form of 'society' composed of aggregate entities like states remains problematic. At best it may be no more than a metatheoretical conception of a far more complex reality; at worst it might constitute a category error; whereby characteristics are attributed to entities which such entities cannot, by their nature, possess.

A further means of evading such difficulties lies in moving from constitutive to functionalist conceptions of 'society': from a concern with the constituents of societies to a consideration of their (beneficial) effects. Hedley Bull thus characterizes societies, in *The Anarchical Society*, as having three purposes:

> First, to ensure that life will be in some measure secure against violence resulting in death or bodily harm. Second ... to ensure that promises, once made, will be kept, or that agreements, once undertaken, will be carried out. Third ... the goal of ensuring that the possession of things will remain stable to some degree, and will not be subject to challenges that are constant and without limit.[5]

At the international level, Bull identifies three purposes additional to those common to all societies at all levels: 'First, there is the goal of preservation of the system and society of states itself. ... Second, there is the goal of maintaining the independence or external sovereignty of individual states. ... Third, there is the goal of peace.'[6]

Bull thus appears to have effected a partial escape from the problems of a possible category error, if only at the expense of an unrestrained plunge into the murky theoretical waters of functionalism and ultra-rationalism. Proceeding further with the argument, it is even possible that 'International Society' may not be a condition that will ever fully materialize in the empirical world, but remain an immanent tendency underlying the more complex, and confusing, reality of day-to-day experience. However, Bull compromises both avenues of possible escape by the statement that:

> A *society of states* (or International Society) exists when a group of states, conscious of certain common interests and common values, form a society in the sense that they conceive themselves to be bound by a common set of rules in their relations with one another, and share in the working of common institutions.[7]

States have again been reified and a serious category error suggested.

If the nature of states, as aggregate entities, often owing as much to legal fictions as to organic foundations, denies them the ability to have the kinds of values, beliefs, understandings and expectations that can direct 'social' behaviour, then it is to the human participants in state structures that such characteristics must be attributed. The acknowledgement of the role of human agency in the generation of anything approximating to an 'International Society' hints at issues that will be developed subsequently in this discussion. It does, however, raise serious questions about the empirical existence of 'International Society' and certainly suggests that any manifestation of 'International Society' is likely to be highly variable, with both time and place.

The 'English School' is troubled by a further difficulty in its treatment of 'International Society'. The various contributors to the 'School' appear to vary considerably in their view as to whether 'International Society' is to be viewed as a simple, empirical phenomenon or a consciously constructed arrangement. The sense apparently conveyed by such advocates of the 'English School' as Hedley Bull[8] or Adam Watson[9] is that International Society can be seen as an empirical condition within international relations. Charles Manning's earlier discussion, however, with its emphasis upon the ideational foundations of international arrangements, suggests more of a constructed character to International Society.[10]

Clarity on the nature and acceptability of the idea of International Society requires careful consideration of three proximate, interrelated issues within the fields of international relations and political studies. The first issue is that of the essential character of human activity and, thereby, the nature of political activity. The second is that of the relationship between normative theory and empirical analysis in the study of political affairs. The third, then, is that of the essentially 'political' character of international relations. Within a reconsideration of the nature of human activity, and a recognition of the organic relationship between empirical and normative analysis within social studies and a suitably extended conception of politics, it might be possible to re-examine the idea of International Society from a sharper and more critical perspective.

The nature of social and political activity

The thrust of much empirical 'social science', from classical economics through to revolutionary Marxist theory, has been the pursuit of timeless universals of human conduct and condition. The notion that true knowledge lies only through the discovery of 'general laws' that generate tested (or unfalsified) propositions has been of considerable attraction to a succession of students of social, economic and political activity.[11] Such epistemological and methodological dispositions have, however, discorded with approaches to human affairs that, as in the work of Max Weber, stress the 'meaningful' foundations of such behaviour.[12] The residual contribution of the recent revival of 'critical theory'[13] within social studies has been to revive doubt about much of the empirical social scientific agenda: revealing the normative bias inherent within such a programme and the relative triviality of many of its findings.

The position adopted in this paper differentiates between human activity and phenomena of the non-human realm (with some possible qualifications in the areas of the higher, and especially aquatic, mammals). The actions of the latter are held to be unaffected by ideas that agents have about themselves or the behaviour that is appropriate to specific circumstances.

Human behaviour, in direct contrast, is held to be largely governed by the ideas that human agents have about themselves, their circumstances, the probable behaviour of others with whom they interact and, most significantly, the values that underlie their aspirations and judgements. The primary source of the ideas that direct individuals lies, moreover, in the society within which those individuals have been nurtured and lived.

That which is timeless and universal in human behaviour is seen, from this perspective, to be obvious and, from the point of view of social studies, relatively trivial: the need to feed, reproduce, etc. Massive variation is to be detected both in the arrangements which various societies have made for the provision of food, reproductive activity and, most centrally, in the burgeoning range of additional purposes towards which an increasing proportion of the energy of human societies is directed and upon which human passion and aspiration is vested. In the explanation of variation and change, a central role is thus attributed to the variability of human ideas about desirable and practicable forms of behaviour.

The core of the human condition is thus to be seen as a 'socially constructed reality',[14] in which the basic values, understandings and expectations of the members of any society generate corresponding patterns of behaviour. The behaviour of the members of the society then manifests a level of consistency sufficient to establish a self-perpetuating 'reality' for all members of that society. The socially constructed reality within any society is robust and enduring to the extent that the underlying set of values, understandings and expectations is widely shared and accepted throughout any society.

The patterning of social life is equally sustained by the mutually supportive understandings and expectations of the individual members of each society. The structuration[15] of social existence thus rests upon such self-reinforcing patterns of inter-subjectivity and it common, to varying degrees, of both *Gemeinschaft* and *Gesellschaft*.

The language system that is common to the members of any society embodies these shared understandings and expectations. Facilitating basic capabilities for comprehension and communication, such language systems condition that which can be readily comprehended and that which must remain literally 'inconceivable'. Language systems thus rest at the heart of the socially constructed reality of any common-language based society.

Idealism, and modern forms of 'discourse' analysis, provide one line of response to the self-encapsulation of propositions about the 'social construction' of knowledge and understanding. For those wishing to adopt a less extreme philosophical position a *paradox of self-reference* may be confronted in the question of what can be the claim to ultimate truth of a proposition that 'truth' is socially generated.

The issue here is whether the propositions of the philosophy or sociology of knowledge are held to be of the same status as the statements made in everyday life. If *all* philosophical and methodological propositions are held to be of a different order from everyday statements and subject to different criteria of truth or falsity then there is no real problem. In terms of set theory we have two distinct sets of propositions and statements. The proposition - P1 - that social knowledge and understanding is socially constructed is a member of a set of philosophical and methodological propositions - Set A - which is not, itself, a member of the set of everyday statements - Set B:

Set A {P1, P2, P3 . . .} *and* Set B {S1, S2, S3 . . .}

However, the proposition that human knowledge and understanding is 'socially constructed' might be held to entail that philosophical proposition is, itself, governed by its own supposed 'truth', that it can be accepted as no more than a 'socially constructed truth'. In this view, there would be more than one set of valid propositions and statements:

Socially constructed 'truths' - {P1, P2, P3 . . . S1, S2, S3 . . .}

and the 'truth' of the statement that social knowledge is socially constructed no more true, or false, than any everyday proposition or statement.

Ultimately, each individual has to answer this question by reference to the degree to which it is believed that discipline and self-critical reflection is capable of generating basic insights and understandings that transcend, to some degree, the constraints and conditioning of the social/intellectual context within which the analyst operates.

The constructed nature of social realities, and the complex of mutually reinforcing dispositions upon which they rest, endow them with a durability that belies the wilder imaginings of philosophical idealists and many 'critical' theorists. Change is possible, under the pressure of external events or internal debate, but such change is often tortuous and traumatic.[16]

Political life is seen, in this discussion, to be a special part of social life; political 'realities' thus being a socially constructed component of the wider 'socially constructed reality' of any community or arena of inter-social activity. Ultimately, the 'political' component of the wider socially constructed reality of a society is concerned with the self-conscious effort to identify that society, define the relationship between the social 'whole' and its parts, and to regulate the behaviour of the members of that society towards one another. Three distinct levels of political life exist: a *foundational level*, identifying the 'legitimate' members of any political order and their 'proper' patterns of interaction; an *institutional* or *constitutional level*, giving form to the fundamental principles of any political order; and a *day-to-day level* of legislation, regulation and myriad actions intended to manage the affairs of the relevant political 'community'. The 'political' remains differentiated from the wider realm of the 'social', moreover, in its embrace of the core of the formal identification and regulation of complex collectivities.

Political analysis – the empirical and the normative

It should be clear from the above discussion that normative components assume a central role in the construction of social and political 'realities'. Core values both direct much of human behaviour and provide a foundation upon which understandings and expectations of the behaviour of others are based. Within such a conception of the nature of political activity, the conventional distinction between empirical and normative theory and analysis is substantially dissolved. The study of empirical 'realities' within the social and political realms must thus involve an examination of the normative foundations of that behaviour; analysis otherwise being confined to the relatively trivial consequences of conditioning forces. Equally, the study of normative social and political theory cannot be conceived as a marginal activity, for appreciative purposes solely. Normative theory becomes central to the realm of critical examination of the actual foundations of empirical social and political activity: with attention devoted equally to the exposure of the normative foundations of current arrangements and practices; and to the examination of the normative and empirical consequences of alternative core values. The remaining division of labour between those traditionally specializing in empirical study and those concentrating upon normative theory might amount to little more than a focus, in the jargon of some critical theorists, upon *deconstruction* of empirical 'realities' in the case of the former and normative *reconstruction* in the case of the latter.

Political analysts are thus, in a sense, both analysts and activists in their public pronouncements. The agendas and languages of the political orders that they study can be accepted, with a conditioning effect upon the priorities and practices consequentially adopted, or they can be resisted and a necessarily critical perspective incorporated into all subsequent study and statements. The political analyst is distinguished from the political activist through the pursuit of an understanding of the contrasting political 'realities', past and present, and in adherence to established academic and intellectual disciplines. Such 'disciplines' are, however, reflective of the norms and understandings of the academic sub-section of wider society. Moreover, as private reflection passes into public pronouncement, the political analyst is faced with the unavoidable choice between acceptance of established political 'realities', and their normative foundations, or rejection within a more critical form of analysis.

Multi-level political analysis

Some of the difficulties of the task confronting students of politics and inter-state politics arise from the complex character of the political behaviour of many actors. While the predominant part of such behaviour is shaped by the prevailing institutional framework, and the fundamental principles upon which it rests, some behaviour that appears initially to be no more than 'daily' politics may actually be directed towards constitutional/institutional change or even pose a challenge to one or more of the fundamental principles of the prevailing political order. The analyst of politics must thus be able to distinguish clearly between 'business as usual' politics, and more challenging forms of political behaviour, if the significance and prospects of any actions, developments or groups are to be effectively evaluated. Moreover, a complex form of analysis may be necessary of the interrelationships between the nature of the prevailing political order and, on the one hand, the emergence of challenges to established principles or institutions and, on the other, the prospects for success of such challenging impulses.

Such multi-level analysis is particularly important in the study and analysis of political change. The pace and extent of change will often be conditioned by the implications of potential changes for the deeper levels of the political order. A change of constitutional arrangements which might appear desirable at one level might have threatening implications for foundational principles. However, important sources of change might also be detected in the gradual emergence of inconsistencies amongst the practices and outcomes of politics at the day-to-day level, institutional structures and foundational principles: tensions building to a point at which ameliorative adjustments are effected at one or other political level.

International Society as a political concept and a politically constructed 'reality'

Political orders exist at all times and in all places; varying, however, in their clarity, cohesiveness and durability. The modern era has, despite repeated challenge and redefinition, witnessed the clear evolution and steady expansion of an inter-state political order. A clear, and deeply embedded, statism, with its embrace of a nominal equality of respect and treatment for all states, has been combined uneasily with a practical acknowledgement of the hierarchy of power and influence amongst extant states.[17] Most of the central features of the prevailing international (inter-state) system, and its institutional arrangement, can be expressed in terms of such a political order, with no reference to notions of 'International Society', as witnessed by the example of Robert Gilpin's contribution to J. D. B. Miller and John Vincent's volume on the work of Hedley Bull.[18]

Given the efficacy of the notion of an international (or inter-state) political order, recourse to the concept of 'International Society' must fulfil some additional function or functions. The first, and most obvious, such function is to denote some special form of inter-state political order to which the notion of society is particularly pertinent. However, the nature of such a particularly 'social' form of international political order is far from self-evident, as is clear from an examination of the writings of those who espouse the concept. This paper has advanced the argument that any political order will constitute a 'politically constructed reality', rather than a simple, naturally given, empirical 'reality'. Central to an examination of any political reality will, therefore, be the questions of who has sought to engender that 'reality', for what purpose and by what means. Such questions complicate, but are central to, any clear purchase upon the notion of 'International Society' and its empirical 'reality'.

Many examinations of the nature, development and provenance of 'International Society' imply the simple empirical existence of such 'International Society' and its inherent 'naturalness'. Thus, Hedley Bull offers an account of 'International Society' as something that has existential status, in the present or past, and that was brought into being by functional forces.[19] Charles Manning, in contrast, furnishes rather more hints of the existentially complex nature of 'International Society' - as a phenomenon that can come into being only if pertinent human actors conceive of arrangements corresponding to such an 'International Society', desire such arrangements and adopt behaviour appropriate to the realization of such a condition in practice.[20]

The attribution of 'International Society' to a functionalist teleology plunges the concept into a well-stirred mire of analytical controversy and philosophical disputation. A 'political constructionist' view of 'International Society', closer to that espoused by Manning, could, however, avoid all such traces of functionalist teleology. The modern state (and the 'nation') can be seen as politically constructed 'realities'. Any subsequent 'International Society' could then be viewed as a second order, political construction. Such a constructed 'International Society' would, however, still manifest some analytically challenging peculiarities.

If successfully constructed, 'International Society' would constitute a most peculiar form of 'society' - being a 'society' of states rather than of real human beings. Any features that went beyond those of any reasonably well-established inter-state political order would have to manifest the cultural characteristics of 'real societies'. Inanimate objects, like states, cannot participate in and project the kinds of linguistically and experientially based cultures that are characteristic of cohesive societies. It is possible to conceive of 'International Society' as a misleading synonym for some deeper, and wider, *world society*, composed or real, sensate human beings whose interactions could constitute a real society. It is clear, however, that, irrespective of any ultimate connection between international and world societies (positive or negative), the 'society' that is of primary theoretical interest to members of the 'English School' is that of states.

'International Society', of the kind theorized by the 'English School', can, in practice, rather than in functionalist theory, be created only by state élites and their diplomatic representatives. It is they who share and propagate common values, understandings, expectations and languages. A form of inter-state society could, therefore, be sustained by the behaviour of a highly restricted number of élite representatives of participating states under special, and highly restrictive, conditions. Such élites, it must be emphasized, initially derive their capacity to act in this 'socially constructive' manner from their roles in their states' apparati. States are thus prioritized in, and by, such a concept of 'International Society'. 'International Society' thus constitutes a politically constructed 'social' facet of a wider, politically constructed international political order. One practical manifestation of such an 'International Society' might be a 'diplomatic society' within, or even underpinning, the wider order.

The conditions which permit the generation of a 'social' component within the inter-state political order are demanding and relatively elusive. The slow evolution of an European-based political order permitted the gradual generation of a diplomatic culture and a reasonably well-established set of guidelines to, and expectations about, the behaviour of the group of European states.[21] With its progressive crystallization at Westphalia (1648), Utrecht (1713–15) and the Congress of Vienna (1815), Europe's 'International Society' may have well suited its purposes and perspectives of its contemporary leaders, but found, and has continued to find, more problematical application beyond the frontiers of the Continent.[22] The destruction of non-European political communities, widespread enslavement of local populations and moral differentiation compromises any claim to a wider 'International Society'. Moreover, in the contemporary world, any serious challenge to the principles, institutions, or practices of the prevailing international political order evidences an absence of 'society' amongst those divided by that challenge.[23] Indeed, as Fred Halliday has been at pains to argue, revolutionary regimes have persistently posed basic challenges to the prevailing order[24] and, hence, any echoes of 'society' internationally.

Of considerable interest, therefore, is the question of why the term 'society' should be so emphasized in the 'English School's' description of the modern inter-state system: a question that suggests a second function of the notion of 'International Society'. The approach developed in this paper would suggest that the term 'International Society' must be a reflection, or possibly an obscuration, of a statist normative order. This statist order, and the inter-state system thus engendered, is presented as a natural, and desirable, 'reality' both by conventional Realists and by theorists of 'International Society'. Many of the trenchant criticisms of this supposed naturalness (and even timelessness) of the Realists' acceptance of the statist order, by writers like Richard Ashley,[25] R. B. J. Walker,[26] Jim George[27] and Ole Wæver,[28] apply with equal force to the realist echoes in many conceptions of 'International Society'. The possibility that both the modern international system and 'International Society' might also have been developed by, and imposed in the interests of, wielders of disproportionate, and even hegemonic, power is also stressed by critical writers like Robert Cox.[29]

The distinctive view of theorists of 'International Society', however, is that the world exhibits, or could exhibit, a statist order, that may be tamed by the (functional) development of 'social' characteristics and constraints. For writers like Martin Wight, therefore, the idea of 'International Society' civilizes an otherwise dismal vision of a world of power-seeking states, which would be otherwise moderated in their impulses and appetites only by such transitory and tenuous 'balances of power' as may wax and wane in the international affairs of humankind.[30] An untamed state system might be fatally unruly; but a 'socialized' inter-state system may allow us to sleep easily in our beds and obviate any further need for critical thought about the ultimate effects of a statist political and world order. Functional and metatheoretical in character, such a notion of 'International Society' serves a plethora of emotional and intellectual needs for its enthusiasts.

For those of a more critical disposition, however, notions of 'International Society' are considerably less reassuring. The embrace of a system of states entailed by 'International Society' perpetuates many of the difficulties generated by such a system. The fragmentation of political authority in such a system may be ameliorated but it is not transcended. The sense of 'otherness' felt by the citizens of one state towards those of any other, will be little diminished by the special sense of participation in an 'International Society' experienced by those of their political leaders and diplomats that have been sufficiently socialized into the norms and understandings. When, indeed, political leadership passes into the hands of those lacking a sense of, or adherence to, 'International Society', then the implications of a system of separated states may make themselves felt with fearsome force. How far the experience of the contemporary international system, or 'International Society', contributes directly to the emergence of such anti-systemic impulses within recalcitrant societies is a critical question, but one which has, with the exception of some of Hedley Bull's later statements,[31] been largely ignored, or even excluded, by mainstream 'International Society' studies.

Considerable intellectual difficulties are also created by the relatively narrow analytical foci of both realist international systems theory and the 'International Society' perspective. Both are extremely limited in the nature of the changes that they can accommodate or explain. Kenneth Waltz's seminal study of international systems offered the only major change of the entire modern era as that between multipolarity and post-1945 bipolarity.[32] Many students of 'International Society', in their turn, focus overwhelmingly on the waxing and waning of 'societal' features as *the* primary, if not exclusive, dimension of change in international relations.

Implications

The central argument in this paper is that studies of international relations that are undertaken without any awareness of the profound significance of the foundational principles of the prevailing order will be seriously flawed. Moreover, it is essential that the principles and institutional foundations of the prevailing political order be disinterred and the 'constructed' character of political orders acknowledged, if a crude and naive empiricism is to be avoided.

A primary effect of incorporating a greater awareness of the politically constructed nature of political orders is to dissolve much of the 'conventional' distinction between positive and normative statements within the study of political affairs. If 'empirical statements' about any political order or significant development within, or arising from, an order are made with a full recognition of the normative principles that underpin the construction of that political order then analysis cannot be confined purely to the supposedly empirical realm: the normative being seen to constitute the basis of much of the empirical. Rigorous analysis will incorporate the display of the normative foundations of empirical phenomena and developments, as a central part of a full account of those phenomena or developments.

Such a constructionist approach should not, however, drift into the analytical dead-end of inter-textual analysis or extreme deconstructionism. The states, systems and 'societies' that are constructed by human agents have a reality of considerable force and durability. Socially and politically constructed 'realities' are no less real for the nature of their origins. The resilience of human institutions, whether formal or informal, is such as to constitute a major influence upon many actions and a substantial constraint upon many of their consequences.[33] Change, in its many forms and effects, may then be stimulated by incompatibilities between the 'realities' that have been constructed in one or more 'domains' of human activity and external 'realities', either socially constructed or environmental.

Discriminating analysis of theories of the 'international system' and 'International Society' thus need to be clear on a number of points: the normative foundations of such a 'system' or 'society'; the institutional expressions of such foundations; their practical consequences in 'daily' inter-state, and indeed domestic, politics; relationships with the constructed 'realities' of the other domains of human activity; and implications for relations with the natural environment within which humanity has to act.

Such an analysis should facilitate a more critical perspective upon those practitioners of inter-state relations who have advocated, or continue to promote, notions of 'International Society'. An enhanced ability to reveal any motives or concerns that might not otherwise be immediately apparent should result, along with a more acute sense of any attendant difficulties in dealing effectively with a range of problems encountered within, or created for, the natural environment.

Finally, a political constructionist analysis of 'International Society' should resolve many of the methodological and conceptual problems encountered by those who have sought to treat it as a simple empirical phenomenon. Acknowledging both international systems and 'International Societies' as constructed 'realities', where they exist, should help to bridge the otherwise awning chasm between contemporary critical theorists and naive realists.

Notes

1 On the concept of *metatheory*, see Castles, F. G., *Politics and Social Insight* (London, Routledge and Kegan Paul, 1971); and on the roles of verification and falsification, see also Ryan, Alan, *The Philosophy of the Social Sciences* (London, Macmillan, 1970).

2 On the existence of such an English School, see Jones, Roy E., 'The English School of international relations: a case for closure', *Review of International Studies*, **7**(1) (January 1981), pp. 1–13; Grader, Sheila, 'The English School of international relations: evidence and evaluation', *Review of International Studies*, **14**(1) (January 1988), pp. 29–44; and Wilson, Peter, 'The English School of international relations: a reply to Sheila Grader', *Review of International Studies* **15**(1) (January 1989), pp. 49–58.

3 Bull, Hedley, 'International theory: the case for a classical approach', in Knorr, K. and Rosenau, J. N., *Contending Approaches to International Politics* (Princeton, NJ, Princeton University Press, 1969), pp. 20–38.

4 See Manning, C. A. W., *The Nature of International Society* (London, G. Bell and Sons Ltd, 1962), especially p. 176; and Luard, Evan, *International Society* (London, Macmillan, 1990), especially p. 2.

5 Bull, Hedley, *The Anarchical Society: A Study of Order in World Politics* (London, Macmillan, 1977).
6 Ibid., pp. 16–19.
7 Ibid., p. 13.
8 Ibid.; see also Bull, Hedley and Watson, Adam (eds), *The Expansion of International Society* (Oxford, Clarendon Press, 1984).
9 Particularly Watson, Adam, *The Evolution of International Society: A Comparative Historical Analysis* (London, Routledge, 1992).
10 Manning, *The Nature of International Society*, especially pp. 1–17.
11 For a discussion of such approaches, see Ryan, *The Philosophy of the Social Sciences*, especially Chs 3 and 4.
12 See, for example, the discussions in Winch, Peter, *The Idea of a Social Science and Its Relation to Philosophy* (London, Routledge and Kegan Paul, 1958); and Hollis, M. and Smith, S., *Explaining and Understanding International Relations* (Oxford, Oxford University Press, 1990), especially Chs 3 and 4.
13 On which, in particular, see Gibbons, M. T. (ed.), *Interpreting Politics* (Oxford, Basil Blackwell, 1987); Hoffman, Mark, 'Critical theory and the inter-paradigm debate', *Millennium: Journal of International Relations*, **16**(2) (1987), pp. 231–49; and see also Jones, R. J. Barry, *Anti-Statism and Critical Theories in International Relations*, Reading Papers in Politics, no. 4 (March 1991), Dept. of Politics, University of Reading, England.
14 See, in particular, Berger, Peter L. and Luckmann, Thomas, *The Social Construction of Reality* (Harmondsworth, Penguin, 1967).
15 On structuration theory, see Giddens, Anthony, *The Constitution of Society: Outline of the Theory of Structuration* (Cambridge, Polity Press, 1984); and Cohen, Ira, *Structuration Theory: Anthony Giddens and the Constitution of Social Life* (London, Macmillan, 1989); and on the application of structuration theory to international relations, see Wendt, Alexander, 'The agent-structure problem in international relations', *International Organization*, **42**(3) (Summer 1987), pp. 335–70.
16 For a venture into the complexities of analysing change in international relations, see Buzan, B. and Jones, R. J. Barry (eds), *Change and the Study of International Relations: The Evaded Dimension* (London, Pinter, 1981).
17 For a discussion of which, see Tucker, Robert W., *The Inequality of Nations*, (London, Martin Robertson, 1977).
18 Gilpin, Robert, 'The global political system', in Miller, J. D. B. and Vincent, R. J. (eds), *Order and Violence: Hedley Bull and International Relations* (Oxford, Clarendon Press, 1990), Ch. 6.
19 Bull, *The Anarchical Society*; Bull and Watson (eds), *Expansion of International Society*.
20 Manning, *The Nature of International Society*.
21 See the discussions in Parts I and II of Bull and Watson (eds), *Expansion of International Society*.
22 See the trenchant criticisms of Jones, 'The English School of international relations: a case for closure', pp. 1–13.
23 See the discussions of the questions of the Third World and 'international society' in Bull and Watson (eds), *Expansion of International Society*, especially Chs 14, 15, 16, 20 and 22; and Miller, J. D. B., 'The Third World', in Miller and Vincent (eds), *Order and Violence*, Ch. 4.

24 Halliday, Fred, '"The sixth great power": on the study of revolution and international relations', *Review of International Studies*, **16**(3) (July 1990), pp. 207–21.

25 See the following works of Richard K. Ashley: 'Political realism and human interests', *International Studies Quarterly*, **25**(2) (June 1981), pp. 204–36; 'The poverty of neorealism', *International Organization* **38**(2) (Spring 1984), pp. 2225–61 (reprinted in Keohane, R. O., *Neorealism and Its Critics* (New York, Columbia University Press, 1986); and 'Untying the sovereign state: a double reading of the anarchy problematique', *Millennium: Journal of International Studies*, **17**(2) (1988), pp. 227–62.

26 Walker, R. B. J., *Inside/Outside: International Relations as Political Theory* (Cambridge, Cambridge University Press, 1993); and Walker, R. B. J., 'History and structure in the theory of international relations', *Millennium: Journal of International Studies*, **18**(2) (1989), pp. 163–83.

27 George, Jim, 'International relations and the search for thinking space: another view of the third debate', *International Studies Quarterly*, **33** (1989), pp. 269–79; and George, Jim, *Discourses of Global Politics: A Critical (Re)Introduction to International Relations* (Boulder, CO, Lynne Rienner, 1994).

28 See Wæver, Ole, 'International society: the grammar of dialogue among states', paper presented to the Workshop on 'The Nature of International Society Reconsidered', ECPR, Limerick, March 1992.

29 See, in particular, Cox, Robert W., 'Gramsci, hegemony and international relations: an essay in method', *Millennium: Journal of International Studies*, **12**(2) (1983), pp. 162–75; and Cox, Robert W., 'Social forces, states and world orders: beyond international relations theory', *Millennium: Journal of International Studies*, **10**(2) (1981), pp. 126–55.

30 For interesting discussions of the work and ideas of Martin Wight, see Bull, Hedley, 'Martin Wight and the theory of international relations: the second Martin Wight Memorial Lecture', *British Journal of International Studies*, **2**(2) (July 1979), pp. 101–16; and Nicholson, Michael, 'The enigma of Martin Wight', *Review of International Studies*, **7**(1) (January 1981), pp. 15–22.

31 For a discussion of this issue, see Miller, 'The Third World'.

32 Waltz, Kenneth, *Theory of International Politics* (Reading, MA, Addison-Wesley, 1979), p. 163.

33 For a fuller discussion of this point, see Jones, R. J. Barry, 'Construction and constraint in the promotion of change in the principles of international conduct', in Holden, B. B. (ed.), *The Ethical Dimensions of Global Change* (London, Macmillan, 1996).

Bibliography

Adler, E. and Barnett, M. (1996) Governing anarchy: a research agenda for the study of security communities, *Ethics and International Affairs*, **10**.

Albert, M. (1997) Towards generative differentiation: the international political system in world society. Paper presented at the workshop 'Identity, Borders, Orders' at New Mexico State University, Las Cruces, New Mexico, 17–19 January.

Alker, H. R. (1990) Rescuing 'reason' from the 'rationalists': reading Vico, Marx and Weber as reflective institutionalists, *Millennium: Journal of International Studies*, **19**(2), 161–85.

Amin, S. (1988) *L'Eurocentrisme: critique d'une ideologie*, Paris, Anthropos.

Archer, C. (1983) *International Organization*, London, George Allen & Unwin.

Aron, R. (1962) *Paix et guerre entre les nations*, Paris, Calmann-Levy.

Aron, R. (1966) *Peace and War*, Florida, Doubleday.

Aron, R. (1967) Peace and war, *Survival*, 371–3.

Ashley, R. K. (1981) Political realism and human interests, *International Studies Quarterly*, **25**(2), 204–36.

Ashley, R. K. (1984) The poverty of neorealism, *International Organization*, **38**(2), 2225–61; reprinted in Keohane, R. O. (1986) *Neorealism and Its Critics*, New York, Columbia University Press.

Ashley, R. K. (1987) The geopolitics of geopolitical space: toward a critical social theory of international politics, *Alternatives*, **12**(4), 403–34.

Ashley, R. K. (1988), Untying the sovereign state: a double reading of the anarchy problematique, *Millennium: Journal of International Studies*, **17**(2), 227–62.

Ashley, R. K. (1989) Imposing international purpose: notes on a problematic of governance, in Czempiel, E.-O. and Rosenau, J. N. (eds), *Global Changes and Theoretical Challenges*, Lexington, MA, Lexington, 251–90.

Ashley, R. K. (1995) The powers of anarchy: theory, sovereignty and the domestication of global life, in Der Derian, J. (ed.), *International Theory: Critical Investigations*, London, Macmillan, 94–128.

Ashley, R. K. (forthcoming) *Statecraft as Mancraft.*

Augelli, E. and Murphy, C. (1988) *America's Quest for Supremacy and the Third World: A Gramscian Analysis*, London, Pinter.

Aune, B. (1970) *Rationalism, Empiricism and Pragmatism*, New York, Random House.

Ayoob, M. (1989) The Third World in the system of states: actor schizophrenia or growing pains? *International Studies Quarterly*, **33**(1), 67–80.

Baldwin, D. A. (ed.) (1993) *Neorealism and Neoliberalism: The Contemporary Debate*, New York, Columbia University Press.

Bandyopadhyaya, J. (1982) *North over South: A Non-Western Perspective of International Relations*, New Delhi, South Asian Publishers.

Beitz, C. R. (1979) *Political Theory and International Relations*, Princeton, NJ, Princeton University Press.

Beitz. C. R. (1979) Bounded morality: justice and the state in world politics, *World Politics*, **33**(3).

Beitz, C. R. (1994) ... in C. Brown (ed.), *Political Restructuring in Europe: Ethical Perspectives*, London and New York, Routledge.

Berger, P. L. and Luckmann, T. (1967) *The Social Construction of Reality*, Harmondsworth, Penguin Press.

Berridge, G. (1980) The political theory and institutional history of states systems, *British Journal of International Studies*, **6**(2), 82-92.

Bhaskar, R. (1979) *The Possibility of Naturalism: A Philosophical Critique of the Contemporary Human Sciences*, Brighton, Harvester Wheatsheaf.

Block, R. (1994) The tragedy of Rwanda, *New York Review of Books*, 20 October.

Boer, P. den, Bugge, P. and Wæver, O. (1993) *The History of the Idea of Europe*, Milton Keynes, Open University Press.

Booth, K. (1991) Security in anarchy: utopian realism in theory and practice, *International Affairs*, **67**(3), 527-46.

Booth, K. (1995) Human rights and international relations, *International Affairs*, **71**(1), 103-26.

Bourdieu, P. (1977) *Outline of a Theory of Practice*, Cambridge, Cambridge University Press.

Bozeman, A. (1960) *Politics and Culture in International History*, Princeton, NJ, Princeton University Press.

Bozeman, A. and Dore, R., (1984) in Bull, H. and Watson, A. (eds), *The Expansion of International Society*, Oxford, Clarendon Press.

Brandt, P. A. (1988) Det semiotiske grundforhold, in Dinesen, A. M. and Jørgensen, K. G. (eds) *Subjektivitet og Intersubjektivitet*, Aalborg, Arbejdspapirer fra Nordisk Sommeruniversitet, **28**, 7-16.

Brice, J. (1922) *International Relations*, London, Macmillan.

Brown, C. (1988) The modern requirement? Reflections on normative international theory in a post-western world, *Millennium: Journal of International Studies*, **17**(2), 339-48.

Brown, C. (1992) *International Relations Theory: New Normative Approaches*, Hemel Hempstead, Harvester Wheatsheaf.

Brown, C. (1995) International theory and international society: the viability of the middle way? *Review of International Studies*, **21**(2), 183-96.

Brown, C. (1996) Back to normal? Some reflections on sovereignty and self-determination after the Cold War, *Global Society*, **10**(1), 11-23.

Bull, H. The European international order, undated paper presented to the British Committee.

Bull, H. Political theory and international relations, Bull Papers.

Bull, H. (1966) International theory: the case for a classical approach, *World Politics*, **18**(3), 361-77.

Bull, H. (1966) The Grotian conception in international society, in Butterfield, H. and Wight, M. (eds), *Diplomatic Investigations: Essays in the Theory of International Politics*, London, George Allen & Unwin, 51-73.

Bull, H. (1966) Society and anarchy in international relations, in Butterfield, H. and Wight, M. (eds), *Diplomatic Investigations: Essays in the Theory of International Politics*, London, George Allen & Unwin, 35-50.

Bull, H. (1969) *The Twenty Years' Crisis* thirty years on, *International Journal*, **24**(4).

Bull, H. (1970) The state's positive role in world affairs, *Daedalus*, **108**(4), 112.

Bull, H. (1972) International law and international order, *International Organization*, **26**(3).

Bull, H. (1972) The theory of international politics 1919-1969, in Porter, B. (ed.), *The Aberystwyth Papers: International Politics 1919-1969*, London, Oxford University Press, 30-55; reprinted in Der Derian, J. (ed.) (1995) *International Theory: Critical Investigations*, London, Macmillan, 181-211.

Bull, H. (1975) Has the sovereign states system a future? Fryer Memorial Lecture, 3 June.

Bull, H. (1976) Martin Wight and the theory of international relations: the second Martin Wight Memorial Lecture, *British Journal of International Studies*, **6**(2), 101-16.

Bull, H. (1977) *The Anarchical Society: A Study of Order in World Politics*, London, Macmillan.

Bull, H. (1977) Introduction: Martin Wight and the study of international relations, in Wight, M. (ed.), *Systems of States*, Leicester, Leicester University Press.

Bull, H. (1978) Review of Donelan, M. (ed.), *The Reason of States*, in *Times Literary Supplement*, 28 April.

Bull, H. (1979) The state's positive role in world affairs, *Daedalus: Journal of the American Academy of Arts and Sciences*, **108**(4).

Bull, H. (1979) Human rights and world politics, in Pettman, R. (ed.), *Moral Claims in World Affairs*, London, Croom Helm.

Bull, H. (1979) Natural law and international relations, *British Journal of International Studies*, **5**.

Bull, H. (1979) The Third World and international society, *The Yearbook of World Affairs*, London, Stevens and Sons.

Bull, H. (1979) The universality of human rights, *Millennium: Journal of International Studies*, **8**(2).

Bull, H. (1980) Someone at BISA said that there was no British School. Nonsense. Talk on 'The appalling state of IR studies', LSE, 17 January.

Bull, H. (1980) Kissinger: the primacy of geopolitics, *International Affairs*, **56**(3).

Bull, H. (1981) Hobbes and the international anarchy, *Social Research*, **48**(4).

Bull, H. (1984) Justice in international relations, in *The 1983-84 Hagey Lectures*, Waterloo, Ontario, University of Waterloo.

Bull, H. (ed.) (1984) *Intervention in World Politics*, Oxford, Clarendon Press.

Bull, H. (1986) Hans Kelsen and international law, in Tur, R. and Twining, W. (eds), *Essays on Kelsen*, Oxford, Oxford University Press.

Bull, H. (1990) The importance of Grotius in the study of international relations, in Bull, H., Kingsbury, B. and Roberts, A. (eds), *Hugo Grotius and International Relations*, Oxford, Clarendon Press.

Bull, H. and Watson, A. (eds) (1984) *The Expansion of International Society*, Oxford, Clarendon Press.

Burton, J. W. (1968) *Systems, States, Diplomacy, and Rules*, Cambridge, Cambridge University Press.

Burton, J. W. (1972) *World Society*, Cambridge, Cambridge University Press.

Burton, J. W. *et al.* (1990) *The Study of World Society: A London Perspective*, as reprinted in Vasquez, J. A. (ed.), *Classics of International Relations*, 2nd edn, Englewoods Cliffs, NJ, Prentice-Hall.

Butterfield, H. (1951) *History and Human Relations*, London, Collins.

Butterfield, H. (1965) The historic states-system. Unpublished paper prepared for the British Committee on the Theory of International Politics.

Butterfield, H. and Wight, M. (eds) (1966) *Diplomatic Investigations: Essays in the Theory of International Politics*, London, George Allen & Unwin.

Butterfield, H. (1966) The balance of power, in Butterfield, H. and Wight, M. (eds), *Diplomatic Investigations: Essays in the Theory of International Politics*, London, George Allen & Unwin, 132–48.

Butterfield, H. (1972) Morality and international order, in Porter, B. (ed.), *The Aberystwyth Papers: International Politics 1919–1969*, London, Oxford University Press, 336–57.

Butterfield, H. (1975) Raison d'état, Martin Wight Memorial Lecture, University of Sussex.

Buzan, B. (1991) *People, States and Fear: An agenda for International Security Studies in the Post-Cold War Era*, 2nd edn, Hemel Hempstead, Harvester Wheatsheaf.

Buzan, B. (1992) The evolution of international society. Paper for the annual workshops of European Consortium for Political Research, Limerick, April.

Buzan, B. (1993) From international system to international society: structural realism and regime theory meet the English School, *International Organization*, **47**(3), 327–52.

Buzan, B. (1996) The present as a historic turning point, *Journal of Peace Research*, **32**(4), 385–98.

Buzan, B. and Jones, R. J. B. (eds) (1981) *Change and the Study of International Relations: the Evaded Dimension*, London, Pinter.

Buzan, B. and Little, R. (1994) Reconceptualising the international system and neorealism: the need to accommodate structural and functional differentiation of units, paper presented to the BISA Conference, University of York, December.

Buzan, B. and Little, R. (1994) The idea of international system: theory meets history, *International Political Science Review* **15**(3), 231–55.

Buzan, B. and Little, R. (1996) Reconceptualising anarchy: structural realism meets world history, *European Journal of International Relations*, **2**(4), 403–38.

Buzan, B. and Wæver, O. (1997) Slippery? Contradictory? Sociologically untenable? The Copenhagen School replies, *Review of International Studies*, **23**(2), March, 143–52.

Buzan, B, Little, R. and Jones, C. (1993) *The Logic of Anarchy: From Neo-realism to Structural Realism*, New York, Columbia University Press.

Buzan, B. *et al.* (1990) *The European Security Order Recast: Scenarios for the Post-Cold War Era*, London, Pinter.

Camilleri, J. A. and Falk, J. (1992) *The End of Sovereignty? The Politics of a Shrinking and Fragmenting World*, Aldershot, Edward Elgar.

Carlsnaes, W. (1992) The agency-structure problem in foreign policy analysis, *International Studies Quarterly*, **36**(3).

Carr, E. H. (1946) *The Twenty Years' Crisis 1919–1939*, London, Macmillan.

Carr, E. H. (1969) *The Twenty Years' Crisis* thirty years on, *International Journal* **24**(4).

Castles, F. G. (1971) *Politics and Social Insight*, London, Routledge and Kegan Paul.

Chase-Dunn, C. (1989) *Global Formation. Structures of the World-economy*, Cambridge, MA, Basil Blackwell.

Clark, G. (1960) *The Seventh Century*, 2nd edn, London, Oxford University Press.

Clark, I. (1989) *The Hierarchy of States: Reform and Resistance in the International Order*, 2nd edn, Cambridge, BISA/Cambridge University Press; 1st edn 1980.

Clausewitz, C. von (1982) *On War*, Harmondsworth, Penguin; first published 1832.

Cochrane, M. (1996) The liberal ironist, ethics and international relations theory. *Millennium*, **25**(1), 29–52.

Cohen, I. (1989) *Structuration Theory: Anthony Giddens and the Constitution of Social Life*, London, Macmillan.

Cohen, R. (1981) *International Politics: The Rules of the Game*, London, Longman.

Cowling, M. (1978) *Conservative Essays*, London, Cassell.

Cox. R. W. (1981) Social forces, states and world orders: beyond international relations theory, *Millennium: Journal of International Studies*, **10**(2), 126–55.

Cox. R. W. (1983) Gramsci, hegemony and international relations: an essay in method, *Millennium: Journal of International Studies*, **12**(2), 165–75.

Cox, R. W. (1987) *Production, Power, and World Order. Social Forces in the Making of History*, New York, Columbia University Press.

Craig, G. A. and George, A. L. (1983) *Force and Statecraft: Diplomatic Problems of Our Times*, Oxford and New York, Oxford University Press.

Cutler, A. C. (1991) The 'Grotian Tradition' in international relations theory: a critique, *Review of International Studies*, **17**(1).

Czempiel, E.-O. (1991) Einmischung ist möglich, *Frankfurter Allgemeine Zeitung*, 20 July.

De Porte, A. W. (1979) *Europe Between the Superpowers: The Enduring Balance*, New Haven, CT, Yale University Press.

Der Derian, J. (1987) *On Diplomacy: A Genealogy of Western Estrangement*, Oxford, Blackwell.

Der Derian, J. (1995) *International Theory: Critical Investigations*, London, Macmillan.

Derrida, J. (1977) Signature Event Context, *Glyph*, **1**, 172–97; first published 1972.

Derrida, J. (1984) Guter Wille zur Macht (I): Drei Fragen an Hans-Georg Gadamer and Guter Will zur Macht (II): Die Unterschriften interpretieren (Nietzsche/Heidegger) in Forget, P. (ed.), *Text und Interpretation*, Munich, Wilhelm Fink Verlag, 56–8 and 62–77.

Donelan, M. (ed.) (1978) *The Reason of State: A Study in International Political Theory*, London, George Allen & Unwin.

Donelan, M. (1990) *Elements of International Political Theory*, Oxford, Clarendon Press.

Doran, C. F. (1991) *Systems in Crisis: New Imperatives of High Politics at Century's End*, Cambridge, Cambridge University Press.

Dunn, J. (1994) *The Nation State and Human Community*. Published in Italian as *Stato Nazionale e Communità Umana*, Milan, Anabasi. Not yet published in English.

Dunne, T. (1991) The genesis and history of the 'English School' of international relations, in Neumann, I. B. (ed.), *The 'English School' of International Relations: A Conference Report*, Oslo, NUPI Report, no. 179, April, 1–17.

Dunne, T. (1993) International relations theory in Britain: the invention of an international society tradition, D.Phil. Thesis, Oxford University.

Dunne, T. (1995) International society: theoretical promises fulfilled?, *Cooperation and Conflict*, **30**(2), 125–54.

Dunne, T. (1995) The social construction of international society, *European Journal of International Relations*, **1**(3), 367–90.

Egido, J. P. (1984) Natural law, in *Encyclopedia of Public International Law*, under the direction of Rudolph Bernhardt, Amsterdam, New York, Oxford, North-Holland Publishing Co. **7**, 344–49.

Elshtain, J. B. (1993) 'Act V: bringing it all back home, again', in Rosenau, J. N. *Global Voices – Dialogues in International Relations*, Boulder, CO, Westview Press, 97–116.

Evans, P. B., Jacobson, H. D. and Putnam, R. D. (eds) (1993) *Double-Edged Diplomacy: International Bargaining and Domestic Politics*, Berkeley, CA, University of California Press.

Evans, T. and Wilson, P. (1992) Regime theory and the English School of international relations: a comparison, *Millennium: Journal of International Relations*, **21**(3), 329-52.

Falk, R. A. (1963) *Law, Morality, and War in the Contemporary World*, New York, Praeger.

Falk, R. A. (1987) *The Promise of World Order*, London, Harvester Wheatsheaf.

Falk, R. A. (1992) *Explorations at the Edge of Time*, Philadelphia, Temple University Press.

Falk, R. A. (1997) The critical realist tradition and the demystification of interstate power, in Gill, S. and Mittelman, J. H. (eds), *Innovation and Transformation in International Studies*, Cambridge, Cambridge University Press.

Farago, B. (1995) L'Europe: empire introuvable? *Le Debat*, **83**, 42–58.

Farer, T. J. (1993) Collectively defending democracy in a world of sovereign states: the western hemisphere's prospect, *Human Rights Quarterly*, **15**.

Ferguson, Y. H. (forthcoming) *Ancient Regimes*, Cambridge, Cambridge University Press.

Ferguson, Y. H. and Mansbach, R. W. (1988) *The Elusive Quest: Theory and International Politics*, Columbia, SC, University of South Carolina Press.

Ferguson Y. H and Mansbach, R. W. (1989) *The State, Conceptual Chaos, and the Future of International Relations Theory*, Boulder, CO, Lynne Rienner.

Ferguson, Y. H. and Mansbach, R. W. (1991) Between celebration and despair: constructive suggestions for future international theory, *International Studies Quarterly*, **35**(4).

Ferguson, Y. H. and Mansbach, R. W. (1996) *Polities: Authority, Identities, and Change*, Columbia, SC, University of South Carolina Press.

Ferguson, Y. H. and Mansbach, R. W. (1996) The past as prelude to the future: changing loyalties in global politics, in Lapid, Y. and Kratochwil, F. (eds), *The Return of Culture and Identity in IR Theory*, Boulder, CO, Lynne Rienner.

Ferguson, Y. H. and Mansbach, R. W. (1996) Beyond inside/outside: political space in a world of politics, *Global Governance*, **2**(2), 261–87.

Fitzpatrick, J. (1989) The 'Image of International Society' in Anglo-American International Relations Theory, paper presented to the joint conference of the International Studies Association (US) and the British International Studies Association, London, March.

Forget, P. (1984), Leitfäden einer unwahrscheinlichen Debatte, in Forget, P. (ed.) *Text und Interpretation*, Munich, Wilhelm Fink Verlag, 7–23.

Foucault, M. (1970) *The Archeology of Knowledge*, New York, Pantheon Books.

Franck, T. M. (1990) *The Power of Legitimacy Among Nations*, New York, Oxford University Press.

Franck, T. M. (1992) The emerging right to democratic governance, *American Journal of International Law*, **86**(1).

Gadamer, H.-G. (1984) Text und Interpretation and Und dennoch: Macht des guten Willens, in Forget P. (ed.), *Text und Interpretation*, Munich, Wilhelm Fink Verlag, 24-55 and 59-61.

Gallarotti, G. M. (1991) The limits of international organization: systematic failure in the management of international relations, *International Organization*, **45**(2), 183-220.

George, J. (1989) International relations and the search for thinking space: another view of the third debate, *International Studies Quarterly*, **33**, 269-79.

George, J. (1994) *Discourses of Global Politics: A Critical (Re)Introduction to International Relations*, Boulder, CO, Lynne Rienner.

Gibbons, M. T. (ed.) (1987) *Interpreting Politics*, Oxford, Basil Blackwell.

Giddens, A. (1984) *The Constitution of Society: Outline of the Theory of Structuration*, Cambridge, Polity Press.

Gilpin, R. (1990) The global political system, in Miller, J. D. B. and Vincent, R. J. *Order and Violence: Hedley Bull and International Relations*, Oxford, Clarendon Press.

Gong, G. W. (1984) *The Standard of 'Civilisation' in International Society*, Oxford, Clarendon Press.

Grader, S. (1988) The English School of international relations: evidence and evaluation, *Review of International Studies*, **14**(1), 29-44.

Grewe, W. G. (1984) *Epochen der Völkerrechtsgeschichte*, Baden-Baden, Nomos.

Grotius, H. (1901) *The Rights of War and Peace*, Washington, DC, M. W. Dunne; first published 1625.

Guzzini, S. (in press) *The History of Realism in IR and IPE: The Continuing Story of a Death Foretold*, London, Routledge.

Haas, E. B. (1990) *When Knowledge is Power: Three Models of Change in International Organizations*, Berkeley, CA, University of California Press.

Halliday, F. (1986) *The Making of the Second Cold War*, London, Verso.

Halliday, F. (1989) *From Kabul to Managua. Soviet-American Relations in the 1980s*, New York, Pantheon Books.

Halliday, F. (1990) 'The sixth Great Power': on the study of revolution and international relations, *Review of International Studies*, **16**(3), 207-22.

Halliday, F. (1992) International society as homogeneity: Burke, Marx, Fukuyama, *Millennium: Journal of International Studies*, **21**(3), 435-61.

Halliday, F. (1994) *Rethinking International Relations*, Basingstoke, Macmillan.

Hampshire, S. (1993) Liberalism: the new twist, *New York Review of Books*, 12 August.

Hanson, D. (1984) Thomas Hobbes' 'Highway to Peace', *International Organization*, **38**(2).

Harris, I. (1993) Order and justice in *The Anarchical Society*, *International Affairs*, **69**(4).

Henkin, L. (1979) *How Nations Behave: Law and Foreign Policy*, New York, Columbia University Press; first published 1968.

Herbst, J. (1992) Challenges to Africa's boundaries in the new world order, *Journal of International Affairs*, **46** (Summer), 17-30.

Herz, J. H. (1950) Idealist internationalism and the security dilemma, *World Politics*, **2**(2), 157-80.

Hinsley, F. H. (1963) *Power and the Pursuit of Peace: Theory and Practice in the History of Relations between States*, Cambridge, Cambridge University Press.

Hinsley, F. H. (1986) *Sovereignty*, 2nd edn, Cambridge, Cambridge University Press; first published 1966.

Hjermind, C. and Jensen L. D. (1996) Den etiske betydning af nye skillelinier efter den kolde krig, exam paper, Institute of Political Science, University of Copenhagen.

Hobbes, T. (1946) *Leviathan*, ed. M. Oakeshott, Oxford, Basil Blackwell.

Hoffman, M. (1987) Critical theory and the inter-paradigm debate, *Millennium: Journal of International Studies*, **16**(2), 231-49.

Hoffmann, S. (1963) Rousseau on war and peace, *American Political Science Review*, **57**(2).

Hoffmann, S. (1966) The fate of the nation state: obstinate or obsolete? *Daedalus* **95**(3), 862-915.

Hoffmann, S. (1977) An American social science: international relations, *Dædalus: Journal of the American Academy of Arts and Sciences*, **106**(3), 41-60.

Hoffmann, S. (1986) International society, *International Affairs*, **62**(2), reprinted (partly revised) in Miller, J. D. B. and Vincent, R. J. (1990) *Order and Violence: Hedley Bull and International Relations*, Oxford, Clarendon Press.

Hoffmann, S. (1986) Hedley Bull's contribution to international relations, *International Affairs*, **62**(2).

Hollis, M. and Smith, S. (1990) *Explaining and Understanding International Relations*, Oxford, Oxford University Press.

Holm, U. (1993) *Det Franske Europa [The French Europe]*, Århus, Århus University Press.

Hont, I. (1995) The permanent crisis of a divided mankind, in Dunn, J. (ed.), *Contemporary Crisis of the Nation-State?* Oxford, Basil Blackwell.

Huntington, S. (1993) The clash of civilisations, *Foreign Affairs*, **72**(3).

Huntington, S. (1993) If not civilisations, what? Paradigms of the post-Cold War world, *Foreign Affairs*, **76**(5).

Hurrell, A. (1990) Kant and the Kantian paradigm in international relations, *Review of International Studies*, **16**(3), 183-206.

Hurrell, A. (1993) International society and the study of regimes: a reflective approach, in Rittberger, V. (ed.), *Regime Theory and International Relations*, Oxford, Clarendon Press, 49-72.

Hurrell, A. (1994) The English School and the liberal problematique, in Neumann, I. B. (ed.), *The 'English School' of International Relations: A Conference Report*, Oslo, NUPI Report no. 179, 34-49.

Hurrell, A. (1994) Order in international society, in Neumann, I. B. (ed.), *The 'English School' of International Relations: A Conference Report*, Oslo, NUPI Report no. 179.

Indyk, M. (1985) The Australian study of international relations, in Aitken, D. (ed.), *Surveys of Australian Political Science*, Sydney, George Allen & Unwin.

Jackson, R. H. (1990) Martin Wight, international theory and the good life, *Millennium: Journal of International Studies*, **19**(2).

Jackson, R. H. (1990) *Quasi-states: Sovereignty, International Relations and the Third World*, Cambridge, Cambridge University Press.

Jackson, R. (1995) The political theory of international society, in Booth, K. and Smith, S. (eds), *International Relations Theory Today*, Oxford, Polity Press.

James, A. (ed.) (1973) *The Bases of International Order*, London, Cambridge University Press.

James. A. (1978) International society, *British Journal of International Studies*, **4**.

James, A. (1980) Diplomacy and international society, *International Relations*, **6**(6).

James, A. (1986) *Sovereign Statehood: The Basis of International Society*, London, George Allen & Unwin.

James, A. (1989) The realism of Realism: the state and the study of international relations, *Review of International Studies*, **1**(3), 215–30.

James, A. (1991) Sovereignty in Eastern Europe, *Millennium: Journal of International Studies*, **20**(1).

James, A. (1992) The equality of states: contemporary manifestations of an ancient doctrine, *Review of International Studies*, **18**(4), 377–92.

James, A. (1993) System or society, *Review of International Studies*, **19**(3), 269–88.

Jervis, R. (1982) Security regimes, *International Organization*, **36**(2), 357–78.

Jones, C. A. (1983) *The North–South Dialogue: A Brief History*, London, Pinter Press.

Jones, R. E. (1981) The 'English School' of international relations: a case for closure, *Review of International Studies*, **7**(1), 1–12.

Jones, R. J. B. (1991) Anti-statism and critical theories in international relations, Reading Papers in Politics, no. 4, Department of Politics, University of Reading.

Jones, R. J. B. (1996) Construction and constraint in the promotion of change in the principles of international conduct, in Holden, B. B. (ed.), *The Ethical Dimensions of Global Change*, London, Macmillan.

Kaldor, M. (1990) *The Imaginary War: Understanding the East–West Conflict*, Oxford, Basil Blackwell.

Kaplan, M. (1966) The great debate: traditionalism vs. science in international relations, *World Politics*, **19**(1), 1–21.

Katzenstein, P. J. (ed.) (1996) *The Culture of National Security: Identity and Norms in World Politics*, New York, Columbia University Press.

Keal, P. (1994) Dual agenda or American agenda? International relations theory and the sociology of international law, paper prepared for the annual conference of British International Studies Association, University of York.

Kegley Jr, C. W. (1993) The neoidealist moment in international studies? realist myths and the new international realities, *International Studies Quarterly*, **37**(2).

Kegley Jr, C. W. (ed.) (1995) *Controversies in International Relations Theory: Realism and the Neoliberal Challenge*, New York, St. Martin's Press.

Kennealy, P. (1988) Talking about autopoiesis – order from noise?, in Teubner, G. (ed.), *Autopoietic Law: A New Approach to Law and Society*, Berlin/New York, Walter de Gruyter/Firenze: European University Institute, Series A, Law, no. 8, 349–68.

Keohane, R. O. (1984) *After Hegemony*, Princeton, NJ, Princeton University Press.

Keohane, R. O. (1988) International institutions: two approaches (1984 ISA Presidential Address), *International Studies Quarterly*, **32**(4); reprinted in Keohane (1989).

Keohane, R. O. (1989) *International Institutions and State Power*, Boulder, CO, Westview Press.

Keohane, R. O. (1992) Book review of Wight, *International Theory*, *American Political Science Review*, **86**(4), 1112.

Keohane, R. O., Nye, J. and Hoffmann, S. (eds) (1993) *After the Cold War: State Strategies and International Institutions in Europe, 1989–1991*, Cambridge, MA, Harvard University Press.

Kingsbury, B. and Roberts, A. (1990) Introduction: Grotian thought in international relations, in Bull, H., Kingsbury, B. and Roberts, A. (eds), *Hugo Grotius and International Relations*, Oxford, Clarendon Press, 1-64.

Kissinger, H. A. (1966) Domestic structure and foreign policy, *Dædalus: Journal of the American Academy of Arts and Sciences*, **95**(2), 503-29.

Kissinger, H. A. (1977) *A World Restored: Castlereagh, Metternich and the Restoration of Peace 1812-1822*, Boston, Houghton Mifflin Company; first published 1957.

Knorr, K. and Rosenau, J. N. (1969) *Contending Approaches to International Politics*, Princeton, NJ, Princeton University Press.

Knudsen, T. B. (1994) *Det Nye Europa: Orden eller Kaos?* MA thesis, University of Aarhus.

Krasner, S. D. (1981) Transforming international regimes. What the Third World wants and why, *International Studies Quarterly*, **25**, 119-48.

Krasner, S. D. (ed.) (1982) International Regimes, a special issue of *International Organization*, **36**(2).

Krasner, S. D. (1993) Westphalia and all that, in Goldstein, J. and Keohane, R. O. (eds), *Ideas and Foreign Policy: Beliefs, Institutions and Political Change*, Ithaca, NY, Cornell University Press, 235-64.

Krasner, S. D. (1994) International political economy: abiding discord, *Review of International Political Economy*, **1**(1), 13-19.

Krasner, S. D. (1995/96) Compromising Westphalia, *International Security*, **20**(3), 115-51.

Kratochwil, F. V. (1989) *Rules, Norms, and Decisions: On the Conditions of Practical and Legal Reasoning in International Relations and Domestic Affairs*, Cambridge, Cambridge University Press.

Kratochwil, F. V. and Ruggie, J. G. (1986) International organization: a state of the art or the art of the state, *International Organization*, **40**(4), 753-76.

Krippendorf, E. (1987) The dominance of American approaches in international relations, *Millennium: Journal of International Studies*, **16**, 207-14.

Laclau, E. and Mouffe, C. (1982) Recasting Marxism: hegemony and new political movements. Interview by D. Plotke, *Socialist Review*, 91-113.

Lane, J. and Ersson, S. O. (1991) *Politics and Society in Western Europe*, London, Sage.

Lewis, I. and Mayall, J. (1996) Somalia, in Mayall, J. (ed.), *The New Interventionism: UN Experience in Cambodia, Former Yugoslavia and Somalia*, Cambridge, Cambridge University Press.

Linklater, A. (1977) The transformation of political community: E. H. Carr, critical theory and international relations, *Review of International Studies*, **23**(3), 321-38.

Linklater, A. (1990) *Men and Citizens in the Theory of International Relations*, London, Macmillan; first published 1982.

Linklater, A. (1990) *Beyond Realism and Marxism*, London, Macmillan.

Linklater, A. (1990) The problem of community in international relations, in *Alternatives*, **15**, 135-54.

Linklater, A. (1992) What is a good international citizen? in Keal, P. (ed.), *Ethics and Foreign Policy*, Canberra, George Allen & Unwin.

Little, R. (1989) Deconstructing the balance of power: two traditions of thought, *Review of International Studies*, **15**(2), 87-101.

Little, R. (1995) Neorealism and the English School: a methodological, ontological and theoretical reassessment, *European Journal of International Relations*, **1**(1), 9-34.

Livingston, S. G. (1992) The politics of international agenda-setting: Reagan and North–South relations, *International Studies Quarterly*, **36**(3), 313-30.

Lose, L. G. (1995) *Conceptualizing International Order: International Society, Regime Theory and Sociological Approaches*, MA dissertation, University of Warwick.

Lotman, Y. M. (1990) *Universe of the Mind: A Semiotic Theory of Culture*, Bloomington, IN, Indiana University Press.

Luard, E. (1977) *Types of International Society*, London, Macmillan.

Luard, E. (1984) *Economic Relationships Among States*, London, Macmillan.

Luard, E. (1986) *War in International Society*, London, I. B. Tauris.

Luard, E. (1990) *International Society*, London, Macmillan.

Luard, E. (1990) *The Globalisation of Politics: The Changed Focus of Political Action in the Modern World*, London, Macmillan.

Luhmann, N. (1990) *Die Wissenschaft der Gesellschaft*, Frankfurt am Main, Suhrkamp.

Luhmann, N. (1990) *Soziologische Aufklurung 5: Konstruktivistische Perspektiven*, Opladen, Westdeutscher Verlag.

Luhmann, N. (1992) Operational closure and structural coupling: the differentiation of the legal system. *Cardozo Law Review*, **13**(5).

Luhmann, N. (1997) *Die Gesellschaft der Gesellschaft* vol. 1–2, Frankfurt am Main, Suhrkamp.

Luke, T. W. (1991) The discipline of security studies and the codes of containment: learning from Kuwait, *Alternatives*, **16**(3), 315-44.

Lyon, P. (1973) New states and international order, in James, A. (ed.) *The Bases of International Order*, London, Oxford University Press.

Mann, M. (1986) *The Sources of Social Power: A History from the Beginning to A.D. 1760*, Cambridge, Cambridge University Press.

Manning, C. A W (1957) Varieties of worldly wisdom, *World Politics*, **9**(2), 149-65.

Manning, C. A W. (1962) *The Nature of International Society*, London, G. Bells and Sons Ltd.

Manning, C. A W. (1972) The legal framework in a world of change, in Porter, B. (ed.), *The Aberystwyth Papers: International Politics 1919–1969*, Oxford, Oxford University Press, 301–35.

Mansbach, R. W. (1997) The past as prelude to the future: changing loyalties in global politics, in Lapid, Y. and Kratochwil, F. V. (eds), *The Return of Culture and Identity in IR Theory*, Boulder, CO, Lynne Rienner.

Mayall, J. (ed.) (1982) *The Community of States: A Study in International Political Theory*, London, George Allen & Unwin.

Mayall, J. (1990) *Nationalism and International Society*, Cambridge, BISA/Cambridge University Press.

Mayall, J. (1991) Non-intervention, self-determination and the 'New World Order', *International Affairs*, **67**(3), 421–30.

Mayall, J. (ed.) (1996) *The New Interventionism: UN Experience in Cambodia, Former Yugoslavia and Somalia*, Cambridge, Cambridge University Press.

Mazruti, A. A. (1990) *Cultural Forces in World Politics*, London, James Currey.

McDougal, M. S. (1953) International law, power, and policy, Academie de Droit International, *Recueil des Cours*, **82**.

McGrew, A. G. and Lewis, P. G. (eds) (1992) *Global Politics. Globalization and the Nation-State*, Cambridge, Polity Press.

Mearsheimer, J. J. (1990) Back to the future: instability in Europe after the Cold War

International Security **15**(1), 5-56.

Mearsheimer, J. J. (1995) The false promise of international institutions, *International Security*, **19**(3), Winter 1994/95, 5-49; with comments by Keohane and Martin, Kupchan and Kupchan, Ruggie, and Wendt, and a reply by Mearsheimer in **20**(1), Summer 1995.

Midgley, E. B. F. (1979) Natural law and the Anglo-Saxons - some reflections in response to Hedley Bull, *British Journal of International Studies*, **5**.

Mill, J. S. (1867) A few words on non-intervention, *Dissertations and Discussions*, London.

Miller, A. J. (1983) The role of deviance in world international society, *Millennium: Journal of International Studies*, **12**(3), 244-59.

Miller, J. D. B. and Vincent, R. J. (eds) (1990) *Order and Violence: Hedley Bull and International Relations*, Oxford, Clarendon Press.

Moravesik, A. (1991) Negotiating the Single European Act: national interests and conventional statecraft in the European Community, *International Organization*, **45**(1). Chicago Press.

Morgenthau, H. J. (1978) *Politics Among Nations: The Struggle for Power and Peace*, 5th edn, New York, Alfred A. Knopf; first published 1947.

Nardin, T. (1983) *Law, Morality and the Relations of States*, Princeton, NJ, Princeton University Press.

Nardin, T. (1992) International ethics and international law, *Review of International Studies*, **18**(1), 19-30.

Nardin, T. and Mapel, D. R. (eds) (1992) *Traditions of International Ethics*, Cambridge, Cambridge University Press.

Navari, C. (ed.) (1991) *The Condition of States: A Study in International Political Theory*, Milton Keynes, Open University Press.

Neumann, I. B. (1995) *Russia and the Idea of Europe: A Study in Identity and International Relations*, London, Routledge.

Neumann, I. B. (1996) Collective identity formation: self and other in international relations, *European Journal of International Relations*, **2**(2), 139-74.

Neumann, I. B. (1997) John Vincent and the English School of international relations, in Neumann, I. B. and Wæver, O. (eds), *The Future of International Relations: Masters in the Making*, London, Routledge, 38-65.

Neumann, I. B., and Welsh, J. M. (1991) The other in European self-definition: an addendum to the literature on international society, *Review of International Studies*, **17**(4), 327-48.

Nicholson, M. (1981) The enigma of Martin Wight, *Review of International Studies*, **7**(1), 15-22.

Northedge, F. S. (1976) *The International Political System*, London, Faber and Faber.

Oakeshott, M. (1990) *On Human Conduct*, Oxford, Clarendon Paperbacks; first published 1975.

Oakeshott, M. (1991) *Rationalism in Politics and Other Essays*, new and expanded edition, Indianapolis, IN, Liberty Press, first published 1962.

Ogley, R. C. (1981) International relations: poetry, prescription or science?, *Millennium: Journal of International Studies*, **10**.

O'Neill, O. (1994) Justice and boundaries, in Brown, C. (ed.), *Political Restructuring in Europe: Ethical Perspectives*, London and New York, Routledge.

Onuf, N. G. (1989) *World of Our Making: Rules and Rule in Social Theory and*

International Relations, Columbia, SC, University of South Carolina Press.

Parkinson, F. (1993) Latin America, in Jackson, R. H. and James, A. (eds), *States in a Changing World*, Oxford, Clarendon Press.

Patomäki, H. (1992) From normative utopias to political dialectics: beyond a deconstruction of the Brown-Hoffman debate, *Millennium: Journal of International Studies*, **21**(1), 53-76.

Philpott, D. (1995) Sovereignty: an introduction and brief history, *Journal of International Affairs*, **48**, 353-68.

Pogge, T. W. (1994) Cosmopolitanism and sovereignty, in Brown, C. (ed.), *Political Restructuring in Europe: Ethical Perspectives*, London and New York, Routledge.

Powell, R. (1994) Anarchy in international relations theory: the neorealist neoliberal debate, *International Organization*, **48**(2).

Puchala, D. J. (1992) Woe to the orphans of the scientific revolution, in Rothstein, R. L. (ed.), *The Evolution of Theory in International Relations*, Columbia, SC, University of South Carolina Press.

Puchala, D. J. and Hopkins, R. F. (1982) International regimes: lessons from inductive analysis, *International Organization*, **36**(2).

Putnam, R. D. (1988) Diplomacy and domestic politics: the logic of two-level games, *International Organization*, **42**(3).

Rae, D, W. and Taylor, M. (1970) *The Analysis of Political Cleavages*, New Haven, CT, Yale University Press.

Rawls, J. (1993) The law of peoples, in Shute, S. and Hurley, S. (eds) *On Human Rights*, London, HarperCollins/New York, Basic Books.

Rengger, N. J. (1990) The fearful sphere of international relations, *Review of International Studies*, **16**(4), 361-8.

Rengger, N. J. (1991) Discovering traditions? Grotius, international society and international relations, *The Oxford International Review*, **3**(1), 47-50.

Rengger, N. J. (1992) A city which sustains all things? Communitarianism and international society, *Millennium: Journal of International Studies*, **21**(3), 353-69.

Rengger, N. J. (1993) No longer a tournament of distinctive knights: systemic transition and the priority of international order, in Brown, R. and Bowker, M. (eds), *Theory and World Politics in the 1980s*, Cambridge, Cambridge University Press.

Richardson, J. L. (1990) The academic study of international relations, in Miller, J. D. B. and Vincent, R. J. (eds), *Order and Violence: Hedley Bull and International Relations*, Oxford, Clarendon Press, 140-85.

Ringmar, E. (1997) Alexander Wendt - a social scientist struggling with history, in Neumann, I. B. and Wæver, O. (eds), *The Future of International Relations: Masters in the Making?* London, Routledge.

Roberts, A. (1991) A new age in international relations?, *International Affairs*, **67**(3), 509-26.

Roberts, A. and Kingsbury, B. (eds) (1993) *United Nations, Divided World*, 2nd edn, Oxford, Clarendon Press.

Rokkan, S. (1977) *Citizens, Elections, Parties*, Oslo, Universitets Forlaget.

Romer, J. (1984) *Détente et rideau de fer*, Paris, Publications de la Sorbonne.

Rorty, R. (1993) Human rights, rationality, and sentimentality, in Shute, S. and Hurley, S. (eds), *On Human Rights*, London, HarperCollins/New York, Basic Books.

Rosenau, J. N. (1990) *Turbulence in World Politics: A Theory of Change and Continuity*, Hemel Hempstead and New York, Harvester Wheatsheaf.

Rosenau, J. N. (1993) *Global Voices: Dialogues in International Relations*, Boulder, CO, Westview Press.

Rosenau, J. N. (1995) Governance in the twenty-first century, *Global Governance*, **1**(1).

Rosenau, J. N. and Czempiel, E.-O. (eds) (1992) *Governance without Government: Order and Change in World Politics*, Cambridge, Cambridge University Press.

Rosenau, J. N. and Durfee, M. (1995) *Thinking Theory Thoroughly: Coherent Approaches to an Incoherent World*, Boulder, CO, Westview Press.

Rossbach, S. (1994) The autopoiesis of the Cold War: an evolutionary approach to international relations?, *EUI Working Papers in Political and Social Sciences* SPS No. 92/23.

Rufin, J.-C. (1991) *L'Empire et les nouveaux barbares*, Paris, Lattès.

Ruggie, J. G. (1975) International responses to technology: concepts and trends, *International Organization*, **29**(3).

Ruggie, J. G. (1983) Continuity and transformation in the world polity: toward a neo-realist synthesis, *World Politics*, **35**, 261–85.

Ruggie, J. G. (1989) International structure and international transformation: space, time and method, in Czempiel, E.-O. and Rosenau, J. N. (eds), *Global Changes and Theoretical Challenges: Approaches to World Politics for the 1990s*, Lexington, MA, Lexington, 21–36.

Ruggie, J. G. (1993) Territoriality and beyond: problematizing modernity in international relations, *International Organization*, **47**, Winter, 139–74.

Ryan, A. (1970) *The Philosophy of the Social Sciences*, London, Macmillan.

Selzer, S. (1975) Letter to Macmillan Publishers, 14 November.

Shapcott, R. (1994) Conversation and coexistence: Gadamer and the interpretation of international society, *Millennium: Journal in International Studies*, **32**(1).

Shaw, M. (1986) *Title to Territory in Africa*, Oxford, Clarendon Press.

Shaw, M. (1992) Global society and global responsibility: the theoretical, historical and political limits of 'international society', *Millennium: Journal of International Studies*, **21**(3), 421–34.

Singham, A. W. and Hune, S. (1986) *Non-alignment in an Age of Alignments*, London, Zed Books.

Slaughter-Burley, A.-M. (1993) International law and international relations theory: a dual agenda, *The American Journal of International Law*, **87**, 205–39.

Smith, S. (1992) The forty years detour: the resurgence of normative theory in international relations, *Millennium: Journal of International Studies*, **21**(3), 489–506.

Smith, S. (1996) Positivists and beyond, in Smith, S., Booth, K. and Zalewsky, M. (eds), *International Theory: Positivism and Beyond*, Cambridge, Cambridge University Press.

Snidal, D. (1991) International cooperation among relative gains maximisers, *International Studies Quarterly*, **35**(4).

Sohn-Rethel, A. (1970) *Geistige und körperliche Arbeit*, Frankfurt, Suhrkamp.

Stopford, J. and Strange, S. (1991) *Rival States, Rival Firms: Competition for World Market Shares*, Cambridge, Cambridge University Press.

Strange, S. (1991) Global patterns of decolonization, 1500–1987, *International Studies Quarterly*, **35**(4), 429–54.

Strange, S. (1991) Anomaly and commonplace in European political expansion:

realist and institutional accounts, *International Organization*, **45**(2).

Strange, S. (1995) The defective state, *Daedalus: Journal of the American Academy of Arts and Sciences*, **124**(2).

Suganami, H. (1983) The structure of institutionalism: an anatomy of British mainstream international relations, *International Relations*, 7(2), 2363–81.

Suganami, H. (1989) *The Domestic Analogy and World Order Proposals*, Cambridge, Cambridge University Press.

Suhr, M. (1996) Keohane: a contemporary classic, in Neumann, I. B. and Wæver, O. (eds), *The Future of International Relations: Masters in the Making?* London, Routledge.

Teubner, G. (1989) How the law thinks: toward a constructivist epistemology of law, *Law and Society Review*, **23**(5), 727–57.

Thompson, J. (1992) *Justice and World Order*, London, Routledge.

Thompson, K. W. (1980) *Masters of International Thought: Major Twentieth-Century Theorists and the World Crisis*, Baton Rouge, LA and London, Louisiana State University Press.

Tucker, R. W. (1977) *The Inequality of Nations*, London, Macmillan.

Tunander, O. (ed.) (1995) *Europa och Muren: Om 'den andre', gränslandet och historiens återkomst i 90-talets Europa (Europe and the Wall: About 'the Other', the Borderland and the Return of History in Europe of the 1990s)*, Aalborg, NSU.

Vasquez, J. A. (1995) The post-positivist debate: reconstructing scientific inquiry and IR theory after Enlightenment's fall, in Booth, K. and Smith, S. (eds), *International Political Theory Today*, Cambridge, Polity Press.

Vincent, R. J. (1974) *Nonintervention and International Order*, Princeton, NJ, Princeton University Press.

Vincent, R. J. (1984) Edmund Burke and the theory of international relations, *Review of International Studies*, **10**(3), 205–18.

Vincent, R. J. (1986) *Human Rights and International Relations*, Cambridge, Cambridge University Press and RIIA.

Vincent, R. J. (ed.) (1986) *Foreign Policy and Human Rights: Issues and Responses*, Cambridge, Cambridge University Press.

Vincent, R. J. (1990) Order in international politics, in Miller, J. D. B. and Vincent, R. J. (eds), *Order and Violence: Hedley Bull and International Relations*, Oxford, Clarendon Press, 38–64.

Wade, R. (1996) Globalization and its limits: the continuing importance of nations and regions, in Berger, S. and Dore, R. (eds), *Convergence or Diversity? National Models of Production and Distribution in a Global Economy*, Ithaca, NY, Cornell University Press.

Wæver, O, (1989) Beyond the 'beyond' of critical international theory, paper for the BISA/ISA Conference, London, March–April, also as *Working Paper* 1989/1 of the Center for Peace and Conflict Research, Copenhagen.

Wæver, O. (1990) Three competing Europes: German, French, Russian, *International Affairs*, **66**(3), 477–93.

Wæver, O. (1990) The language of foreign policy (a review essay on Carlsnaes), *Journal of Peace Research*, **27**(3), 335–48.

Wæver, O. (1991) Territory, authority and identity: the late 20th century emergence of neo-medieval political structures, paper presented at the first general conference of EUPRA, European Peace Research Association, Florence, November.

Wæver, O. (1992) International society: the grammar of dialogue among states, paper presented to the workshop on 'The Nature of International Society Reconsidered', European Consortium Political Research, Limerick, March.

Wæver, O. (1992) *Introduktion til studiet af international politik*, Copenhagen: Forlaget Politiske Studier.

Wæver, O. (1992) International society: theoretical promises unfulfilled? *Cooperation and Conflict*, **27**(1), 147–78.

Wæver, O. (1994) Resisting the temptation of post foreign policy analysis, in Carlsnaes, W. and Smith, S. (eds), *European Foreign Policy: The EC and Changing Perspectives in Europe*, European Consortium Political Research/Sage, 238–73.

Wæver, O. (1995) Identity, integration and security: solving the sovereignty puzzle in EU studies, *Journal of International Affairs*, **48**(2), 389–431.

Wæver, O. (1996) The rise and fall of the inter-paradigm debate, in Smith, S., Booth, K. and Zalewski, M. (eds), *Theorising International Relations: Positivism and After*, Cambridge, Cambridge University Press.

Wæver, O. (1996) Europe's three empires: a Watsonian interpretation of post-wall European security, in Fawn, R. and Larkins, J. (eds), *International Society After the Cold War: Anarchy and Order Reconsidered*, London, Macmillan (in association with *Millennium: Journal of International Studies*), 220–60.

Wæver, O. (1996) European security identities, *Journal of Common Market Studies*, **34**(1), March, 103–32.

Wæver, O. (1996) Figures of international thought: introducing persons instead of paradigms, in Neumann, I. B. and Wæver, O. (eds), *The Future of International Relations: Masters in the Making?* London, Routledge.

Wæver, O. (1998) Insecurity, security and asecurity in the West European non-war community, in Adler, E. and Barnett, M. (eds), *Governing Anarchy: Security Communities in Theory, History and Comparison*, Cambridge, Cambridge University Press.

Wæver, O. (forthcoming) Governance and emancipation: the order/justice dilemma again – only worse?, in Ciprut, J. V. (ed.), *From Past Imperfect to Future Conditional: International Relations in the Decades Ahead.*

Wæver, O. (in preparation) *The Politics of International Structure.*

Wæver, O., Holm, U. and Larsen, H. (in preparation) *The Struggle for 'Europe': French and German Concepts of State, Nation and European Union.*

Walker, R. B. J. (1989) History and structure in the theory of international relations, *Millennium: Journal of International Studies*, **18**(2), 163–83.

Walker, R. B. J. (1989) Ethics, modernity and the theory of international relations, working paper, Princeton University.

Walker, R. B. J. (1990) Security, sovereignty, and the challenge of world politics, *Alternatives*, **15**(1), 3–28.

Walker, R. B. J. (1993) *Inside/Outside: International Relations as Political Theory*, Cambridge, Cambridge University Press.

Waltz, K. N. (1979) *Theory of International Politics*, Reading, MA, Addison Wesley.

Waltz, K. N. (1992) Realist thought and neorealist theory, in Rothstein, R. L. (ed.), *The Evolution of Theory in International Relations*, Columbia, SC, University of South Carolina Press.

Watson, A. (1964) *The War of the Goldsmith's Daughter*, London, Chatto and Windus.

Watson, A. (1983) *Diplomacy: The Dialogue Between States*, New York, McGraw-Hill.

Watson, A. (1987) Hedley Bull, state systems and international studies, *Review of International Studies*, **13**(2), 99–109.

Watson, A. (1990) Systems of states, *Review of International Studies*, **16**(2), 99–110.

Watson, A. (1992) *The Evolution of International Society: A Comparative Historical Analysis*, London, Routledge.

Watson, A. (1995) Foreword to Der Derian, J. (ed.) *International Theory: Critical Investigations*, London, Macmillan, ix–xvii.

Weber, C. (1992) Reconsidering statehood: examining the sovereignty/intervention boundary, *Review of International Studies*, **18**(3), 199–216.

Wendt, A. E. (1987) The agent-structure problem in international relations theory, *International Organization*, **41**(3), 335–70.

Wendt, A. E. (1992) Levels of analysis versus agents and structures, *Review of International Studies*, **18.**

Wendt, A. E. (1992) Anarchy is what states make of it, *International Organization*, **46**(2), 391–425.

Wendt, A. E. (1994) Collective identity formation and the international state, *American Political Science Review*, **88**(2), 384–96.

Wendt, A. E. and Duvall, R. (1989) Institutions and international power, in Czempiel, E.-O. and Rosenau, J. N. (eds.), *Global Changes and Theoretical Challenges: Approaches to World Politics for the 1990s*, Lexington, MA, Lexington, 51–74.

Wesson, R. G. (1967) *The Imperial Order*, Berkeley, CA, University of California Press.

Wesson, R. G. (1978) *State Systems: International Pluralism, Politics and Culture*, London, Collier Macmillan.

Wheeler, N. J. (1992) Pluralist or solidarist conceptions of international society: Bull and Vincent on humanitarian intervention, *Millennium: Journal of International Studies*, **21**(3), 463–87.

Wheeler, N. J. (1993) Human rights and security: beyond non-intervention, in Rees, W. (ed.), *International Politics in Europe: The New Agenda*, London, Routledge.

Wheeler, N. J. (1996) Guardian angel or global gangster: a review of the ethical claims of international society, *Political Studies*, **44**(1), 123–35.

Wheeler, N. J. and Dunne, T. (1996) Hedley Bull's pluralism of the intellect and solidarism of the will, *International Affairs*, **72**(1), 91–107.

Who can police the world? *New York Review of Books*, 12 May 1994.

Wight, G. and Porter, B. (eds) (1991) *International Theory: The Three Traditions*, London, Leicester University Press for the RIIA.

Wight, M. (1966) Why is there no international theory?, reprinted in Butterfield, H. and Wight, M. (eds), *Diplomatic Investigations: Essays in the Theory of International Politics*, London, George Allen & Unwin, 17–34; first published 1960.

Wight, M. (1966) Western values in international theory? in Butterfield, H. and Wight, M. (eds), *Diplomatic Investigations: Essays in the Theory of International Politics*, London, George Allen & Unwin, 89–131.

Wight, M. (1977) *Systems of States*, Leicester, Leicester University Press.

Wight. M. (1977) 'De systematibus civitatum' and 'International legitimacy', in Wight, M. (ed.), *Systems of States*, Leicester, Leicester University Press.

Wight. M. (1986) *Power Politics*, 2nd edn, Penguin Books for RIIA.

Wight, M. (1987) An anatomy of international thought, *Review of International Studies*, **13.**

Williamson, J. and Haggard, S. (1994) The political conditions for economic reform, in Williamson, J. and Haggard, S. (eds), *The Political Economy of Policy Reform*, Washington, DC, International Institute for Economics.

Wilson, P. (1989) The English School of international relations: a reply to Sheila Grader, *Review of International Studies*, **15**(1), 49–58.

Winch, P. and Kegan, P. (1958) *The Idea of a Social Science and its Relation to Philosophy*, London, Routledge.

Wind, M. (1996) Onuf - the rules of anarchy, in Neumann, I. B. and Wæver, O. (eds), *The Future of International Relations: Masters in the Making?*, London, Routledge, 236–68.

Wright, P. M. (1984) Central but ambiguous: states and international theory, *Review of International Studies*, **10**, 233–7.

Wright, P. M. (ed.) (1986) *Rights and Obligations in North–South Relations: Ethical Dimensions of Global Problems*, London.

Zacher, M. W. (1992) The decaying pillars of the Westphalian temple: implications for international order and governance, in Czempiel, E.-O. and Rosenau, J. N. (eds), *Governance with Government: Order and Change in World Politics*, Cambridge, Cambridge University Press.

Zhang, Y. (1991) China's entry in international society: beyond the standard of civilisation, *Review of International Studies*, **17**(1), 3–16.

Index